Theatre in the Twentieth Century

Theatre in the Twentieth Century

EDITED BY

Robert W. Corrigan

GROVE PRESS, INC.
NEW YORK

The material in *Theatre in the Twentieth Century* appeared in the *Tulane Drama Review* during the years 1956 to 1961.

Library of Congress Catalog Card Number: 61-11768

First Printing

Manufactured in the United States of America

FOR MONROE LIPPMAN
AND ROBERT M. LUMIANSKY

*whose vision, encouragement, and support
have made this book possible.*

Contents

Theatre in the Twentieth Century

Introduction:
The Theatre in Search
of a Fix

BY ROBERT W. CORRIGAN

ONE OF THE MOST AMAZING recent phenomena in our theatre is the discovery and gradual acceptance by audiences and critics of the plays of Beckett, Ionesco, Adamov, Genet, and Ghelderode. With a prudishness that is just about par for the course, we have tended to reject these plays and label their authors opprobriously as *avant-garde*. But somehow—in spite of our rejection—these plays keep reasserting themselves; they have a mysterious hold on our sensibilities. We find ourselves going to them, being moved or amused by them, and applauding them—fully aware that we don't always know what they mean or what their authors intend. For all their seeming unintelligibility and simplicity, these plays possess a vitality we have missed, and more important, in their boldly experimental nature they are symptomatic of the unrest which prevails in the contemporary theatre. These playwrights want to "fix" the theatre, and their plays suggest ways that have been taken to revitalize it.

Each of the writers in this movement shares the conviction that the theatre must express the senselessness and irrationality of all human actions. They believe the theatre must confront audiences with that sense of isolation—the sense of man's being encircled in a void—which is an irremediable part of the human condition. In such a universe communication with others is almost impossible, and the language of these plays is symptomatic of their authors' belief in man's inability to

11

communicate and express his basic thoughts and feelings. This has prompted Wallace Fowlie to say that "all of these plays give the impression of being autopsies of our unacknowledged, invisible manias." All that happens in them is beyond rational motivation, happening at random or through the "demented caprice of an unaccountable idiot fate." And so critics, using Ionesco's definition of the "absurd" as "that which has no purpose, or goal, or objective," have come to label the theatre of these playwrights "The Theatre of the Absurd."

But in reducing the human situation to its ultimate absurdity, Beckett, Ionesco, *et al.* realize that the stereotyped dramatic progressions of our determinism-oriented naturalistic theatre will no longer satisfy. They are searching for a new form, new techniques—techniques that are expressive of the central fact of their world: that man's unconscious is no more help to him than his intelligence in solving time's inscrutable ironies.

Now, to revolt against naturalism is not very new; but with the possible exception of Alfred Jarry—and he had so little impact he hardly counts—none of the theatre's revolutionaries beginning with Ibsen and Strindberg have ever resolved so systematically to undermine and destroy not only the superstructure of naturalism, the elaborate settings, the contrived plot, the socially recognizable characters with their all-too-familiar problems, but the very foundation of the naturalistic vision: the laws of logic.

For the Absurdists, tragedy and comedy are both manifestations of despair, of the act which *exists*, exists alone in its own unmotivated isolation, unmeaningful and absurd. The recognizable hero, the logically motivated heroine, the well-knit plot all give *meaning*—a spurious, illusory, distorting meaning—to the act, and so rob it of its elemental import, which lies in its irreducible absurdity. For the Absurdist playwrights, as for Sartre and Camus, the absurd alone bears the stamp of truth; logic is a pattern imposed by a dishonest philosophy pandering to the comfort of those who dare not face reality.

This attitude toward the so-called natural logic of the universe has had tremendous effects on the dramaturgy of the Absurdist playwrights. The first of these is manifested in their thinking about tragedy and comedy. Tragedy doesn't seem to flourish in the world of the absurd. As early as 1939, Eugene O'Neill sensed the impossibility of his life-long ambition to write a tragedy, when he remarked:

It's struck me as time goes on, how something funny, even farcical can suddenly, without apparent reason, break up into something gloomy and tragic. . . . A sort of unfair *non sequitur,* as though events, though life, were manipulated just to confuse us. I think I'm aware of comedy more than I ever was before—a big kind of comedy that doesn't stay funny very long.

When man is forced to admit that the absurd is more than ever inherent in human existence, when he sees his existence as essentially governed by the irrational, the inexplicable, and the nonsensical, he moves into the realm of the comic. For comedy supposes an unformed world, a world being made and turned upside down. In our Punch and Judy world no one is guilty or responsible. As Gautier put it, "comedy is the logic of the absurd," and thus it can admit the disorderly, the absurd, and the improbable into the realm of Art. As Dostoevski, Joyce, and Kafka have so adequately shown in the novel, the fragmentary, schizoid lives that we live are an existential comedy. They suggest that modern man lives in the midst of so many irreconcilable forces that the only way they can be given form is by religious faith or comedy. But it is a special kind of comedy, the "comedy of the grotesque." Our world is similar to the one represented in the apocalyptic paintings of Hieronymus Bosch. The grotesque is a means whereby art can encompass the paradoxical and express the form of the unformed, "the face of a world without a face." However, this grotesque comedy, so aware of the absurdity of experience, is also extremely conscious of its sufferings, struggle, and failure. It is best described as a kind of tragicomedy. It is a vision of life that may be summed up by the closing prayer of Joyce's *Finnegan's Wake:*

> Loud, heap miseries upon us yet entwine
> Our arts with laughters low. In the name
> Of the former and of the latter and of
> Their holocaust, All men.

Or as Ionesco put it: "It all comes to the same thing anyway; comic and tragic are merely two aspects of the same situation, and I have now reached the stage when I find it hard to distinguish one from the other."

The most striking thing about the plays of the avant-garde dramatists is that on the surface they seem to be either unintelligible or simple to the point of absurdity. Yet these plays are the result of serious attempts to give dramatic form to all the complexities of our world. Today we must embrace the idea of paradox in our art as well as our foreign policy. As Duerrenmatt has suggested, "Our world seems still to exist only because the atom bomb exists: out of fear of the bomb."

In *Waiting for Godot,* for instance, Beckett has created an image of man searching for relationship—with himself, with his fellow men, and with his God—only to shatter this image by questioning the validity of the quest. Is there, after all, any ultimate and objective truth? How can we know it? Is it possible that we may be wrong? Is it true for all of us? Prove it! Why bother? In short, what's the use of living anyway?

As John R. Moore has pointed out in his essay, "A Farewell to Something," *Waiting for Godot* ends not in a tragic resolution but in a comic impasse. This is what is so new and important about it. Beckett has rejected the heritage of the French (and probably the Western) theatre; Descartes' *cogito, ergo sum* (I think, therefore I am) has become *vomeo, ergo sum* (I retch, therefore I am); the lyric deliberations of Corneille and Racine on the wonder of the human will have been reduced to an emotionally charged shorthand; the Pascalian dialectic of reason and passion has been mocked to absurdity—or as Anouilh put it, *"Waiting for Godot* was the *Pensées* acted out by circus clowns." But Gogo and Didi, two irreducible specimens of humanity, remain comically, tragically, ambiguously alive with the courage of their hallucinations. They affirm that man can still, albeit fearfully, stick his tongue out at the universe. Like Henry James' Bostonian, they have "the ability to dare and endure, to know and not to fear reality, to look the world in the face and take it for what it is."

But for all its concern for man's ontological solitude, the Theatre of the Absurd is not a theatre of ideas. Ionesco makes this point very strongly when he writes:

> The theatre is not the language of ideas. When it tries to become the vehicle of ideologies, it can only become their popularizer. It simplifies them dangerously. . . . Every ideological theatre risks being only a theatre of patronage. What would be, not only its usefulness, but its proper function, if the theatre were condemned to do the work of philosophy, or theology, or politics, or pedagogy? A psychological theatre is insufficiently psychological. It is better to read a treatise on psychology. An ideological theatre is insufficiently philosophical. Instead of going to see the dramatic illustration of such and such a political theory, I prefer to read my usual daily, or listen to a speech by the candidate of my party.

Rather than ideas, then, these playwrights are trying to deal directly with the themes—emptiness, frustration, change, despair, and death—that obsess them. They believe that the theatre of naturalism either does not treat such themes, or if it does, it presents man in a reduced and estranged perspective. "Truth is in our dreams, in the imagination," says Ionesco. This is the clue to his theatre. All of the Absurdists want a theatre "which progresses not through a predetermined subject and plot, but through an increasingly intense and revealing series of emotional states."

But action, which alone can create movement and bring a play to life, is normally provided by the plot. It is the plot that unites ideas, character and language; yet the plot depends upon the close relationship of all three. We are now dealing with a dislocated drama; its traditional elements have been given a violent wrench. So we find that the plot has been twisted into a situation that is to reveal an emotional state. There are many dramatic situations in a plot; here the situation has been stretched to take the place of the plot. This inflation of the *situation* into the source of dramatic action, so that it replaces the plot, is the vital secret of the Theatre of the Absurd. It is the most exciting and the most disturbing aspect of this theatre. Exciting because the dramatic situation is the essence of the theatre; disturbing because it has serious limitations. It is no accident that most of Beckett's, Ionesco's, Adamov's, and Ghelderode's plays are written in one act; a plot is capable of endless ramifications largely because character changes circumstances. Once you have fixed your characters, their psychological reactions are no longer of interest. The situation assumes full command.

But if this is so, then what happens to character in the Theatre of the Absurd? None of these playwrights has created a character who can stand alone as a great individual. Traditionally, one of the most successful ways for a dramatist to express a profound truth about life, philosophy, or human nature has been for him to create a great character, a great individual in whom the audience can recognize a universal truth. In the Theatre of the Absurd the characters are types; they have no individuality and often not even names. Sometimes they are interchangeable, as for example in *Godot*, when Pozzo and Lucky change roles; or the same name, in a Kafka-like manner, is used in several plays—as is the case of Berenger in Ionesco's *The Killer* and *Rhinoceros*.

But once you do away with a character's individuality, it is impossible for the dramatist to make individual judgments, for there can be no sequence of acts—no real interaction of character and situation—leading to a judgment. We never feel that the question of whether Gogo and Didi, Hamm and Clov, the Old Man and Woman are good or evil is raised or even pertinent; they are pathetic victims of a nothing which is so much. There are no value judgments or distinctions in values in the world of the Absurd. In Adamov's *Ping-Pong*, the aesthetic, economic, and philosophic implications of pinball machines are discussed with religious fervor. In Ionesco's *Jack or the Submission* the whole action is to convince Jack to accept the family's chief value: "I love potatoes with bacon."

In such a world, human action and self-sacrifice have no meaning. The most horrible aspect of Ionesco's *The Chairs* is the fact that the old couple's immolation at the end of the play is so meaningless. Ionesco presents us with an inverted Messiah and the end of the world in his "salvation." As the Orator signs autographs and the Old Woman sobs, the Old Man begins his final soliloquy:

> Our existence can come to an end in this apotheosis. . . . My mission is accomplished. I will not have lived in vain, since my message will be revealed to the world. . . . Our corpses will fall far from each other, and we will rot in an aquatic solitude. . . .

Confident that their message will save the world, they dive into the sea. The professional orator, who is to deliver their message, takes the podium and turns out to be a deaf-mute; he can only squawk and write two words on a blackboard—"Angelfood" and "Adieu." Ionesco seems to be saying that enriched cake flour is a significant token of farewell for our age; it is the perverted apocalypse of our civilization.

One of the most significant results of the Absurdists' rebellion against the natural laws of logic has been their rejection of the psychologically oriented play. Each of these playwrights is vehement in maintaining that with our almost morbid concern with psychology—particularly here in America—we are denying the theatre's historical nature. For most of this century the remedy that our theatre offered for the mystery of evil was: "Change the society!" Since 1945 it has been: "Get a doctor!" Now, there is no denying that the increased concern for psychology on the part of our dramatists has had salutary effects on the theatre. But it has gotten to the point where every so-called serious play has become a clinical case history, and this is more detrimental than beneficial.

To begin with, it is a severely limited view of man. When all human actions are explainable in terms of some kind of psychological cause and effect, the possibility of deliberative and moral choice is dissolved. There is an old saw about no man being a hero to his valet. The same is true of his psychoanalyst. And ultimately, the same is true of the dramatic artist. For example, as David Daiches has suggested, Oedipus remains a hero with great stature so long as he is not suffering from an Oedipus complex. But once we learn to explain him in terms of repressed hopes and fears, or traumatic childhood experiences, or a vitamin deficiency in infancy, he may remain interesting—in fact, he will gain a new kind of interest as Cocteau's *The Infernal Machine* attests—but he loses stature. For, to use another old saw, "To understand all, is to forgive all." But when we can do both of these things all men are reduced to a common level. Which of us can understand a Hamlet, or a Lear? And which of us can forgive an Othello or a Macbeth? But it is precisely the fact that they are greater than our understanding, that there is a mysterious greatness about them, that makes them the heroes they are. And it is this mystery that makes them great; it is this mysterious quality in men which passeth all understanding that affirms man and his universe.

Maxwell Anderson has written that "from the point of view of the playwright, the essence of a tragedy, or even a serious play, is the spiritual awakening, or regeneration of his hero." But the problem is to know what we mean by the heroic in our time and also what we mean when we speak of spiritual awakening or regeneration. To begin with, it is certainly safe to say that society, as a force for good or evil, plays a larger and more essential role in the modern theatre than in the great plays of earlier periods. Consequently, the typical hero of modern drama will be different. In what ways?

The hero is always best described in terms of those forces which urge him to spiritual redemption. The first important shift in attitude concerning the nature of heroism in the modern drama takes place in *Faust*. When Goethe made Faust settle down to the practical activity of cultivating a strip of land for the purpose of establishing a prosperous (and generalized) society, he created an heroic type whose spiritual state and spiritual concern radically differ from those of Oedipus or Lear. Humanitarianism, no matter how well motivated and beneficent, is not the same thing as the kind of realization that makes Oedipus gouge out his eyes, or makes Lear's flawed heart "Burst smilingly, 'twixt two extremes of passion, joy and grief." As the late Theodore

Spencer put it, "Humanitarian devotion is not in itself necessarily a spiritual act." For example, Dr. Stockman in Ibsen's *An Enemy of the People* is not a spiritual figure. Solness in *The Master Builder* is. The discovery Dr. Stockman makes is not of a new dimension inside himself but of an evil in the society outside him. Although Stockman fights that evil heroically, it is not a spiritual struggle.

Here we find it necessary to distinguish between moral and spiritual values. In our time, society has come to exert more and more pressure on us as individuals; as a result, we have come to think of society as an agent of Destiny. But when we identify society with Destiny, we feel that Destiny has diminished. Any mind capable of spiritual aspiration must find in the actions of the dramatic hero that which affirms the vitality of the free will in any given situation. Man's free will may be defeated by the forces of Destiny—in fact, the great plays have always testified that the destroying forces of Destiny are as much a part of the hero's character as his free will—it may be paralyzed and thus incapable of action, it may be submerged by the battle in such a way as to become part of that Destiny, it may even turn out to be an illusion; but it must always be an active force if we are to believe that we are partaking in human greatness. Such a Destiny must be greater than an aggregate of human beings or an expression of social patterns.

The playwright who has been influenced by a deterministic view of human nature is certain sooner or later to fail in distinguishing between the hero and the victim, Destiny and society. The consequence in the twentieth century has been a theatre of steadily diminishing stature. This is related to another aspect of psychology which has had even more profound effects on the drama. The modern playwright cannot help but have absorbed a great deal that psychology has made known. He knows all about the relationship of infantile frustration and adult neuroses; he has learned about the psychosomatic aspects of illness; and above all he knows that all human actions—even the greatest and most selfless of them—spring from some deep and hidden but nonetheless selfish motivation. Doesn't he feel that there is a danger in passing a moral judgment on individuals? In fact, how can there be a moral pattern to human experience in such a world? For example: A man may commit a murder; but wait, we know that he saw something horrible in the barn when he was a child; we discover that he was brought up on the lower East Side without orange juice and cod-liver oil, and that his mother was a whore. How can we blame him for this murder that he was eventually driven to commit? Oh, yes, we can put him in a jail or an asylum; we can even take his life. But this is because he is dangerous to society and does not necessarily involve moral condemnation. If, then, our moral judgments can be dissolved by psychological understanding, how can the dramatist pattern a tragedy or create characters with stature; finally, how can there be drama at all? If there is no possibility for an appraisal of personality as such, why should Hamlet's death be any more significant than that of Rosencrantz or Guildenstern?

The trouble with so much of the modern theatre—particularly in this country—is that the playwright has come to assume that if he explains his characters he has written a play. He has forgotten that a dramatic situation requires not that we should *understand* a character but simply that we should *believe* in him. Dramatic action always leads to a judgment; it requires that something shall happen to and through the characters; something that is embodied in the events of which the characters are a part. Whenever the personality of the character, rather than the action of which the character should be a part, becomes the playwright's chief concern, the range of the theatre is drastically reduced if not unalterably damaged.

Now, obviously we can't return to the womb of some hypothetical pre-Freudian existence. It will be impossible for us ever again to view man without some degree of psychoanalytic prejudice; but the important issue is whether the theatre will be so dominated by psychology that it is blinded to those older and more valuable insights of a social, moral, and spiritual nature which have been the basis of theatre from the very beginning. The Theatre of the Absurd is revolting against the kind of theatre in which all action is conceived in terms of psychological plausibility, a theatre in which actions are dissolved by psychological explanation or by those mists of fantasy which are at one with the spectator's moral evasions.

But more important than the avant-garde's concern with man's ontological solitude and its rebellion against psychology is its attitude toward language. Each of these playwrights is revolting against the tyranny of words in the modern theatre. As a result, their plays—at least until very recently—have no "message"; the dialogue is not a monologue apportioned out to several characters; they are packed with symbols, but these symbols don't mean anything in particular and they suggest many things. Their characters lead their own lives, talk their own thoughts.

Their speeches impinge on each other and glance away. There is none of the planted line and heavy-handed cross references we are so accustomed to. There doesn't seem to be any central theme, only many related ideas, to these dramatic St. Vitus' dances. But as the plays draw to a close—they don't end in any Aristotelian sense—each of these ideas is subtly recaptured and made to work for an overall impact. Finally, and most important, in all of their plays there is an insistent demand that the gestures of pantomime are the theatre's most appropriate and valuable means of expression; the insistence that the mimetic gesture precedes the spoken word and that the gesture is the true expression of what we feel, while words only describe what we feel. In fact, these writers assert that in objectifying the feeling in order to describe it, words kill the very feeling they would describe.

It is no wonder, then, that these playwrights feel a great affinity to the mimes—Etienne Decroux, Marcel Marceau, and Jacques Tati; no wonder that they turn for inspiration to the early films of Charlie Chaplin, Buster Keaton, the Keystone Cops, Laurel and Hardy, and the Marx Brothers; no wonder, finally, that they are all under the influence of Jacques Copeau and Antonin Artaud. It is only with the recent translation into English of Artaud's book, *The Theatre and Its Double* (the earlier and more seminal work of Copeau has not as yet been translated), that most of us have been able to discover what the aesthetic of this whole avant-garde theatre movement is.

Artaud's basic premise is that it is a mistake in the theatre to assume that "In the beginning was the word." And our theatre does make just that assumption. For most of us, critics as well as playwrights, the word is everything; there is no possibility of expression without it; the theatre is thought of as a branch of literature, and even if we admit a difference between the text spoken on the stage and the text read by the eyes, we have still not managed to separate it from the idea of a *performed text*. Artaud and the playwrights who have followed him maintain that our modern psychologically oriented theatre denies the theatre's historical nature. For them, as Artaud put it, "the stage is a concrete physical place which must speak its own language—a language that goes deeper than spoken language, a language that speaks directly to our senses rather than primarily to the mind as is the case with the language of words."

This is the most significant thing about the avant-garde theatre—it is a theatre of gesture. "In the beginning was the Gesture!" Gesture is not a decorative addition that accompanies words; rather it is the source, cause, and director of language, and insofar as language is dramatic it is gestural. It is this insistence on restoring the gestural basis to theatre that has resulted in the renascence of pantomime in such plays as *The Chairs, Waiting for Godot, Ping-Pong, Endgame, The Balcony,* and *Escurial.* But how different this pantomime is from pantomime as most moderns conceive it! For most of us, pantomime is a series of gestures which represent words or sentences—a game of charades. But this is not the pantomime of history. For the great mimes, as Artaud points out, gestures represent ideas, attitudes of mind, aspects of nature which are realized in an effective, concrete way, by constantly evoking objects or natural details in a manner much like that Oriental language which represents night by a tree on which a bird that has already closed one eye is beginning to close the other.

Now, up to a point this attitude is valid and certainly it is a much needed antidote to the worn-out and expressionless language and structure of most modern plays in the well-made-play tradition of naturalism. However, as is the case with most revolutionaries, the cause is just, but they go too far.

In the first place, for all the noise, the debates, the angry articles, the thumping of the "young Turks," there is nothing really very new in this. Ionesco's essays say nothing that Mallarmé didn't say in his long essay on the theatre seventy years ago. Artaud, the high priest of the Absurdists, says nothing in *The Theatre and Its Double* that Appia, Craig, and Copeau didn't say before him. It is all well and good to say that we should do away with stereotyped plots and concern ourselves with expressing emotional states, but Maeterlinck and the Symbolists were doing this at the turn of the century—and where did Mityl and Tityl get the theatre? It is grand to say that the theatre has a language prior to words, and so Beckett and Ionesco write (is "write" the correct word?) Acts Without Words; but how different is this from Jacques Bernard's "Theatre of Silence" of the twenties?

More important—and we tend to forget this—is the fact that it was the desire for more expressive language that caused realistic dialogue to be introduced into the theatre in the first place. Ibsen, Strindberg, and Chekhov didn't write the way they did because they had theories about language; they wrote realistic dialogue partly in reaction to the hollow rhetoric of the romantic play, but chiefly because they had created characters who could best express themselves with this kind of speech.

The Absurdists, in turn, are reacting against the arid language of naturalism. They insist, although I am not sure what they mean by the distinction, that the real content of a play lies in the action and not in the words. As a result, in some of their plays—Beckett's *Act Without Words*, and Ionesco's *The New Tenant*—they have discarded language altogether. However, the answer to the problem doesn't lie in the defiant rejection of language, but rather in the revitalization of it. The big question, then, is how to make the language of the theatre once again dramatic.

The most valuable service the Absurdists have rendered the modern theatre may well be their demand that the language of the theatre be gestural in nature. By insisting that language be gestural, that it be considered as something more than a means of conducting human characters to their external ends, they have forced our playwrights to see beyond the simple distinction that language is made of words and gesture is made of motion, to the reverse distinction: "Words are made of motion, made of action or response; and gesture is made of language —made of the language beneath or beyond or alongside of the language of words." We are becoming aware once again, as R. P. Blackmur has pointed out, that "when the language of words most succeeds it *becomes* gesture in its words." It is this quality that must be carried into language whenever the context is imaginative or dramatic. This quality alone makes the language of the stage appear as necessity, as a result of a series of compressions, collisions, scenic frictions, and evolutions. Such language "creates meaning as conscience creates judgment, by feeling the pang, the inner bite, of things forced together," and this is the conflict we call dramatic, the conflict most at home in the theatre.

Now, the basic dramatic gesture of poetry is the metaphor. A metaphor is a "*connector*," and it links two antagonistic or disparate worlds by finding some similarity between the two which permits the soaring of the poet's imagination toward a clearly conceived picture image. A metaphor then implies an imaginative perception on the part of the poet of a similarity, or a common power, which exists between two dissimilar worlds. Furthermore, when a given metaphor is repeated often enough, symbolic image patterns are created, and these metaphoric configurations are used by the playwright to express the meaning of the dramatic action.

This is the kind of "connection" that I think we are going to have to rediscover if we are ever going to "fix" the theatre. But this won't be

easy; for apart from the tendency toward artificiality, which characterizes so much of our so-called "poetic drama," there are two other
obstacles to overcome. The first is the effect that the movies and TV
have had on our audiences. We must face the fact that these two mass
media have stepped in between the theatre and the popular imagination. They have seized upon the daydreams of wealth, love, physical
beauty, luxury, and adventure that haunt the emotionally starved and
financially pinched millions of our civilization. The movies and television, while they appease these longings, at the same time create a whole
mythology for them. And this world of fantasy cannot but influence
the playwright, since it forms a part of the world picture which confronts the modern sensibility, and since it contributes to the patterns
of speech and the reservoir of visual imagination from which the writer
draws his metaphors and images. But more important than this is the
audience's loss of *imaginative power,* its inclination not so much to
share in a dramatic experience as to have it served up as diversion. The
consequence of this dulling effect is that more and more of our audiences find it difficult to comprehend anything but the most colloquial
and explicit dialogue. They tend to reject anything that demands an
active effort or response. One reason for this, I suppose, is that the
language of visual images is easier to assimilate but more equivocal than
that of words. It allows for that blurring of emotion and situation which
is so characteristic of modern plays. We are led up to some psychological
climax and then the situation is left inarticulate. We are given some
cliché of gesture, a shrug, and a fadeout as a substitute for an artistic
solution. One is reminded of *Tea and Sympathy, Dark at the Top of
the Stairs, Two for the Seesaw,* and *Look Homeward Angel.*

This leads to the second obstacle: the firmly entrenched convention
of inarticulateness in our theatre. The rebels of naturalism were right in
rejecting the romantic verse drama with its purple passages, soliloquies,
and asides for "real" dramatic speech. But the convention of colloquial
speech may be as restricting as any other. The drama is so much more
confined in time and space than the novel that it must live by finding
short cuts to the imagination. If speech is limited to the flat level of
"natural" conversation, the dramatist will find it hard to penetrate any
distance below the surface of character and situation, and harder still
to "place" his play in relation to the wider universe of thought and
experience, which lies behind its physical setting. Finally, the reticence,
inarticulateness, and homely idiom of our theatre is no longer a healthy

reaction but a lazy abdication, an inarticulateness which is not dramatically significant but is the inarticulateness of characters who have nothing to say.

If we are to "fix" the theatre, we must make the case of articulateness and imagination, for it will be done only by the dramatist who uses metaphor and imagery, whether in verse or prose, to achieve intensity and depth of meaning. We must have plays that are essentially true to human nature, but don't attempt to convince the audience that they are watching a piece of real life. People do not rage in the phrases of Lear or make love in the words of Romeo, though they may wish they could. Dramatic poetry or real dramatic prose is not lifelike; it is larger than life, it employs all the resources of language to illuminate the short hour of experience in which the dramatist has caught his figures and which may bring to a climax the events of a lifetime. In language what the dramatist seeks above all is concentration. Imagery and metaphor, by appealing to our memory or our senses, by relating the concrete to the abstract, are the most highly charged forms of language he can use. And more important, they enable the dramatist to solve the most difficult of his problems: those revelations of the inner life of his characters which may not relate directly to the action of the plot, but are nonetheless significant parts of the play.

It is for this reason that our playwrights need to realize again the basis of their art—the living word. Of all language, that which I've called imaginative is the fullest and most intense, and unless the theatre relates itself to the most vital expression of the modern sensibility it will become as it too often has—superficial. As I have said, such language is not necessarily lifelike, yet it offers the richest and most fully *articulate* expression of human experience; it is the only language which can give the full expression to that balance of human faculties which characterizes the art of the theatre.

In their use of language the Absurdists would deny this, and it is very possible that the theatre they would revive will turn out to be stillborn. I am sure they would counter this by saying that what they write is in accordance with the "facts of life." If the dialogue in their plays consists of meaningless clichés and stereotyped phrases, they would insist that this is the way we talk. If their characters are constantly changing their personalities, these playwrights would point out that no one today is really consistent or truly integrated. If the people in their plays seem to be helpless puppets without any will of their own, the Absurdists would argue that we are all passively at the mercy of blind fate and meaningless circumstance; that their theatre is the true theatre of our time. If that is the case, then: *Hail to the Ultra-Naturalists!*

But if it is true—and I believe it is—that man is a creature of his language, that by his use of it he defines himself, then ours is a civilization that has lost its nerve. It has lost its trust in the possibility of words to communicate meaningfully. I am sure the Absurdists would agree with this, and their plays are persuasive documents of the fact. Whenever an age loses its nerve, more and more it reduces its language to the verb, that verbal expression which denotes action in its simplest and most concrete form. On the other hand, a more confident age uses nouns and adjectives—those verbal forms which express the quality of action. This is the irony and the danger of the avant-garde theatre. They would "fix" our theatre by "connecting" it with the vital theatre of former ages; but they forget that the source of vitality of this enduring theatre is in that language which they would deny.

By all means let's revitalize the theatre and its language. But we must never forget that the theatre in its most embracing form begins with the play, and if you eliminate the spoken language, the play will not exist. It can be admitted that words are limited in what they can express, but they are finally all we've got. Yes, the language of our stage has become stagnant, but the answer is not to throw it out, but rather—and this I believe is the obligation of all writers—to revitalize language so it can more fully express man's feeling. Only an increased trust in the possibility of words to communicate meaningfully will bring about the renaissance of our theatre.

The Theatre of the Absurd has done us a great service by experimenting with nonverbal techniques. In this it has broken down many of Naturalism's restrictions and in so doing has opened up the theatre. But the final irony is appropriately directed to the playwrights themselves. They are seeking ways to link the contemporary theatre with the traditional theatre, and the traditional theatre is first and foremost a celebration of life, that life which the Absurdists would deny.

The real answer to the despair of the Absurdists, and this is the affirmation of our theatre, is that our playwrights—and I include Beckett, Ionesco, and Adamov—still find human action significant, still find it necessary to *write* plays, and in the very writing attest to the miracle of life that their philosophy would deny. As Yeats put it: "The fiddles are tuning all over the world." For those of us who cannot make such a commitment, these "fiddlers" urge us—and it is important that they do—to maintain as best we can that courtesy of the spirit which accepts the absence of spiritual consolations without complaint and is content to wait in stillness.

1. The Playwright: Vision and Method

The Playwright and the Atomic World

BY ARTHUR MILLER

I OBVIOUSLY CAN HAVE NO special competence in the field of foreign policy. I only know what I read in the papers and the fact that I am a creative writer does not make my opinions either wiser or more persuasive than those of any other man. But it seems to me that there might be some good purpose in one of my profession expressing himself on this kind of problem. A certain awareness of attitudes outside our borders has been forced on me over the past ten years. My plays are regularly produced on the stages of Europe, Asia, Australia, and other areas. I have not traveled extensively abroad for some seven years now, but I do receive a steady mail from artists, producers, and audiences in foreign countries; there are visits and a steady correspondence with them and frequent newspaper reviews and articles concerning my work.

From all these sources I have a certain group of impressions, especially of Europe, which have at least one rather unusual basis, namely, the comparative foreign reaction to works written for the American audience.

Through these varying reactions to the same object, national attitudes can be examined in a perspective less turbulent and possibly of more lasting truth than purely political studies will elicit. In a theatre, people are themselves; they come of their own volition; they accept or reject, are moved or left cold not by virtue of reason alone or of emotion alone, but as whole human beings.

A communion through art is therefore unusually complete; it can be a most reliable indication of a fundamental unity; and an inability to commune through art is, I think, a stern indication that cultures have not yet arrived at a genuine common ground. Had there been no Flaubert, no Zola, no Proust, de Maupassant, Stendhal, Balzac, Dumas; had there been no Mark Twain, or Poe, Hawthorne, Emerson, Hemingway, Steinbeck, Faulkner, or the numerous other American artists of the first rank, our conviction of essential union with France and of France with us would rest upon the assurances of the two Departments of State and the impressions of tourists. I think that had there been no Tolstoy, no Gogol, no Turgenev, no Chekhov or Dostoevski, we should have no assurance at all nor any faint hope that the Russian heart was even ultimately comprehensible to us. Recently the new government of Ceylon which has just replaced the avowedly pro-British, pro-American regime, was and is still thought to be anti-American. The program is to nationalize foreign-owned plantations and for the first time in history they will exchange Ambassadors with Moscow and Peking. The Prime Minister, an Oxford graduate, took pains to correct the idea he was anti-Western. He said, "How could I be against a country that produced Mark Twain?"

There is more than a literary appreciation behind this remark, I think. Literature of the first rank is a kind of international signaling service, telling all who can read that wherever that distant blinker is shining live men of a common civilization.

Now, at the outset, I want to make clear that I disagree with those who believe the United States has entirely failed in its foreign policy since the close of World War II. But I think that the values this country has stood for in the past, more than in the present, have helped to keep alive a promise of a democratic future for the world. I do not believe, however, that our policy has stopped communism. I think that our armament has been a deterrent. But that is all. A policy of merely deterring anything is negative. I believe the time is upon us, and has been for some time now, when an entirely new approach has to be taken to the whole problem of what the future is to be. I base this upon the assumption that the atomic and armament stalemate is an historic fact which will remain for an indefinite period. In short, the policy was justified, if it was at all, on the basis of an imminence of war. I am proceeding on the ground that there will not be a war and cannot be. I summarize these conclusions at the outset so that the criticisms I may level now will be taken as they are intended—as guides to a positive foreign policy, and not an exercise in sarcasm. For good or ill, what the government has done in the world we have done; equally, what it will do in the future must represent, more than ever before, the real feelings and the judgments of the people. My quarrel, in fact, is that our policy has ceased to reflect the positive quality of the American people, and rests basically on their fears, both real and imaginary. We are much more than our fears, but the world does not often know that. And now to certain observations from my experience as a dramatist.

To begin with, I have often been struck, in foreign reviews of my plays, by the distinct difference in the foreign critic's attitudes toward meaning in a play, toward the theatre as an institution. Here our critics and most of the people in our audiences are pragmatists. As in our scientific tradition, our industrial tradition, in most of the things we do, we are almost wholly absorbed by the immediate impact of an idea or an invention. A thing is judged almost exclusively by whether it works, or pays, or is popular. In the scientific fields, my understanding is that this has been both an advantage and a liability, because our traditionally meager interest in theoretical, pure science has held back our scientific advance. At the same time, of course, our concentration upon practical, applied science has helped to give us a highly developed industry and a profusion of consumers' goods. The roster of those scientists who developed the atomic bomb is, as we know, very heavily weighted with foreign names, for this was a child of pure research. The opposing emphasis here and abroad is probably accounted for by the smallness of the European market for the products of applied science, for one thing. From this lack they have in this case made a virtue. But the irony remains that despite our enormous scientific establishment and our admitted superiority in many applied fields, there is evidently an impression abroad, founded until recently on fact, that we have little intellectual interest in science. I believe there is now a consciousness here of that need which is long past due.

In the field of the drama the same sort of irony prevails, and I think its operating principle has a certain effect upon a rather wide sector of European opinion. On the one hand, one feels the European writer, the critic, and from my mail the audience too, are more interested in the philosophic, moral, and principled values of the play than we are. One senses that they rather look askance at our lack of interest in these matters, and I often think that for this among other reasons they so often regard us as essentially a people without seriousness. The truth is that while our plays move much more rapidly than theirs do, are less likely to dwell on long conversations woven around piquant paradox and observation for its own sake, and while they strive more to be actions than thoughts, it is often admitted that if there is a leadership in the contemporary play since the Second World War, at least in terms of international public appeal, America has it. Put simply, we write plays for people and not for professors or philosophers; the people abroad accept and love many of our plays, and in some cases, even the philosophers do too. The point I would make here is that without any special consciousness of the attempt, we have created in the past few decades a kind of American dramatic style. We have also created an American movie style, an American style of dress, and probably architecture, and a style of shopping, and a style of comic books, and a style of novel writing and popular music—in a word, we have spontaneously created methods of reaching the great mass of the people whose effectiveness and exportability, if one may use an ugly word, are not equalled anywhere else.

This has had a multiple effect and it is not easy to separate the good from the bad. But I know, for instance, that there is great resentment among thinking people in Europe at the inroads made by *Reader's Digest* and comic books. One finds Dick Tracy all over the place. As a result of this particular kind of export, we are unwittingly feeding the idea that we incline ever so slightly to the moronic. The idea, for instance, of publishing an abridged novel is barbaric to them, and I'm not sure they're wrong. At the same time, however, our best writers are in many cases their secret or admitted models.

It is time to interject here some word about the importance of what is vaguely called culture in our foreign relations, a matter to which our government, to put it gently, is stupendously indifferent. In 1950 I was interviewed by the press in Copenhagen. It was an entirely literary interview. But when the reporters had left, one man stayed behind. Unlike the others who were of an intellectual sort, he wanted to know where I lived, what sort of a house, whether I played with my children, owned a car, dressed for dinner, and so forth. He turned out to have been from a tabloid paper which was read mainly by what he termed shopgirls. Now, I have yet to be interviewed by the *New York Daily News*, for instance, so I asked him what interest his readers could have in a person who wrote such morose and dreary plays. "It is very important for them to know that there are writers in America," he said. I could hardly believe they doubted that. "Oh yes," he said, "they will be very surprised to read about you, that you exist." But if they were that ignorant, I said, what difference would it make to them whether writers exist in America? What importance could the whole question have for them? "Very important," he said. "They are not intellectuals, but they think anyway that it is necessary for a country to have intellectuals. It will make them more sympathetic to America."

This is but one of many similar incidents which have made me wonder whether we are struggling, unknowingly, with a difference in cultural attitudes which may even warp and change purely political communication at any particular moment.

It is not that we are a people without seriousness. It is that we measure seriousness in an entirely different way than they do. They are the inheritors of a culture which was established, and I believe still exists, on an essentially aristocratic concept, which is to say, out of societies whose majority was nearly illiterate; education was for the few and the artist a kind of adornment to the political state, a measure of its glory and its worth. The artist for us, even as we may pay him much better than they do and cheat him much less, is more of an odd duck, and even among his fellow artists here he does not really exist except when he gains a great popular following. Again, our pragmatism is at work. I think that more Americans than not concede an artist his importance in proportion to his ability to make money with what he creates, for our measure of value is closely attuned to its acceptance by the majority. The artistic product has traditionally had little if any intrinsic justification for most of us. And this has presented our artists with a very lonely and frustrating life on the one hand, but on the other with a worthy if nearly impossible challenge. We regard it as our plain duty to make high art, if we are able, but to make it for all the people. More often than not, however, the art that *is* made sacrifices art for popularity partly because popularity pays fabulously among us. But the challenge is the right one anyway, I believe. The thing of importance now, however, is that even as we have produced some of the best works of literature of this era, we yet stand accused with perfect sobriety of being a mindless country. In this area the Russians have an inherited advantage over us. Despite all their differences from the Western tradition, their inherited attitude toward the artist and the intellectual has essentially the same sort of consciousness as that of the European. I think, for instance, of the time Dostoevski died. The entire Russian nation went into mourning for a novelist. I think of the endless lines of people who came to sit at Tolstoy's feet in his later years. I think too of the time a few years ago when I visited the Royal Dramatic Theatre in Stockholm and saw an announcement of a forthcoming cycle of Strindberg's plays. I asked the director whether Strindberg was a popular writer in his native Sweden, and the director said he was not. Still for at least one period in each season, Strindberg's plays are regularly produced. "But why do you do this if he is not very popular?" I asked. "That isn't the point," he said. "He was our greatest dramatist and one of the best in the world; it is up to us to keep his plays alive and before the public." Later, we walked through the vast dressing room area of the theatre, and there was one which, he said, is not often used. It belonged to a great actor who was now too aged to play. Yet, they kept his dressing room solely for his use just in case he might drop in to rest of an afternoon. They needed dressing rooms badly, but it was inconceivable to take this once-great actor's name off his door until he had died.

This is not the occasion to examine the right and wrong of that system; I only wish to say that there is in Europe at least the strong remnant of the idea that the artist is the vessel of his country's selfhood, the speaker who has arisen among his countrymen to articulate if not to immortalize their age. I believe, as well, that because this reverence remains, it leads them to believe that they care more for art than we do, and that it follows we have no real life of the spirit but only a preoccupation with commodities. I would go even further and say that often our immense material wealth is the cue for them to believe that we care less for people than for things. I will not comment here on how much we care for people or how little; I am trying to avoid the question of the civilizing value of this kind of reverence for art. I will only say that at least in one country, Germany, its alleged pride in its artists did not seem to mitigate its ferocity in two world wars. But this is not the whole story either, and I leave it to go on with my observations.

In the different attitudes toward art can be detected attitudes which may be of significance politically. The reviews and comments upon my own play, *Death of a Salesman*, are of interest in this connection. When the play opened in New York it was taken for granted that its hero, the Salesman, and the story itself were so American as to be quite strange if not incomprehensible to people of other nations; in some countries there is, for instance, no word that really conveys the idea of the salesman in our sense. Yet, wherever it has been shown there seems to have been no difficulty at all in understanding and identifying with the characters, nor was there any particular notice taken of the hero's unusual occupation. It seems to me that if this instantaneous familiarity is any guide, we have made too much of our superficial differences from other peoples. In Catholic Spain where feudalism is still not a closed era, among fishermen in Norway at the edge of the Arctic Circle, in Rome, Athens, Tokyo, there has been an almost disappointing similarity of reaction to this and other plays of mine in one respect at least. They all seem to feel the anxieties we do; they are none of them certain of how to dissolve the questions put by the play, questions like: What ultimate point can there be for a human life? What satisfaction really exists in the ideal of a comfortable life surrounded by the gadgets we strive so hard to buy? What ought to be the aim for a man in this kind of a world? How can he achieve for himself a sense of genuine fulfillment and an identity? Where, in all the profusion of materiality we have created around us, is the cup where the spirit may reside? In short, what is the most human way to live?

I have put these questions because the commentators around the world have put them, but also because they do inform the play and I meant them to. Yet, no American reviewer actually brought up any of these questions. A play is rarely discussed here as to its philosophic meanings, excepting in a most cursory way; yet the basic effect upon us and the effect upon foreign audiences is evidently very similar. What I am trying to point out, again, is that it is less often the fact itself, the object itself about which we differ, than our unwillingness to rationalize how we feel. I sense that even as we do create the things of the spirit it seems to them rather an accident, rather a contradiction of our real character. I would add that had my plays not worked in Europe, which is to say that had they really been only philosophical works and not infused with the American pragmatic need for scenes to move with a pace and with characters made clear and familiar, the European would not be likely to be interested in them either.

I think it is true to say that for the most part as a nation we do not understand, we do not see that art, our culture itself, is a very sinew of the life we lead. Truly, we have no consciousness of art even as it has changed our tastes in furniture, in the houses we buy, in the cars we want. Only as it is transformed into things of daily use have we the least awareness of its vital functioning among us, and then it is only as its by-products appear in the most plain aspects of usefulness. As an example, even while abstract art is gazed at without comprehension, if not with hatred, its impact upon our linoleum designs, our upholsteries, our drapes, our women's dresses, our buildings, our packages, our advertising—these uses or misuses are quickly accepted without a thought. We have made in real life a most modern environment in many cases and have little conscious awareness of modernity; they have kept an outmoded environment in many cases and have a heightened awareness of what is modern.

This whole antipathy for theorizing, of knowing intellectually what we are doing, has very often crippled our ability to appraise reality. We so often become drowned in our own actions. For instance, it seems to me that this government has acted time and again as though its reasons would be automatically accepted without question or suspicion. In recent months we have armed Pakistan, a nation imbedded in the Indian nation, and one with which India has some potentially explosive disagreements. The reason given for arming Pakistan was security against Russia and China. For the Indian Government, however, there could only be one result of this arming and it would be to strengthen Pakistan against India. To defend our act by claiming naïveté will simply not do under the circumstances. We intended the arms for defense against Russia and China, therefore that is all they will be used for. To rise above our immediate action and interest, to see beyond the moment and through the eyes of another country—this requires a kind of imagination which, to be sure, is not very difficult to achieve, but one must be accustomed to using it. In general, it seems to me, speaking as an artist and not a politician, this government has proceeded at times quite as though individual actions could have no larger meaning; quite as though, in dramatic terms, each moment of the play we are writing were to be judged for itself and separately from the play as whole.

This evident inability to see a context behind an action does not stop at politics. I think it is part of our method of seeing life. Again, I will use the theatre as an example. Our critics will be inclined to see the hero of a play as a psychological figure, as an individual, a special case always, and their interest flags beyond that point. It is even said that, strictly speaking, it is not their business as to the larger significance of a character portrayed on the stage. They are present to discern whether he is interesting, logically formed, persuasive as a fiction, and so forth. The European, however, while interested in the character's manifest surface, is equally intent upon discovering what generality he represents. It is not the business of our critics to decide or most often to even discuss whether a play is built upon a tattered and outworn idea; if an old and worn idea is made to work on the stage once again in terms of effects and suspense and so forth, it is enough. In the European review one will inevitably find some estimate of the value of the concept behind the play. In other words, it is assumed to begin with that a thing is always made with an intention and that the intention is as important to evaluate as the effects it manages to create.

Thus it is that we find ourselves unable to meet the suspicions of Europeans in many situations, and find ourselves puzzled and even angered as a result. For instance, it is no secret to anyone in Europe that our borders are, in effect, sealed. And when, as happened recently, a writer of the eminence of Graham Greene is denied entry here for a visit in transit to the Far East, I am sure that most Americans cannot find the slightest patriotic interest in the situation. It happens that for a short time some decades ago, Mr. Greene, a converted Catholic, belonged to the Communist Party and has been an anti-Communist ever since. More importantly, his works are known around the world, and they are regarded by tens of thousands of people as sincere attempts to wrestle with some of the most serious moral and religious and ethical problems of this age. I can only ascribe his exclusion to a complete unwillingness, perhaps even an inability, to admit that Mr. Greene is not any Greene but a very particular Greene existing in a definite Red context; that being a writer of his stature is not a fact of any consequence but a politically important consideration; that for millions of people in the world his profession and the high seriousness with which he has practiced it lend him a certain dispensation, the dispensation of the truth-seeker; and finally, that to refuse him entry into this country implied that this country feared what he might see here. I am sure that given these considerations, our officials would reply that the law is the law; that a writer is only another name to them. Yet it is impossible not to conclude that the real interests of the United States, to say nothing of its dignity, are transgressed by such an action.

I believe that this attitude toward culture is a disservice to us all because it lays us open to extremely dangerous suspicions which can spread out to stain our whole effort to preserve the democratic idea in the world, especially when we have had to create so large a military machine. A display of force is always a generator of fear in others, whether it be in private or public, local or international affairs. We consent to the policeman's carrying a gun not because we have lost our fear of the bullet but because we have agreed to suspend that fear on the assurance that the policeman carrying it is acculturated with us, that he shares our values, that he holds high what we hold high. But at the same time he must be willing to use that gun, he must be psychologically able to commit violence if we are to believe in his protection, and his willingness to slay, if it is not securely hedged about by his very clearly displayed respect for our values, quickly becomes a fearful thing. It is no different with a nation which would convince the world of its peaceful intentions even as it is heavily armed and its troops are stationed around the world. In the final analysis a reliance on force is always a confession of moral defeat, but in the affairs of nations it is tragically necessary sometimes to confess that defeat and to gather and rely on force. But to forget even for a moment that only the most persuasively demonstrated belief in civilized values can keep the image of force from being distorted into a menacing image—to forget this is to invite the easy demolition of our efforts for peace.

To prove an assertion whose implications are so vast is impossible, yet I must say that in a very profound way the differences I have indicated in our attitudes toward culture itself have often made it possible for Russian propaganda to raise fear of us in foreign peoples.

In passing, I should like to touch for a moment on a minor but I think indicative paradox inherent here. A recent article in the *New York Times Magazine* on Russian education and another group of photographs in *Life* described the high seriousness of the Russian college students, their evident dedication to their work, a picture so intense as to throw up in the mind the counter-image of so many American students for whom college is quite another thing. Unless I am entirely mistaken, the same article and the same photographs would not appear extraordinary to the European. What would be strange to him and cause him to wonder on his community with us, would be pictures of some of the shenanigans indulged in by some of our students. What I am trying to indicate here again is that there are superficial differences in our attitudes to culture in his particular area which show us to be less intimately connected to the European than the Russian is. The same is true of our kind of theatre as contrasted with the German, let us say, and the Russian. I emphasize that the official attitude toward these manifestations of culture is extremely weighty outside this country. Yet the fact remains, and I believe it to be a demonstrable fact, that with all our absence of apparent awe, we have produced more than a decent quota of cultural works in the past two decades. The crucial importance of the image we cast in the world is not appreciated among us and in my opinion is one of the wounds through which the blood of our influence and our dignity is constantly seeping out. I go back once again to the image of our force. If our enormous power to destroy—and whatever else it is, military force is a destructive force—if we are content to allow it to appear in the hands of a people who make nothing of culture, who are content to appear solely as businessmen, technicians, and money-makers, we are handing to the Russian, who appears to make so much of culture, an advantage of regiments. And the further irony is that the serious Russian, both student and artist, has been so hamstrung by the tyrannical strictures on thought in his country, that his intellectual production has in recent years been brought to nearly a standstill excepting in those scientific pursuits connected with militarily valuable science. It is, in their case, an irony which does not escape the notice of the world; in fact, it is precisely their tyranny that has kept nations out of their grasp. I believe, in short, that if we could only recognize and admit to our successes in culture, if the policy of our government and our people toward the things of the mind and the spirit were especially conscious and made serious, we have at hand a means of coming into closer harmony with other people who at bottom share our basic values.

But lest I seem to advocate a new advertising campaign let me quickly correct the impression. To be sure, the object of a business or a nation in its relations with the world outside is to show its best qualities. More precisely, the obvious thing to do is to exhibit to the world whatever the world will most easily take to its heart for its own, those things which will make other peoples fear us less and love us more, those things with which they can identify themselves. For it is easier to misunderstand and hate that which seems alien and strange.

Our most popular, most widely seen cultural export is the American movie. It is a powerful convincer because hardly anybody in the world doesn't like to go to the movies. More importantly, however, it is spontaneously made, it appears without an ulterior political motive. So the man who sees it does so voluntarily and with his resistance down.

The trouble with the movies, however, is the same sort of trouble which Americans themselves often create when they go to Europe. Our movies draw the affections of people, their admiration, and envy for the opulence they generally portray, and also their disgust—as for instance, when a woman douses a cigarette in a perfectly good, uneaten, fried egg. At the same time, the movie star is beloved, his private life is followed with the interest long ago reserved for the minor gods. As such, we can only be glad so many foreigners like to see our pictures.

But even as we gain by them we lose something of tremendous importance. Most movies are admittedly and even proudly brainless. When you have as much destructive power as we do, it is of the first importance that the world be continuously made aware not merely of how silly we can be, and at times how vulgar, but of how deep an attachment the American people has for the nicest cultivation of humane values.

It is in our novels, our poems, our dance, our music, and some of our plays, primarily, that we can and do reveal a better preoccupation. Yet, I can say from personal experience and from the experiences of other writers, that the work of art in which we really examine ourselves, or which is critical of society, is not what this government regards as good propaganda. I am not aware, for instance, that the export of any comic book has been interfered with, but only recently a nonfiction book was refused a Congressional appropriation for inclusion in our overseas libraries because it showed a dust storm and a picture of an old-time country schoolhouse. In my opinion, it is not only not bad to show such things, nor bad to send our critical works around the world, but a necessity. For it is clearly one of our handicaps that we somehow insist at least officially that we have no inkling of a tragic sense of life. We posture before the world at times as though we had broken with the entire human race and had hold of a solution to the enigma of existence which was beyond questioning. As a dramatist I know that until the audience can identify itself with the people and the situations presented on the stage, it cannot be convinced of anything at all; it sits before an utterly incomprehensible play of shadows against an unseeable wall. Thus, when a work or an action or a speech or a declaration to the world is presented without a trace of decent humility before the unsolved problems of life, it is not only that we do not really reflect our real selves, but that we must inevitably alienate others. For the truth is that we have not discovered how to be happy and at one with ourselves, we have only gone far in abolishing physical poverty, which is but one single element in the solution. And by harping only on that, we in effect declare a want of spirituality, a want of human feeling, a want of sympathy in the end. I believe we have solutions for poverty which the world must eventually come to adopt or adapt to other conditions, and we are obligated to demonstrate always what we have accomplished, obligated not only to ourselves but to humanity which hungers for ways to organize production and create material wealth. But along with our success we have created a body of art, a body of literature which is markedly critical, which persists in asking certain human questions of the patterns we have created, and they are questions whose ultimate answers will prove or disprove our claims to having built a genuine civilization and not merely a collection of dominating inventions and bodily comforts. We are too often known abroad as dangerous children with toys that can explode the planet for us to go on pretending that we are not conscious of our underlying ethical and moral dilemmas.

It is no disgrace to search one's soul, nor the sign of fear. It is rather the first mark of honesty and the pool from which all righteousness flows. The strength of a Lincoln as he appeared in the eye of the world was not compounded of a time-bound mastery of military force alone, nor of an image monolithic and beyond the long reach of doubt. That man could lead and in our best moments leads us yet because he seemed to harbor in his soul an ever-renewing tear for his enemies and an indestructible desire to embrace them all. He commanded armies in the cruelest kind of war between brothers, yet his image is of a peaceful man. For even as history cast him as a destroyer of men, as every leader in war must always be, he seemed never to have lost that far-off gaze which cannot obliterate the tragic incompleteness of all wisdom and must fill with sympathy the space between what we know and what we have to do. For me, it is a reassuring thing that so much attention and appreciation is shown our novels and plays of high seriousness, for it signifies, I think, that others wish to see us more humanly and that the world is not as satisfied as we sometimes wish to appear that we have come to the end of all philosophy and wonderment about the meaning of life. It is dangerous to be rich in a world full of poverty. It is dangerous in obvious ways and in ways not so obvious.

During the war I worked for some time in the Brooklyn Navy Yard repairing and building ships for our fleet. The ships of many allied nations were often repaired there and we got to know many of the foreign crews. I remember one afternoon standing on the deck of a

British destroyer with a British sailor at my side, when alongside us an American destroyer was passing out into the harbor. It was a boiling hot summer day. As the American ship moved slowly beside us a sailor appeared on her deck and walked over to a water cooler on the deck and drank. On British destroyers a thirsty man went below to a tap and drank lukewarm water; when he bathed it was out of a portable basin, the same one he washed his clothes in. I glanced at the British seaman sweating on the deck beside me and I said, "That's what you guys ought to have, eh?" "Oh," he said, with an attempt at a sneer, "your ships are built for comfort." It was not that he couldn't bear the idea of ice water on a hot day. I feel reasonably sure he would not have joined a demonstration against the British Admiralty had a water cooler been installed on his deck. But the mere fact that we had coolers on our decks did not at once overwhelm him with a reverence for our superiority. The essential emotion in his mind was a defense of his own dignity and the dignity of his country in the face of what ought to have been a promising hope for himself but was taken as a challenge, if not a kind of injury to his own pride. I am not saying we ought not to have water coolers, either in our ideas or on our ships, but a foreign policy based solely on water coolers and water coolers alone may create as much envy, distrust, and even hatred as anything else. As a matter of fact, his deprivation he made into a positive virtue. It was common to hear Britishers say that their fleet was made to fight, unlike ours, that they had no comforts, no shower baths, plenty of cockroaches and what to us would be miserable food, because they had no time and ought to have no time, for anything but their guns, and because a ship of the fleet had no right to be anything but a floating gun platform. And finally, they convinced themselves that we couldn't hit anything anyway.

It is important for us to recall that there was a time not long ago when the positions were almost exactly reversed. It was the time of our frontier, the time when for the European, America was an uncomfortable place, without the amenities of his civilization. And at that time a stock situation in our plays and novels and our folklore was the conflict between the elegant but effete European or Englishman being outwitted or mocked or in some other way overcome morally by the inelegant, poor, roughhewn Yankee the mark of whose superiority was his relative poverty, an inability to spell, and a rugged, even primitive jealousy of his own independence. I was reminded of this irony by the latest novel of the aforementioned Graham Greene called *The Quiet*

American. This is the story of an American working in Asia for a cloak and dagger bureau in Washington, and his friendship and conflict with a British newspaperman. One is struck time and again by the Britisher's resentment of the American's precautions against disease or dirt—a veritable phobia of contamination—quite like the old literature in which the Englishman appears in tweeds and cap to shoot buffalo in the West, his sandwich hamper neat and ready, the napkin included. It is not merely the resentment which is important, but Greene's evident conviction that the American's relative wealth insulates him from any interest or insight into the realities around him, particularly the stubborn problem of the meanings of existence, meanings which transcend the victory over material want. And Greene reflects as well a kind of grudging admiration for the Asiatic Communists compared to the smooth-faced, naïve American, for the Communist, he says, knows how to talk to his fellow poor. In contrast, the Americans are prosperous and spiritually blank-eyed; they walk with the best of intentions in the impenetrable delusion that theirs is the only civilized way to live; in this book they walk in a closed circle outside of which the alien millions of the world, especially the poor, lead a life unknown and unknowable to them, and they are forced, the Americans are in this book, finally to rely upon devious policies of political opportunism and terroristic force. I will add that there is a pronounced quality of caricature in this book, a caricature which quite astounded me coming from the pen of Graham Greene. It is easy to cast a stone at him and walk away, but there it is, a book which evidently appears quite accurate to the British and presumably to the European, whose reviewers took no note of the caricature in it; the work of a man who has not shown himself to be a fool in the past and is surely not against democracy.

It is time, I think, for us to step back and with open eyes, and a dignified humility, to look at where we are. How does it come to pass that so successful a system and so free should so steadily lose its hold upon the hearts of men over a single decade, when its competition is a tyranny whose people live in comparative poverty and under the rule of men instead of law. Is it truly possible that everything can be laid to the success of Communist propaganda? If that is true, then I think the jig is up, for then history is truly made of words, and words that lie. But it is demonstrably untrue, for there has never been a Communist revolution in a country with parliamentary government, except for Czechoslovakia, which was a revolution under Russian bayonets. Nevertheless, there is a sense in the world that somehow we are helpless, except for our armament, against a positive ideology which moves forward as we stand still or move backward. The conviction grows, it seems, that we have nothing really to say that we haven't said, and nothing to do except to stand by our guns.

I would make certain simple and self-evident observations and leave the largest conclusions to you. There is a revolution going on every single day in this era. Sometimes it erupts only in North Africa, sometimes in Iran, sometimes in a less obvious way in Greece, sometimes in the heart of Africa itself. By and large the foreign policy of the United States has gone on the assumption that things ought to remain as they are. By and large we have adopted a posture of resistance to change and have linked our fate and our dignity and our idea of safety to those regimes and forces which are holding things down. It is as though the misery of most of the world would not exist had the Communists not given it a name. We have, in more ways than one, made them into magicians. We had a Point Four program. We were going to buy the friendship of peoples with a few hundred million dollars. But the basic conditions of misery, the basic setup under which this misery is perpetuated and will continue to be perpetuated—for this we have no official word. The deepest hope, and we must come to admit it, was that they would take our aid and stop shouting. As a consequence, even by our own admission, enormous amounts of our aid have made the rich richer, as in Greece, and the poor no better off. Nor is this entirely our fault in a technical sense. It is not our fault that thieves steal for themselves, but there is a possibility which lies in another direction, a possibility which costs money to realize, but in my view presents our one great hope. One, but only one element in it, involves our resolution as a people and as a government that abject poverty and human freedom cannot coexist in the world. It is the desperation born of poverty that makes freedom a luxury in men's minds. Were this country to place as the first object in its foreign policy a resolution, a call, a new dedication to the war on poverty, a new wind would, I think, begin to blow through the stifled atmosphere of international relations.

I believe such a program set at the very forefront of our work in the world would have not economic consequences alone, but ultimately political and institutional changes would occur. There ought to be in training here technicians and experts for loan wherever they are needed, an army of them ready to move into any land asking for them. We ought to be building as many atomic power reactors as we can build, and we ought to be offering them to any nation asking for them. And above all, we ought to make clear that there are no strings attached.

The objection will be that we have already tried this and what have we got in return? I say that we have not tried it unpolitically. In India, in Italy, in Greece and other places we have given aid on conditions of political fealty and there is no blinking that fact. We have said, in effect, your misery does not move our hearts if you do not believe as we do. I say that it is the peoples of the world more than their governments who must be reached and raised up, and if that is the aim, if the love of the American people and their sympathy is permitted to surround this aid, instead of the fear of the American people turning all help into a species of bribery, we shall have reason for hope. Nehru is not suspicious of America because we have given India help in the past but because we have withheld it at times and threatened to at others when he says something we don't like. We ought to make it absolutely clear to the world that we are precisely what has never been before, a nation devoting itself now to the international onslaught on poverty, a nation eager for change, not in fear of it. Certainly we shall be greeted with cynicism, but if we adopt cynicism we are falling into the trap set for us, as we so often have over the past ten years.

But along with economic and technical aid on a scale far beyond that of the past, our entire attitude toward cultural matters must be revolutionized. There ought to be an army of teachers in training here for foreign service, people who can teach languages, mathematics, science, and literature. We ought to appear in the world as the source and pool from which the nations may draw for the new age that is to come. Our own gates must be thrown open to the musicians, the players, the writers, the literature of these countries, and our own artists must be invited to perform wherever there is an audience for them. And what do we get in return? Nothing. Nothing but the slow, but I believe inevitable, understanding of the peoples of the world, nothing but the gradual awakening to the fact that we are not a fearful country, nor a country that knows all the answers, but a country with an understanding for the poor, a country which has such an abundance of materials and talents that it wishes to reach out its hand to others less favored.

But whatever the technical aspects of this approach, however difficult they may be to put into force, they are simple compared to the change in spirit required of us. I think the single most important alteration that has occurred among us since the second World War is an insidious infusion of cynicism. No more were we going to be naïve, not again taken in by large visions and give-aways and the whole social-worker, Rooseveltian panorama of idealism. We were dealing now with sharks and we must know how.

Yet, when was it that we held our undisputed moral leadership in the world? When did we start to lose it? It is simply no good laying the blame on Communist propaganda because it was no more wily after the war than before. We have lost sight of the context in which we are living. We have come to imagine that because there are two major powers there can only be one of two ways the social and economic organization of the world can materialize. But already there are three. There is Tito's Yugoslavia, striving to remain independent, trying to establish a kind of socialism and at the same time to put forth at least a root from which may grow a tradition of civil liberty. And there are four. There is India, insistent upon social planning and a high degree of government supervision of economic life, yet tolerant of private property and private business, but rejecting the American system of unrestricted private enterprise. And there are five, with Israel mixing completely socialized villages and farms with a private economy developing in the cities. And there will probably be six, seven, eight, or a dozen different combinations of social and economic forces in as many areas before the next decade is finished. Only one rule can guide us if we are to be wise, and it is, again, that misery does not breed freedom but tyranny.

We have long since departed from any attempt to befriend only democratic nations and not others. The police states included by us in what we call the Free World are too numerous to mention. The Middle East and certain states in South America are not noteworthy for their respect for civil rights, nor is Franco Spain or the Union of South Africa. All these states promise only one thing in common—an allegiance to the West. But if we are not to be taken in by our own propaganda we shall have to see that they have other less amiable traits in common. They are economically backward and their regimes have vested interests in backwardness. Why then do we include them in the Free World? Because they claim in common a hatred of socialism and a willingness to fight with our side in case of war. But what if there is not to be war in our generation? Then we have only collected deserts that might have been watered but were not.

This brings me to my final point and it is the most vital and the most debatable of all. I believe that the world has now arrived, not at a moment of decision, but two minutes later. When Russia exploded her atom bomb the decision of history was made, and it was that diplomacy based either on the fear or the confidence that the final decision would be made by war, is no longer feasible. I believe the arms stalemate is with us for an indefinite time to come, and that to base a foreign policy upon an ingathering of states willing to side with us in war is to defeat ourselves in the other contest, the main contest, the crucial contest. I believe that the recent shift of Russian emphasis to economic, social, and cultural penetration rather than revolutionary tactics issuing in ultimate war, is based on this new situation. I believe that literally the hands, or more precisely, the fists, of the nations are tied if they only knew it, and that it is their hearts and minds which are left with the struggle. I believe that in its own devious way history has placed the nations squarely in a moral arena from which there is no escape.

But the implications go even further. The whole concept of Russian-type socialism and American capitalism competing for the allegiance of mankind is going to fall apart. There will be no pure issue from this struggle. There will be so many mutations and permutations of both systems, that it will be impossible to untangle them and call them one or the other.

The danger, I believe, is that the Communist idea will, in fact, be able to accommodate itself to the new complexity, but that we shall not, because we shall have refused to see that great social changes can be anything but threats to us. The danger is that without our participation in the reorganization of the backward sections of the world, our central value, the dignity of the human being based upon a rule of law and civil liberty, will never become part of the movement of peoples striving to live better at any cost.

For that and that alone ought to be our mission in this world. There are many mansions not only in heaven but on earth. We have or ought to have but one interest, if only for our safety's sake, and it is to preserve the rights of man. That ought to be our star and none other. Our sole aim in the past ten years was the gathering in of states allied against the Soviet Union, preparing for an attack from that source. As from some fortress town of the Middle Ages, we have seen the world. But now as then history is making fortresses ridiculous, for the movement of man is outside and his fate is being made outside. It is being made on his farm, in his hut, in the streets of his cities, and in his factories.

In the period of her so-called naïveté, America held the allegiance of people precisely because she was not cynical, because her name implied love and faith in people, and because she was the common man's country. In later years we have gone about forgetting our simplicity while a new ideology has risen to call for justice, however cynically, and imparting the idea that Russia stood for the working man. Meanwhile in a small voice we have spoken of justice and in a big voice of arms and armaments, wars and the rumors of wars. Now we must face ourselves and ask—what if there is to be no more war? What is in us that the world must know of? When we find this, the essence of America, we shall be able to forge a foreign policy capable of arousing the hopes and the love of the only force that matters anymore, the force that is neither in governments nor armies nor banks nor institutions, the force that rests in the heart of man. When we come to address ourselves to this vessel of eternal unrest and eternal hope, we shall once again be on our way.

Problems of the Theatre

BY FRIEDRICH DUERRENMATT

BEHOLD THE DRIVE FOR PURITY in art as art is practiced these days. Behold this writer striving for the purely poetic, another for the purely lyrical, the purely epic, the purely dramatic. The painter ardently seeks to create the pure painting, the musician pure music, and someone even told me, pure radio represents the synthesis between Dionysos and Logos. Even more remarkable for our time, not otherwise renowned for its purity, is that each and every one believes he has found his unique and the only true purity. Each vestal of the arts has, if you think of it, her own kind of chastity. Likewise, too numerous to count, are all the theories of the theatre, of what is pure theatre, pure tragedy, pure comedy. There are so many modern theories of the drama, what with each playwright keeping three or four at hand, that for this reason, if no other, I am a bit embarrassed to come along now with my theories of the problems of the theatre.

Furthermore, I would ask you not to look upon me as the spokesman of some specific movement in the theatre or of a certain dramatic technique, nor to believe that I knock at your door as the traveling salesman of one of the philosophies current on our stages today, whether as existentialist, nihilist, expressionist or satirist, or any other label put on the compote dished up by literary criticism. For me, the stage is not a battlefield for theories, philosophies and manifestos, but rather an instrument whose possibilities I seek to know by playing with it. Of course, in my plays there are people and they hold to some belief or

---

This version of *Problems of the Theatre* was prepared for publication (Vlg. der Arche, Zurich, 1955) from the manuscript of a lecture delivered by Friedrich Duerrenmatt in the fall of 1954 and the spring of 1955 in different cities of Switzerland and West Germany.

philosophy—a lot of blockheads would make for a dull piece—but my plays are not for what people have to say: what is said is there because my plays deal with people, and thinking and believing and philosophizing are all, to some extent at least, a part of human nature. The problems I face as playwright are practical, working problems, problems I face not before, but during the writing. To be quite accurate about it, these problems usually come up after the writing is done, arising out of a certain curiosity to know how I did it. So what I would like to talk about now are these problems, even though I risk disappointing the general longing for something profound and creating the impression that an amateur is talking. I haven't the faintest notion of how else I should go about it, of how not to talk about art like an amateur. Consequently I speak only to those who fall asleep listening to Heidegger.

What I am concerned with are empirical rules, the possibilities of the theatre. But since we live in an age when literary scholarship and criticism flourish, I can not quite resist the temptation of casting a few side glances at some of the theories of the art and practice of the theatre. The artist indeed has no need of scholarship. Scholarship derives laws from what exists already; otherwise it would not be scholarship. But the laws thus established have no value for the artist, even when they are true. The artist can not accept a law he has not discovered for himself. If he can not find such a law, scholarship can not help him with one it has established; and when the artist does find one, then it does not matter that the same law was also discovered by scholarship. But scholarship, thus denied, stands behind the artist like a threatening ogre, ready to leap forth whenever the artist wants to talk about art. And so it is here. To talk about problems of the theatre is to enter into competition with literary scholarship. I undertake this with some misgivings. Literary scholarship looks on the theatre as an object; for the dramatist it is never something purely objective, something separate from him. He participates in it. It is true that the playwright's activity makes drama into something objective (that is exactly his job), but he destroys the object he has created again and again, forgets it, rejects it, scorns it, overestimates it, all in order to make room for something new. Scholarship sees only the result; the process, which led to this result, is what the playwright can not forget. What he says has to be taken with a grain of salt. What he thinks about his art changes as he creates his art; his thoughts are always subject to his mood and the moment. What alone really counts for him is what he is doing at a given moment; for its sake he can betray what he did just a little while ago. Perhaps a writer should not talk about his art, but once he starts, then it is not altogether a waste of time to listen to him. Literary scholars who have not the faintest notion of the difficulties of writing and of the hidden rocks that force the stream of art into oft unsuspected channels run the danger of merely asserting and stupidly proclaiming laws that do not exist.

Doubtless the unities of time, place and action which Aristotle—so it was supposed for a long time—derived from Greek tragedy constitute the ideal of drama. From a logical and hence also esthetic point of view, this thesis is incontestable, so incontestable indeed, that the question arises if it does not set up the framework once and for all within which each dramatist must work. Aristotle's three unities demand the greatest precision, the greatest economy and the greatest simplicity in the handling of the dramatic material. The unities of time, place and action ought to be a basic dictate put to the dramatist by literary scholarship, and the only reason scholarship does not hold the artist to them is that Aristotle's unities have not been obeyed by anyone for ages. Nor can they be obeyed, for reasons which best illustrate the relationship of the art of writing plays to the theories about that art.

The unities of time, place and action in essence presuppose Greek tragedy. Aristotle's unities do not make Greek tragedy possible; rather, Greek tragedy allows his unities. No matter how abstract an esthetic law may appear to be, the work of art from which it was derived is contained in that law. If I want to set about writing a dramatic action which is to unfold and run its course in the same place inside of two hours, for instance, then this action must have a history behind it, and that history will be the more extensive the fewer the number of stage characters there are at my disposal. This is simply an experience of how the theatre works, an empirical rule. For me a history is the story which took place before the stage action commenced, a story which alone makes the action on the stage possible. Thus the history behind Hamlet is, of course, the murder of his father; the drama lies in the discovery of that murder. As a rule, too, the stage action is much shorter in time than the event depicted; it often starts out right in the middle of the event, or indeed toward the end of it. Before Sophocles' tragedy could begin, Oedipus had to have killed his father and married his mother, activities that take a little time. The stage action must compress an event to the same degree in which it fulfills the demands of Aristotle's unities. And the closer a playwright adheres to the three unities, the more important is the background history of the action.

It is, of course, possible to invent a history and hence a dramatic action that would seem particularly favorable for keeping to Aristotle's unities. But this brings into force the rule that the more invented a story is and the more unknown it is to the audience, the more careful must its exposition, the unfolding of the background be. Greek tragedy was possible only because it did not have to invent its historical background, because it already possessed one. The spectators knew the myths with which each drama dealt; and because these myths were public, ready coin, part of religion, they made the feats of the Greek tragedians possible, feats never to be attained again; they made possible their abbreviations, their straightforwardness, their stichomythia and choruses, and hence also Aristotle's unities. The audience knew what the play was all about; its curiosity was not focused on the story so much as on its treatment. Aristotle's unities presupposed the general appreciation of the subject matter—a genial exception in more recent times is Kleist's *The Broken Jug*—presupposed a religious theatre based on myths. Therefore as soon as the theatre lost its religious, its mythical significance, the unities had to be reinterpreted or discarded. An audience facing an unknown story will pay more attention to the story than to its treatment, and by necessity then such a play has to be richer in detail and circumstances than one with a known action. The feats of one playwright can not be the feats of another. Each art exploits the chances offered by its time, and it is hard to imagine a time without chances. Like every other form of art, drama creates its world; but not every world can be created in the same fashion. This is the natural limitation of every esthetic rule, no matter how self-evident such a rule may be. This does not mean that Aristotle's unities are obsolete; what was once a rule has become an exception, a case that may occur again at any time. The one-act play obeys the unities still, even though under a different condition. Instead of the history, the situation now dominates the plot, and thus unity is once again achieved.

But what is true for Aristotle's theory of drama, namely its dependency upon a certain world and hence its validity relative to that world, is also true of every other theory of drama. Brecht is consistent only when he incorporates into his dramaturgy that *Weltanschauung,* the communist philosophy, to which he—so he seems to think—is committed; but in doing so he often cuts off his own nose. Sometimes his plays say the very opposite of what they claim they say, but this lack of agreement can not always be blamed on the capitalistic audience. Often it is simply a case where Brecht, the poet, gets the better of Brecht, the dramatic theorist, a situation that is wholly legitimate and ominous only were it not to happen again.

Let us speak plainly. My introducing the audience as a factor in the making of a play may have seemed strange to many. But just as it is impossible to have theatre without spectators, so it is senseless to consider and treat a play as if it were a kind of ode, divided into parts and delivered in a vacuum. A piece written for the theatre becomes living theatre when it is played, when it can be seen, heard, felt, and thus experienced immediately. This immediacy is one of the most essential aspects of the theatre, a fact so often overlooked in those sacred halls where a play by Hofmannsthal counts for more than one by Nestroy, and a Richard Strauss opera more than one by Offenbach. A play is an event, is something that happens. In the theatre everything must be transformed into something immediate, something visible and sensible; the corollary to this thought, however, is that not everything can be translated into something immediate and corporeal. Kafka, for example, really does not belong on the stage. The bread offered there gives no nourishment; it lies undigested in the iron stomachs of the theatre-going public and the regular subscribers. As luck would have it, many think of the heaviness they feel not as a stomach ache, but as the heaviness of soul which Kafka's true works emanate, so that by error all is set aright.

The immediacy sought by every play, the spectacle into which it would be transformed, presupposes an audience, a theatre, a stage. Hence we would also do well to examine the theatres for which we have to write today. We all know these money-losing enterprises. They can, like so many other institutions today, be justified only on an idealistic basis: in reality, not at all. The architecture of our theatres, their seating arrangements and their stages, came down from the court theatre or, to be more precise, never got beyond it. For this reason alone, our so-called contemporary theatre is not really contemporary. In contrast to the primitive Shakespearean stage, in contrast to this "scaffold" where, as Goethe put it, "little was shown, everything signified," the court theatre made every effort to satisfy a craving for naturalness, even though this resulted in much greater unnaturalness. No longer was the audience satisfied to imagine the royal chamber behind the "green curtain"; every attempt was made to show the chamber. Characteristic of such theatre is its tendency to separate audience and stage, by means both of the curtain as well as having the spectators sit in the dark facing a well-lit stage. This latter innovation was perhaps the most treacherous of all, for it alone made possible the solemn atmosphere in which our theatres suffocate. The stage became a peep show. Better lighting was constantly invented, then a revolving stage, and it is said they have even invented a revolving house! The courts went, but the court theatre stayed on. Now to be sure, our time has discovered its own form of theatre, the movies. But no matter how much we may emphasize the differences, and how important it may be to emphasize them, still it must be pointed out that the movies grew out of theatre, and that they can at last achieve what the court theatre with all its machinery, revolving stages and other effects only dreamed of doing: to simulate reality.

The movies, then, are nothing more nor less than the democratic form of the court theatre. They intensify our sense of intimacy immeasurably, so much so that the movies easily risk becoming the genuinely pornographic art. For the spectator is forced into being a "voyeur," and movie stars enjoy their immense popularity because those who see them come also to feel that they have slept with them; that is how well movie stars are photographed. A larger-than-life picture is an indecency.

Just what then is our present-day theatre? If the movies are the modern form of the old court theatre, what is the theatre? There is no use in pretending that the theatre today is anything much more than a museum in which the art treasures of former golden ages of the drama are put on exhibition. There is no way of changing that. It is only too natural at a time like ours, a time which, always looking toward the past, seems to possess everything but a living present. In Goethe's time the ancients were rarely performed, Schiller occasionally, but mostly Kotzebue and whoever else they were. It is worthwhile to point out that the movies preempt the theatre of its Kotzebues and Birch-Pfeiffers, and it is hard to imagine what sort of plays would have to be put on today, if there were no movies and if all the scriptwriters wrote for the legitimate stage.

If the contemporary theatre is to a large extent a museum, then this has definite effects on the actors which it employs. They have become civil servants, usually even entitled to their pensions, permitted to act in the theatre when not kept busy making movies. The members of this once despised estate have settled down now as solid citizens—a human gain, an artistic loss. And today actors fit into the order of professional rank somewhere between the physicians and small industrialists, surpassed within the realm of art only by the winners of the Nobel prize, by pianists and conductors. Some actors are visiting professors of sorts, or independent scholars, who take their turn appearing in the museums or arranging exhibitions. The management, of course, takes this into account when it arranges its playbill more or less with an eye to its guest-stars; says the management: what play should we put on when this or that authority in this or that field is available to us at such and such a date? Moreover actors are forced to move about in many different acting styles, now in a baroque style, now in a classical one, today acting naturalism, tomorrow Claudel. An actor in Molière's day did not have to do that. The director, too, is more important, more dominant than ever, like the conductor of an orchestra. Historical works demand, and ought to demand, proper interpretation; but directors as yet dare not be as true to the works they put on as some conductors are quite naturally to theirs. The classics often are not interpreted but executed, and the curtain falls upon a mutilated corpse. But then, where is the danger in it all? There is always the saving convention by which all classical things are accepted as perfection, as a kind of gold standard in our cultural life, with all things looked upon as gold that shine in Modern Library or Temple classics. The theatre-going public goes to see the classics, whether they be performed well or not; applause is assured, indeed is the duty of the educated man. And thus the public has legitimately been relieved of the task of thinking and of passing judgments other than those learned by rote in school.

Yet there is a good side to the many styles the present-day theatre must master, although it may at first glance appear bad. Every great age of the theatre was possible because of the discovery of a unique form of theatre, of a particular style, which determined the way plays were written. This is easily demonstrable in the English or Spanish theatre, or the Vienna National Theatre, the most remarkable phenomenon in the German-speaking theatre. This alone can explain the astounding number of plays written by Lope de Vega. Stylistically a play was no problem for him. But to the degree that a uniform style of theatre does not exist today, indeed can no longer exist, to that extent is writing for the theatre now a problem and thus more difficult. Therefore our contemporary theatre is two things: on one hand it is a museum, on the other an experimental field, each play confronting the author with new challenges, new questions of style. Yes, style today is no longer a common property, but highly private, even particularized from case to case. We have no style, only styles, which puts the situation in art today in a nutshell. For contemporary art is a series of experiments, nothing more nor less, just like all of our modern world.

If there are only styles, then, too, we have only theories of the art and practice of the theatre, and no longer one dramaturgy. We now have Brecht's and Eliot's, Claudel's and that of Frisch or of Hochwaelder: always a new theory of drama for each dramatic offering. Nevertheless one can conceive of a single theory of drama, a theory that would cover all particular instances, much in the same way that we have worked out a geometry which embraces all dimensions. Aristotle's theory of drama would be only one of many possible theories in this dramaturgy. It would have to be a new *Poetics*, which would examine the possibilities not of a certain stage, but of the stage, a dramaturgy of the experiment itself.

What, finally, might we say about the audience without which, as we have said before, no theatre is possible? The audience has become anonymous, just "the paying public," a matter far worse than first strikes the eye. The modern author no longer knows his public, unless he writes for some village stage or Caux, neither of which is much fun. A playwright has to imagine his audience; but in truth the audience is he himself—and this is a danger which can neither be altered now nor circumvented. All the dubious, well-worn, politically misused notions which attach themselves to the concepts of "a people" and "society," to say nothing of "a community," have perforce also crept into the theatre. What points is an author to make? How is he to find his subjects, what solutions should he reach? All these are questions for which we may perhaps find an answer once we have gained a clearer notion as to what possibilities still exist in the theatre today.

In undertaking to write a play I must first make clear to myself just where it is to take place. At first glance that does not seem like much of a problem. A play takes place in London or Berlin, in the mountains, a hospital or on a battlefield, wherever the action demands. But it does not work out quite that way. A play, after all, takes place upon a stage which in turn must represent London, the mountains or a battlefield. This distinction need not, but can be made. It depends entirely on how much the author takes the stage into account, how strongly he wants to create the illusion without which no theatre can exist, and whether he wants it smeared on thickly with gobs of paint heaped upon the canvas, or transparent, diaphanous and fragile. A playwright can be deadly serious about the place: Madrid, the Ruetli, the Russian steppe, or he can think of it as just a stage, the world, his world.

How the stage is to represent a given place is, of course, the task of the scene designer. Since designing scenes is a form of painting, the developments which have taken place in painting in our time have not failed to touch the theatre. But the theatre can really neither abstract man nor language, which is in itself both abstract and concrete, and scenery, no matter how abstract it would pretend to be, must still represent something concrete to make sense, and for both of these reasons, abstraction in scenic design has essentially failed. Nevertheless the "green curtain" behind which the spectators have to imagine the place, the royal chamber, was reinstituted. The fact was recalled that the dramatic place and the stage were not one and the same, no matter how elaborate, how verisimilar the stage setting might be. The fact is the place has to be created by the play. One word: we are in Venice; another: in the Tower of London. The imagination of the audience needs but little support. Scenery is to suggest, point out, intensify, but not describe the place. Once more it has become transparent, immaterialized. And similarly the place of the drama to be shown on the stage can be made immaterial.

Two fairly recent plays which most clearly illustrate the possibility referred to as immaterializing the scenery and the dramatic place are Wilder's *Our Town* and *The Skin of Our Teeth*. The immaterializing of the stage in *Our Town* consists of this: the stage is nearly empty; only a few objects needed for rehearsals stand about—some chairs, tables, ladders and so on; and out of these everyday objects the place is created, the dramatic place, the town, all out of the word, the play, the wakened imagination of the spectators. In his other play Wilder, this great fanatic of the theatre, immaterializes the dramatic place: where the Antrobus family really lives, in what age and what stage of civilization, is never wholly clear; now it is the ice age, now a world war. This sort of experiment may be met quite often in modern drama; thus it is indefinite where in Frisch's play, *Graf Oederland,* the strange Count Wasteland abides; no man knows where to wait for Godot, and in *The Marriage of Milord Mississippi* (*Die Ehe des Herrn Mississippi*) I expressed the indefiniteness of the locale (in order to give the play its spirit of wit, of comedy) by having the right window of a room look out upon a northern landscape with its Gothic cathedral and apple tree, while the left window of the same room opens on a southern scene with an ancient ruin, a touch of the Mediterranean and a cypress. The really decisive point in all this is that, to quote Max Frisch, the playwright is making poetry with the stage, a possibility which has always entertained and occupied me and which is one of the reasons, if not the main one, why I write plays. But then—and I am thinking of the comedies of Aristophanes and the comic plays of Nestroy—in every age poetry has been written not only *for,* but *with* the stage.

Let us turn from these incidental problems to more basic ones. What do the particular problems look like, which I—to cite an author whom I know at least to some, though not the whole extent—have faced? In *The Blind Man* (*Der Blinde*) I wanted to juxtapose the word against the dramatic place, to turn the word against the scene. The blind duke believes he is living in his well-preserved castle whereas he is living in a ruin; he thinks he is humbling himself before Wallenstein, but sinks to his knees before a Negro. The dramatic place is one and the same, but by means of the pretense carried on before the blind man, it plays a dual role: the place seen by the audience and the place in which the blind man fancies himself to be. So also, when in my comedy, *An Angel Comes to Babylon* (*Ein Engel kommt nach Babylon*), I picked for my dramatic locale the city in which the Tower was built, I had essentially to solve two problems. In the first place the stage had to express the fact that there were two places of action in my comedy, heaven and the city of Babylon; heaven, which was the secret point of origin of the action, and Babylon the locale, where that action ran its course.

Well, I suppose heaven could have been simply represented by a dark background to suggest its infinity, but since I wanted to convey in my comedy the idea that heaven was not something infinite, but something incomprehensible and altogether different, I asked for the stage background, the heaven above the city of Babylon, to be occupied entirely by the Great Nebula in Andromeda, just as we might see it through the telescope on Mt. Palomar. What I hoped to achieve thereby was that heaven, the incomprehensible and inscrutable, would take on form, gain, as it were, its own stage presence. In this wise also heaven's rapprochement with the earth was to be brought out, reiterating the coming together of the two that is expressed in the action through the angel's visiting Babylon. Thus, too, a world was constructed in which the result of the action, namely the building of the tower of Babylon, became possible.

In the second place I had to think of how to make the stage represent Babylon, the place in which the action unfolds. I found the idea of Babylon challenging because of its timeliness, its Cyclopean big-city character, its New-York-look with its skyscrapers and slums, and by having the first two acts take place along the banks of the Euphrates I wished to hint at Paris. Babylon, in brief, stands for the metropolis. It is a Babylon of the imagination, having a few typically Babylonian features, but as a modernized parodied version, with its modernities— for instance the convenience of electric street-lights. Of course the execution of the scenery, the building of the stage itself, is a job for the scene designer, but the playwright must always decide himself just what kind of stage he wants.

I love a colorful stage setting, a colorful theatre, like the stage of Theo Otto, to mention an admirable example. I have little use for a theatre that uses black curtains as was the fashion once upon a time, or for the tendency to glory in threadbare poverty which some stage designers seem to aim for. To be sure the word is important above all else in the theatre; but note: above all else. For after the word there are many other things, which also rightfully belong to the theatre, even a certain wantonness. Thus when someone asked me quite thoughtfully with respect to my play *Mississippi*, where one of the characters enters through a grandfather's clock, whether or not I thought a four-dimensional theatre possible, I could only remark that I had not thought of Einstein when I did it. It is just that in my daily life it should give me great pleasure if I could enter into a company and astonish those present by coming into the room through a grandfather's clock or by floating in through a window. No one should deny us playwrights the opportunity to satisfy such desires now and then at least on the stage, where such whims can be fulfilled. The old argument of which came first, the chicken or the egg, can be transformed in art into the question of whether the egg or the chicken, the world as potential or as rich harvest, is to be presented. Artists might very well be divided then into those favoring the egg and those favoring the chicken. The argument is a lively one. Alfred Polgar once said to me, it was odd that while in the contemporary Anglo-Saxon drama everything came out in the dialogue, there was always much too much happening on the stage in my plays and that he, Polgar, would sometimes like to see a simple Duerrenmatt play. Behind this truth, however, lies my refusal to say that the egg came before the chicken, and my personal prejudice of preferring the chicken to the egg. It happens to be my passion, not always a happy one perhaps, to want to put on the stage the richness, the manifold diversity of the world. As a result my theatre is open to many interpretations and appears to confuse some. Misunderstandings creep in, as when someone looks around desperately in the chicken coop of my plays, hoping to find the egg of Columbus which I stubbornly refuse to lay.

But a play is bound not only to a place, but also to a time. Just as the stage represents a place, so it also represents a time, the time *during* which the action takes place as well as the time *in* which it occurs. If Aristotle had really demanded the unity of time, place and action, he would have limited the duration of a tragedy to the time it took for the action to be carried out (a feat which the Greek tragedians nearly achieved), for which reasons, of course, everything would have to be concentrated upon that action. Time would pass "naturally," everything coming one after the other without breaks. But this does not always have to be the case. In general the actions on the stage follow one another but, to cite an example, in Nestroy's magical farce, *Death on the Wedding Day* (*Der Tod am Hochzeitstag*), there are two acts taking place simultaneously and the illusion of simultaneity is skillfully achieved by having the action of the second act form the background noise for the first, and the action of the first act the background noise for the second. Other examples of how time is used as a theatrical device could be easily recalled. Time can be shortened, stretched, intensified, arrested, repeated; the dramatist can, like Joshua, call to his heaven's orbits, "Theatre-Sun, stand thou still upon Gibeon! And thou, Theatre-Moon, in the valley of Ajalon!"

It may be noted further that the unities ascribed to Aristotle were not wholly kept in Greek tragedy either. The action is interrupted by the choruses, and by this means time is spaced. When the chorus interrupts the action, it achieves as regards time—to elucidate the obvious like an amateur—the very same thing the curtain does today. The curtain cuts up and spreads out the time of an action. I have nothing against such an honorable device. The good thing about a curtain is that it so clearly defines an act, that it clears the table, so to speak. Moreover it is psychologically often extremely necessary to give the exhausted and frightened audience a rest. But a new way of binding language and time has evolved in our day.

If I cite Wilder's *Our Town* once again, I do so because I assume that this fine play is widely known. You may recall that in it different characters turn toward the audience and talk of the worries and needs of their small town. In this way Wilder is able to dispense with the curtain. The curtain has been replaced by the direct address to the audience. The epic element of description has been added to the drama. For this reason, of course, this form of theatre has been called the epic theatre.

Yet when looked at quite closely, Shakespeare's plays or Schiller's *Goetz von Berlichingen* are in a certain sense also epic theatre. Only in a different, less obvious manner. Since Shakespeare's histories often extend over a considerable period of time, this time span is divided into different actions, different episodes, each of which is treated dramatically. *Henry IV, Part I,* consists of nineteen such episodes, while by the end of the fourth act of *Goetz* there already are no less than forty-one tableaux. I stopped counting after that. If one looks at the way the over-all action has been built up, then, with respect to time, it is quite close to the epic, like a movie that is run too slowly, so that the individual frames can be seen. The condensation of everything into a certain time has been given up in favor of an episodic form of drama.

Thus when an author in some of our modern plays turns toward the audience, he attempts to give the play a greater continuity than is otherwise possible in an episodic form. The void between the acts is to be filled; the time gap is to be bridged, not by a pause, but by words, by a description of what has gone on in the meanwhile, or by having some new character introduce himself. In other words, the expositions are handled in an epic manner, not the actions to which these expositions lead. This represents an advance of the word in the theatre, the attempt of the word to reconquer territory lost a long time ago. Let us emphasize that it is but an attempt; for all too often the direct address to the audience is used to explain the play, an undertaking that makes no sense whatever. If the audience is moved by the play, it will not need prodding by explanations; if the audience is not moved, all the prodding in the world will not be of help.

In contrast to the epic, which can describe human beings as they are, the drama unavoidably limits and therefore stylizes them. This limitation is inherent in the art form itself. The human being of the drama is, after all, a talking individual, and speech is his limitation. The action only serves to force this human being on the stage to talk in a certain way. The action is the crucible in which the human being is molten into words, must become words. This, of course, means that I, as the playwright, have to get the people in my drama into situations which force them to speak. If I merely show two people sitting together and drinking coffee while they talk about the weather, politics or the latest fashions, then I provide neither a dramatic situation nor dramatic dialogue, no matter how clever their talk. Some other ingredient must be added to their conversation, something to add pique, drama, double meaning. If the audience knows that there is some poison in one of the coffee cups, or perhaps even in both, so that the conversation is really one between two poisoners, then this little coffee-for-two idyl becomes through this artistic device a dramatic situation, out of which and on the basis of which dramatic dialogue can develop. Without the addition of some special tension or special condition, dramatic dialogue can not develop.

Just as dialogue must develop out of a situation, so it must also lead into some situation, that is to say, of course, a new situation. Dramatic dialogue effects some action, some suffering, some new situation, out of which in turn new dialogue can again develop, and so on and so forth.

However, a human being does more than just talk. The fact that a man also thinks, or at least should think, that he feels, yes, more than anything feels, and that he does not always wish to show others what he is thinking or feeling, has led to the use of another artistic device, the monologue. It is true, of course, that a person standing on a stage and carrying on a conversation with himself out loud is not exactly natural; and the same thing can be said, only more so, of an operatic aria. But the monologue (like the aria) proves that an artistic trick, which really ought not be played, can achieve an unexpected effect, to which, and rightly so, the public succumbs time and again; so much so that Hamlet's monologue, "To be or not to be," or Faust's, are among the most beloved and most famous passages in the theatre.

But not everything that sounds like a monologue is monologue. The purpose of dialogue is not only to lead a human being to a point where he must act or suffer, but at times it also leads into a major speech, to the explanation of some point of view. Many people have lost the appreciation of rhetoric since, as Hilpert maintains, some actor who was not sure of his lines discovered naturalism. That loss is rather sad. A speech can win its way across the footlights more effectively than any other artistic device. But many of our critics no longer know what to make of a speech. An author, who today dares a speech, will suffer the same fate as the peasant Dicaeopolis; he will have to lay his head upon the executioner's block. Except that instead of the Acharnians of Aristophanes, it will be the majority of critics who descend on the author—the most normal thing in the world. Nobody is more anxious to bash out someone's brains than those who haven't any.

Moreover, the drama has always embodied some narrative elements; epic drama did not introduce this. So, for instance, the background of an action has always had to be related, or an event announced in the form of a messenger's report. But narration on the stage is not without its dangers, for it does not live in the same manner, is not tangible the way an action taking place on the stage is. Attempts have been made to overcome this, as by dramatizing the messenger, by letting him appear at a crucial moment, or by making him a blockhead from whom a report can only be extracted with great difficulties. Yet certain elements of rhetoric must still be present if narration is to succeed on the stage. Stage narratives can not exist without some exaggeration. Observe, for instance, how Shakespeare elaborates on Plutarch's description of Cleopatra's barge. This exaggeration is not just a characteristic of the baroque style, but a means of launching Cleopatra's barge upon the stage, of making it visible there. But while the speech of the theatre can not exist without exaggeration, it is important to know when to exaggerate and above all, how.

Furthermore, just as the stage characters can suffer a certain fate, so also their language. The angel that came to Babylon, for example, grows more and more enthusiastic about the earth's beauty from act to act, and hence his language must parallel this rising enthusiasm until it grows into a veritable hymn. In the same comedy the beggar Akki relates his life in a series of *makamat*, passages of a rich and stately prose interspersed with rhymes, refined in grammar, rhetoric, poetic idiom and tradition, that come from the Arabic and flourished a thousand years ago. In this way I try to convey the Arabic character of this personage, his joy in inventing stories and in duelling and playing with words, without at the same time wandering off into another form, the chanson. The *makamat* or anecdotes of Akki are nothing less than the most extreme possibilities offered by his language, and therefore they intensify his being. Through the *makamat* Akki has become all language and this is just what an author must always strive for, so that there are moments in his plays in which the characters he has created with the written word become living language and nothing less.

A danger lurks here, too, of course. Language can lead a writer astray. The joy of being able all of a sudden to write, of possessing language, as it came over me, for instance, while I was writing *The Blind Man*, can make an author talk too much, can make him escape from his subject into language. To keep close to the subject is itself a great art, achieved only by masterful control of the impetus to talk. Dialogue, like playing on words, can also lead an author into byways, take him unawares away from his subject. Yet ideas flash into his mind again and again, ideas which he ought not resist, even if they disrupt his carefully laid plans. For in addition to being on guard against some of these tempting flashes of ideas, a writer must also have the courage to follow some of them.

These elements and problems of place, time, and action, which are all, of course, interwoven and are but hinted at here, belong to the basic material, to the artistic devices and tools of the craft of the drama. But let me make it clear here and now, that I make war upon the notion of "the craft of the drama." The very idea that anyone who makes a sufficiently diligent and steadfast endeavor to achieve something in that art will succeed in the end or even that this craft can be learned is a notion we thought discarded long ago. Yet it is still frequently met with in critical writings about the art of play-writing. This art is supposed to be a sound-and-solid, respectable and well-mannered affair. Thus, too, the relationship between a playwright and his art is considered by some to be like a marriage in which everything is quite legal when blessed with the sacraments of esthetics. For these reasons, perhaps, critics often refer to the theatre, much more than to any other form of art, as a craft which, depending on the particular case, has been more or less mastered. If we investigate closely what the critics really mean by "the craft of the drama," then it becomes obvious that it is little else but the sum of their prejudices. There is no craft of the theatre; there is only the mastery of the material through language and the stage or, to be more exact, it is an overpowering of the material, for any creative writing is a kind of warfare with its victories, defeats and indecisive battles. Perfect plays do not exist except as a fiction of esthetics in which, as in the movies, perfect heroes may alone be found. Never yet has a playwright left this battle without his wounds; each one has his Achilles' heel, and the playwright's antagonist, his material, never fights fairly. It is cunning stuff, often not to be drawn out of its lair, and it employs highly secret and low-down tricks. This forces the playwright to fight back with every permissible and even non-permissible means, no matter what the wise exhortations, rules and adages of the masters of this craft and their most honored trade may say. Best foot forward won't get an author anywhere in the drama, not even his foot in the doorway. The difficulties in writing for the drama lie where no one suspects them; sometimes it is no more than the problem of how to have two people say hello, or the difficulty in writing an opening sentence. What is sometimes considered to be the craft of the drama can be easily learned inside half an hour. But how difficult it is to divide a given material into five acts and how few subjects there are which can be divided that way, how nearly impossible it is to write today in iambic pentameter, those things are hardly ever suspected by the hack writers who can slap a play together anytime and without trouble, who can always divide any subject into five acts, and who have always written and still write with facility in iambic pentameter. They really pick their material and their language in the way some critics think this is done. They are not so much amateurs when they talk about art as when they tailor art to their talk. No matter what the material is like, they always fashion the same bathrobe to be sure the audience will not catch cold and that it will sleep comfortably. There is nothing more idiotic than the opinion that only a genius does not have to obey those rules prescribed for writers of talent. In that case I should like to be counted among the geniuses. What I want to emphasize strongly is that the art of writing a play does not necessarily start out with the planning of a certain child, or however else a eunuch thinks love is made; but it starts out with lovemaking of which a eunuch is incapable. Though really the difficulties, pains and also fortunes of writing do not lie within the realm of things we mean to talk about or even can talk about. We can only talk about the craft of the drama, a craft that exists only when one *talks* of drama, but not when one writes plays. The craft of the drama is an optical illusion. To talk about plays, about art, is a much more utopian undertaking than is ever appreciated by those who talk the most.

Employing this—really non-existent—craft, let us try and give shape to a certain material. Usually there is a central point of reference, the hero. In theories of the drama a difference is made between a tragic hero, the hero of tragedy, and a comic hero, the hero of comedy. The qualities a tragic hero must possess are well known. He must be capable of rousing our sympathy. His guilt and his innocence, his virtues and his vices must be mixed in the most pleasant and yet exact manner, and administered in doses according to well-defined rules. If, for example, I make my tragic hero an evil man, then I must endow him with a portion of intellect equal to his malevolence. As a result of this rule, the most sympathetic stage character in German literature has turned out to be the devil. The role of the hero in the play has not changed. The only thing that has changed is the social position of the character who awakens our sympathy.

In ancient tragedy and in Shakespeare the hero belongs to the highest class in society, to the nobility. The spectators watch a suffering, acting, raving hero who occupies a social position far higher than their own. This continues still to impress audiences today.

Then when Lessing and Schiller introduced the bourgeois drama, the audience saw itself as the suffering hero on the stage. But the evolution of the hero continued. Buechner's Woyzeck is a primitive proletarian who represents far less socially than the average spectator.

But it is precisely in this extreme form of human existence, in this last, most miserable form, that the audience is to see the human being also, indeed itself.

And finally we might mention Pirandello who was the first, as far as I know, to render the hero, the character on the stage, immaterial and transparent just as Wilder did the dramatic place. The audience watching this sort of presentation attends, as it were, its own dissection, its own psychoanalysis, and the stage becomes man's internal milieu, the inner space of the world.

Of course, the theatre has never dealt only with kings and generals; in comedy the hero has always been the peasant, the beggar, the ordinary citizen—but this was always in comedy. Nowhere in Shakespeare do we find a comic king; in his day a ruler could appear as a bloody monster but never as a fool. In Shakespeare the courtiers, the artisans, the working people are comic. Hence, in the evolution of the tragic hero we see a trend toward comedy. Analogously the fool becomes more and more of a tragic figure. This fact is by no means without significance. The hero of a play not only propels an action on, he not only suffers a certain fate, but he also represents a world. Therefore we have to ask ourselves how we should present our own questionable world and with what sort of heroes. We have to ask ourselves how the mirrors which catch and reflect this world should be ground and set.

Can our present-day world, to ask a concrete question, be represented by Schiller's dramatic art? Some writers claim it can be, since Schiller still holds audiences in his grip. To be sure, in art everything is possible when the art is right. But the question is if an art valid for its time could possibly be so even for our day. Art can never be repeated. If it were repeatable, it would be foolish not just to write according to the rules of Schiller.

Schiller wrote as he did because the world in which he lived could still be mirrored in the world his writing created, a world he could build as a historian. But just barely. For was not Napoleon perhaps the last hero in the old sense? The world today as it appears to us could hardly be encompassed in the form of the historical drama as Schiller wrote it, for the reason alone that we no longer have any tragic heroes, but only vast tragedies staged by world butchers and produced by slaughtering machines. Hitler and Stalin can not be made into Wallensteins. Their power is so enormous that they themselves are no more than incidental, corporeal and easily replaceable expressions of this power; and the misfortune associated with the former and to a considerable extent also with the latter is too vast, too complex, too horrible, too mechanical and usually simply too devoid of all sense. Wallenstein's power can still be envisioned; power as we know it today can only be seen in its smallest part for, like an iceberg, the largest part is submerged in anonymity and abstraction. Schiller's drama presupposes a world that the eye can take in, that takes for granted genuine actions of state, just as Greek tragedy did. For only what the eye can take in can be made visible in art. The state today, however, can not be envisioned for it is anonymous and bureaucratic; and not only in Moscow and Washington, but also in Berne. Actions of state today have become *post hoc* satiric dramas which follow the tragedies executed in secret earlier. True representatives of our world are missing; the tragic heroes are nameless. Any small-time crook, petty government official or policeman better represents our world than a senator or president. Today art can only embrace the victims, if it can reach men at all; it can no longer come close to the mighty. Creon's secretaries close Antigone's case. The state has lost its physical reality, and just as physics can now only cope with the world in mathematical formulas, so the state can only be expressed in statistics. Power today becomes visible, material only when it explodes as in the atom bomb, in this marvelous mushroom which rises and spreads immaculate as the sun and in which mass murder and beauty have become one. The atom bomb can not be reproduced artistically since it is massproduced. In its face all of man's art that would recreate it must fail, since it is itself a creation of man. Two mirrors which reflect one another remain empty.

But the task of art, insofar as art can have a task at all, and hence also the task of drama today, is to create something concrete, something that has form. This can be accomplished best by comedy. Tragedy, the strictest genre in art, presupposes a formed world. Comedy—insofar as it is not just satire of a particular society as in Molière—supposes an unformed world, a world being made and turned upside down, a world about to fold like ours. Tragedy overcomes distance; it can make myths originating in times immemorial seem like the present to the Athenians. But comedy creates distance; the attempt of the Athenians to gain a foothold in Sicily is translated by comedy into the birds undertaking to create their own empire before which the gods and men will have to capitulate. How comedy works can be seen in the most primitive kind of joke, in the dirty story, which, though it is of very dubious value, I bring up only because it is the best illustration of what I mean by creating distance. The subject of the dirty story is the purely sexual, which because it is purely sexual, is formless and without objective distance. To be given a form the purely sexual is transmuted, as I have already mentioned, into the dirty joke. Therefore this type of joke is a kind of original comedy, a transposition of the sexual onto the plain of the comical. In this way it is possible today in a society dominated by John Doe, to talk in an accepted way about the purely sexual. In the dirty story it becomes clear that the comical exists in forming what is formless, in creating order out of chaos.

The means by which comedy creates distance is the conceit. Tragedy is without conceit. Hence there are few tragedies whose subjects were invented. By this I do not mean to imply that the ancient tragedians lacked inventive ideas of the sort that are written today, but the marvel of their art was that they had no need of these inventions, of conceits. That makes all the difference. Aristophanes, on the other hand, lives by conceits. The stuff of his plays are not myths but inventions, which take place not in the past but the present. They drop into their world like bomb shells which, by throwing up huge craters of dirt, change the present into the comic and thus scatter the dirt for everyone to see. This, of course, does not mean that drama today can only be comical. Tragedy and comedy are but formal concepts, dramatic attitudes, figments of the esthetic imagination which can embrace one and the same thing. Only the conditions under which each is created are different, and these conditions have their basis only in small part in art.

Tragedy presupposes guilt, despair, moderation, lucidity, vision, a sense of responsibility. In the Punch-and-Judy show of our century, in this back-sliding of the white race, there are no more guilty and also, no responsible men. It is always, "We couldn't help it" and "We didn't really want that to happen." And indeed, things happen without anyone in particular being responsible for them. Everything is dragged along and everyone gets caught somewhere in the sweep of events. We are all collectively guilty, collectively bogged down in the sins of our fathers and of our forefathers. We are the offspring of children. That is our misfortune, but not our guilt: guilt can exist only as a personal achievement, as a religious deed. Comedy alone is suitable for us. Our world has led to the grotesque as well as to the atom bomb, and so it is a world like that of Hieronymus Bosch whose apocalyptic paintings are also grotesque. But the grotesque is only a way of expressing in a tangible manner, of making us perceive physically the paradoxical, the form of the unformed, the face of a world without face; and just as in our thinking today we seem to be unable to do without the concept of the paradox, so also in art, and in our world which at times seems still to exist only because the atom bomb exists: out of fear of the bomb.

But the tragic is still possible even if pure tragedy is not. We can achieve the tragic out of comedy. We can bring it forth as a frightening moment, as an abyss that opens suddenly; indeed many of Shakespeare's tragedies are already really comedies out of which the tragic arises.

After all this the conclusion might easily be drawn that comedy is the expression of despair, but this conclusion is not inevitable. To be sure, whoever realizes the senselessness, the hopelessness of this world might well despair, but this despair is not a result of this world. Rather it is an answer given by an individual to this world; another answer would be not to despair, would be an individual's decision to endure this world in which we live like Gulliver among the giants. He also achieves distance, he also steps back a pace or two who takes measure of his opponent, who prepares himself to fight his opponent or to escape him. It is still possible to show man as a courageous being.

In truth this is a principal concern of mine. The blind man, Romulus, Uebelohe, Akki, are all men of courage. The lost world order is restored within them; the universal escapes my grasp. I refuse to find the universal in a doctrine. The universal for me is chaos. The world (hence the stage which represents this world) is for me something monstrous, a riddle of misfortunes which must be accepted but before which one must not capitulate. The world is far bigger than any man, and perforce threatens him constantly. If one could but stand outside the world, it would no longer be threatening. But I have neither the right nor the ability to be an outsider to this world. To find solace in poetry can also be all too cheap; it is more honest to retain one's human point of view. Brecht's thesis, that the world is an accident, which he developed in his street scene where he shows how this accident happened, may yield—as it in fact did—some magnificent theatre; but he did it by concealing most of the evidence! Brecht's thinking is inexorable, because inexorably there are many things he will not think about.

And lastly it is through the conceit, through comedy that the anonymous audience becomes possible as an audience, becomes a reality to be counted on, and also, one to be taken into account. The conceit easily transforms the crowd of theatre-goers into a mass which can be attacked, deceived, outsmarted into listening to things it would otherwise not so readily listen to. Comedy is a mousetrap in which the public is easily caught and in which it will get caught over and over again. Tragedy, on the other hand, predicated a true community, a kind of community whose existence in our day is but an embarrassing fiction. Nothing is more ludicrous, for instance, than to sit and watch the mystery plays of the Anthroposophists when one is not a participant.

Granting all this there is still one more question to be asked: is it permissible to go from a generality to a particular form of art, to do what I just did when I went from my assertion that the world was formless to the particular possibility for writing comedies today? I doubt that this is permissible. Art is something personal, and something personal should never be explained with generalities. The value of a work of art does not depend on whether more or less good reasons for its existence can be found. Hence I have also tried to avoid certain problems, as for example the argument which is quite lively today, whether or not plays ought to be written in verse or in prose. My own answer lies simply in writing prose, without any intentions of thereby deciding the issue. A man has to choose to go one way, after all, and why should one way always be worse than another? As far as my concepts of comedy are concerned, I believe that here, too, personal reasons are more important than more general ones that are always open to argument. What logic in matters of art could not be refuted! One talks best about art when one talks of one's own art. The art one chooses is an expression of freedom without which no art can exist, and at the same time also of necessity without which art can not exist either. The artist always represents his world and himself. If at one time philosophy taught men to arrive at the particular from the general, then unlike Schiller who started out believing in general conclusions, I can not construct a play as he did when I doubt that the particular can ever be reached from the general. But my doubt is mine and only mine, and not the doubt and problems of a Catholic for whom drama holds possibilities non-Catholics do not share. This is so even if, on the other hand, a Catholic who takes his religion seriously is denied those possibilities which other men possess. The danger inherent in this thesis lies in the fact that there are always those artists who for the sake of finding some generalities to believe in accept conversion, taking a step which is the more to be wondered at for the sad fact that it really will not help them. The difficulties experienced by a Protestant in writing a drama are just the same difficulties he has with his faith. Thus it is my way to mistrust what is ordinarily called the building of the drama, and to arrive at my plays from the unique, the sudden idea or conceit, rather than from some general concept or plan. Speaking for myself, I need to write off into the blue, as I like to put it, so that I might give critics a catchword to hang onto. They use it often enough, too, without really understanding what I mean by it.

But these matters are my own concerns and hence it is not necessary to invoke the whole world and to make out as if what are my concerns are the concerns of art in general (lest I be like the drunk who goes back to Noah, the Flood, original sin and the beginning of the world to explain what is, after all, only his own weakness). As in everything and everywhere, and not just in the field of art, the rule is: No excuses, please!

Nevertheless the fact remains (always keeping in mind, of course, the reservations just made) that we now stand in a different relationship to what we have called our material. Our unformed, amorphous present is characterized by being surrounded by figures and forms that reduce our time into a mere result, even less, into a mere transitional state, and which give excessive weight to the past as something finished and to the future as something possible. This applies equally well to politics. Related to art it means that the artist is surrounded by all sorts of opinions about art and by demands on him which are based not upon his capacities, but upon the historical past and present forms. He is surrounded therefore by materials which are no longer materials, that is possibilities, but by materials which have already taken on shape, that is some definitive form. Caesar is no longer pure subject matter for us; he has become the Caesar whom scholarship made the object of its researches. And so it happened that scholars, having thrown themselves with increasing energy not only upon nature but also upon the intellectual life and upon art, establishing in the process intellectual history, literary scholarship, philology and goodness knows what else, have created a body of factual information which can not be ignored (for one can not be conscious of these facts and at the same time pretend to be so naïve that one need pay no attention to the results of scholarship). In this way, however, scholars have deprived the artist of materials by doing what was really the artist's task. The mastery of Richard Feller's *History of Berne* precludes the possibility of an historical drama about the city of Berne; the history of Berne was thus given shape before some literary artist could do it. True, it is a scholastic form (and not a mythical one which would leave the way open for a tragedian), a form that severely limits the field for the artist, leaving to art only psychology which, of course, has also become a science. To rewrite such a history in a creative literary manner would now be a tautology, a repetition by means which are not suitable or fitting, a mere illustration of scholarly insights; in short, it would be the very thing science often claims literature to be. It was still possible for Shakespeare to base his Caesar upon Plutarch, for the Roman was not a historian in our sense of the word but a storyteller, the author of biographical sketches. Had Shakespeare read Mommsen he could not have written his Caesar because he would of necessity have lost the supremacy over his materials. And this holds true now in all things, even the myths of the Greeks which, since we no longer live them but only study, evaluate, investigate them, recognizing them to be mere myths and as such destroying them, have become mummies; and these, bound tightly round with philosophy and theology, are all too often substituted for the living thing.

Therefore the artist must reduce the subjects he finds and runs into everywhere if he wants to turn them once more into real materials, hoping always that he will succeed. He parodies his materials, contrasts them consciously with what they have actually been turned into. By this means, by this act of parody, the artist regains his freedom and hence his material; and thus material is no longer found but invented. For every parody presupposes a conceit and an invention. In laughter man's freedom becomes manifest, in crying his necessity. Our task today is to demonstrate freedom. The tyrants of this planet are not moved by the works of the poets. They yawn at a poet's threnodies. For them heroic epics are silly fairy tales and religious poetry puts them to sleep. Tyrants fear only one thing: a poet's mockery. For this reason then parody has crept into all literary genres, into the novel, the drama, into lyrical poetry. Much of painting, even of music, has been conquered by parody, and the grotesque has followed, often well camouflaged, on the heels of parody: all of a sudden the grotesque is there.

But our times, up to every imaginable trick there is, can handle all that and nothing can intimidate it: the public has been educated to see in art something solemn, hallowed and even pathetic. The comic is considered inferior, dubious, unseemly; it is accepted only when it makes people feel as bestially happy as a bunch of pigs. But the very moment people recognize the comic to be dangerous, an art that exposes, demands, moralizes, it is dropped like a hot potato, for art may be everything it wants to be so long as it remains *gemütlich*.

We writers are often accused of art that is nihilistic. Today, of course, there exists a nihilistic art, but not every art that seems nihilistic is so. True nihilistic art does not appear to be nihilistic at all; usually it is considered to be especially humane and supremely worthy of being read by our more mature young people. A man must be a pretty bungling sort of nihilist to be recognized as such by the world at large. People call nihilistic what is merely uncomfortable. Then also people say, the artist is supposed to create, not to talk; to give shape to things, not to preach. To be sure. But it becomes more and more difficult to create "purely" or however people imagine the creative mind should work. Mankind today is like a reckless driver racing ever faster, ever more heedlessly along the highway. And he does not like it when the frightened passengers cry out, "Watch out" and "There's a warning sign! Slow down" or "Don't kill that child!" What is more, the driver hates it even worse when he is asked, "Who is paying for the car?" or "Who's providing the gas and oil for this mad journey?," to say nothing of what happens when he is asked for his driver's license. What unpleasant facts might then come to light! Maybe the car was stolen from some relatives, the gas and oil squeezed from the passengers, and really not gas and oil but the blood and sweat of us all; and most likely he wouldn't even have a driver's license and it would turn out that this was his first time driving. Of course, it would be embarrassing if such personal questions were to be asked. The driver would much prefer the passengers to praise the beauty of the country-side through which they are traveling, the silver of the river and the brilliant reflection of the ice-capped mountains in the far distance, would even prefer to have amusing stories whispered into his ear. Today's author, however, can no longer confine himself with good conscience to whispering pleasant stories and praising the beautiful landscape. Unfortunately, too, he can not get out of this mad race in order to sit by the wayside, writing the pure poetry demanded of him by all the non-poets. Fear, worry, and above all anger open his mouth wide.

How very nice it would be if we could end now on this emphatic note. It would be a conclusion that could be considered at least partially safe and not wholly impossible. But in all honesty we must ask ourselves at this point if any of this makes sense today, if it were not better if we practiced silence. I have tried to show that the theatre today is, in the best sense of the word to be sure, in part a museum, and in part a field of experimentation. I have also tried to show here and there what these experiments are. Is the theatre capable of fulfilling this, its latter destiny? Not only has the writing of plays become more difficult today but also the rehearsing and performing of these plays is harder. The very lack of time results at best in only a decent attempt, a first probing, a slight advance in what might be the right direction. A play that is to be more than a merely conventional piece, that is really to be an experiment, can no longer be solved at the writing desk. Giraudoux's fortune was that he had Jouvet. Unhappily this happens only once or twice. The repertory theatre of Germany can afford less and less to experiment. A new play must be gotten rid of as quickly as possible. The museum's treasures weigh too heavily in the scales. The theatre, our whole culture, lives on the interest of the well invested intellect, to which nothing can happen any more and for which not even royalties have to be paid. Assured of having a Goethe, Schiller or Sophocles at hand, the theatres are willing now and then to put on a modern piece —but preferably only for a premiere performance. Heroically this duty is discharged, and sighs of relief are breathed all around when Shakespeare is performed next time. What can we say or do? Clear the stages completely! Make room for the classics! The world of the museum is growing and bursts with its treasures. The cultures of the cave dwellers have not yet been investigated to the nth degree. Let the custodians of the future concern themselves with our art when it is our turn. It does not make much difference then if something new is added, something new is written. The demands made of the artist by esthetics increase from day to day. What is wanted is the perfection which is read into the classics. And let the artist even be suspected of having taken one step backwards, of having made a mistake, just watch how quickly he is dropped. Thus a climate is created in which literature can be studied but not made. How can the artist exist in a world of educated and literate people? This question oppresses me, and I know no answer. Perhaps the writer can best exist by writing detective stories, by creating art where it is least suspected. Literature must become so light that it will weigh nothing upon the scale of today's literary criticism: only in this way will it regain its true worth.

Translation by GERHARD NELLHAUS

Discovering the Theatre

BY EUGENE IONESCO

WHEN I AM ASKED: "WHY do you write plays?" I always feel very embarrassed, and am at a loss for an answer. It seems to me sometimes that I started to write for the theatre because I hated it. I read literary works and essays, or went to the movies with pleasure. From time to time I listened to music, or visited art galleries; but for all practical purposes I never went to the theatre.

When, quite by chance, I saw a play, it was in order to accompany someone, or because I had not been able to refuse an invitation, because I had been obliged to go.

I derived no pleasure from it, and did not participate in it. The playing of the actors disturbed me: I was embarrassed for them. The situations seemed arbitrary to me. There was something false in it all, I thought.

The theatrical event had no magic for me. It all seemed a bit ridiculous, rather painful. I didn't understand how anyone could be an actor, for instance. It seemed to me that the actor was doing something inadmissible, censurable. He was renouncing himself, abandoning himself, changing skin. How could he accept being someone else, playing a role, being someone that he was not? It was for me a kind of coarse trickery, extremely obvious, inconceivable.

The actor, however, did not really become someone else; he simply pretended to, which was worse, I thought. It seemed painful to me, and somehow dishonest. "How well he acts," said the spectators. For me, he acted badly, and it was bad to act.

To go to the theatre meant for me to go and see apparently serious people make a spectacle of themselves. And yet I am not an entirely prosy person. I am not an enemy of the imagination. Indeed, I have

77

always thought that the truth of fiction is more profound, more charged with meaning than everyday reality. Realism, whether it be socialist or not, falls short of reality. It shrinks it, attenuates it, falsifies it; it does not take into account our basic truths and our fundamental obsessions: love, death, astonishment. It presents man in a reduced and estranged perspective. Truth is in our dreams, in the imagination; everything, at each instant, confirms this statement. Fiction preceded science. All that we dream, that is to say, all that we desire, is true. (The truth of Icarus preceded aviation, and if Ader or Blériot flew, it is because all men have dreamed of flying.) Only myth is true: history, attempting to realize it, disfigures it, half ruins it; history is imposture, mystification, when it claims that it has "succeeded." All that we dream is capable of realization. Reality, on the other hand, does not have to be capable of realization: it is only what it is. It is the dreamer, or the thinker, or the scientist, who is the revolutionary; it is he who tries to change the world.

Fiction did not disturb me at all in novels, and I was willing to admit of it in films. Novelistic fiction, as well as my own dreams, imposed themselves upon me quite naturally, as possible reality. The playing of film actors did not provoke in me that indefinable uneasiness, that embarrassment produced by a theatrical performance.

Why could I not accept theatrical reality? Why did its truth appear false to me? And why did the false seem to want to parade as true, substitute for truth? Was it the fault of the actors, or of the text, or was it my own? I believe now that what disturbed me in the theatre was the presence on the stage of characters of flesh and blood. Their material presence destroyed the fiction. It was as though there were present two levels of reality, the concrete reality, impoverished, empty, limited, of these banal living men, moving and speaking upon the stage, and the reality of the imagination. And these two realities faced each other, unmasked, irreconcilable: two antagonistic universes which could not succeed in unifying and blending.

This is indeed what was the matter: each gesture, each attitude, each speech spoken upon the stage destroyed for me the universe which that gesture, that attitude, that speech was precisely trying to evoke; destroyed it before even evoking: it was for me a real abortion, a kind of failure, a sort of foolishness. If you stop your ears in order not to hear the dance music played by an orchestra, but continue to watch the dancers, you can see how ridiculous they appear, and how meaningless their movements become; just so, if someone found himself for the first time at the performance of a religious ceremony, it would appear incomprehensible and absurd to him.

It was with a sort of desacralized awareness that I attended the theatre, and that is why I did not like it, feel it, or believe in it.

A novel is a story which is told to you; whether it is imaginary or not has no importance; nothing prevents you from believing it. A film is an imaginary story which is being shown to you. It is a novel in pictures, an illustrated novel; a film is therefore also a story told, visually of course, but that changes nothing in its nature; one can believe in it. Music is a combination of sounds, a story of sounds, auditory adventures. A picture is an organization, or disorganization, of forms, colors, perspectives; there is no question of believing it or not believing it; it is there; it is real. It is enough if its elements correspond to the ideal exigencies of composition, of pictorial expression. Novel, music, painting, these are pure fiction, containing no heterogeneous elements; that is why they stand alone, and are admissible. The cinema itself can stand alone, since it is a series of images; it also is pure, whereas the theatre seemed to me essentially impure: fiction was mingled with elements foreign to it; it was imperfectly fiction, a raw material which had not undergone an indispensable transformation, a mutation. On the whole everything in the theatre exasperated me. When I saw actors identify themselves completely with their roles and weep real tears, for example, it was unbearable; I found it literally indecent.

When, on the other hand, I saw the actor too much master of his role, outside of it, dominating it, separating himself from it, as Diderot or Jouvet would have had it, or according to the theories of alienation of Brecht, which are not at all revolutionary, it displeased me equally. That also seemed an inacceptable mixture of the true and the false, for I felt a need for that indispensable transformation of the real—the real in its narrowest sense—into fiction. That indispensable transformation is not in fact realized by Brecht, because of his didacticism which goes against the spirit of all art: it remains heavily attached to the level of the sub-ideology. I did not like the actor, the star, whom I considered an anarchical ingredient, breaking up, destroying, to his own advantage, the unity of scenic organization, and pulling everything to himself to the detriment of the coherent integration of the various elements of the performance. But the dehumanization of the actor, as practiced by Piscator or Brecht (that disciple of Piscator), who made of the actor a simple pawn in the chess game of the performance, a lifeless instrument, without fire, without participation or personal invention, this time for the benefit of the *mise en scène* which in turn pulled everything after it—that primacy of the organization exasperated me equally, literally gave me a feeling of stifling: to nullify the initiative of the actor, to kill him, is to kill the life of the performance.

Later, that is to say, quite recently, I realized that Jean Vilar in his productions had been able to find in an ingenious way the indispensable proportions, respecting the necessity of scenic cohesion without dehumanizing the actor, giving thus to the performance its unity, and to the actor his freedom, halfway between the style of the Odéon (therefore even beyond the declamatory exaggerations in the style of Sarah Bernhardt or Mounet-Sully) and the Brechtian or Piscatoresque barracks. But with Vilar it is not a question of expressing theatrical theories, nor immutable dogmas—it is an affair of tact, of an instinctive sense of the theatre.

However, that did not entirely fit my temperament either: I saw no way out, no way to reconcile freshness, spontaneity, naïveté, that is to say, creative authenticity, with theatrical thought, with preconceived ideas, dogmatic and stifling.

Nor did I see how one could escape this very real uneasiness caused by an unawareness of the impurity of the performed play. I was truly not an agreeable spectator, but rather, surly, grumpy, always dissatisfied. Was it because of an illness peculiar to me, or was the theatre responsible?

*   *   *

Even the texts of plays which I had read displeased me. Not all! For I was not blind to Sophocles or Aeschylus, nor to Shakespeare, nor afterwards to certain plays of Kleist or of Büchner. Why? Because all of these plays, I thought, are extraordinary in the reading, for literary qualities which perhaps are not specifically theatrical. In any case, since Shakespeare and Kleist I do not think I have derived pleasure from any plays. Strindberg seemed insufficient and clumsy. Molière himself bored me. These tales of misers, hypocrites, cuckolds, did not interest me. His metaphysical spirit displeased me. What do these stories of people matter to me, or these characters and customs seen in such a narrow perspective? Shakespeare questions the totality of the condition and destiny of man. The problems of Molière seemed to me, in the last analysis, relatively secondary, sometimes sad, certainly even dramatic, but never tragic: for they can all be resolved. There is no solution to the intolerable, and only that which is intolerable is truly theatrical.

On the other hand, the plays of Shakespeare in their grandeur seemed diminished in presentation. No Shakespearean performance captivated me so much as the reading of *Hamlet, Othello, Julius Caesar,* etc. Perhaps, since I rarely went to the theatre, I did not see the best Shakespearean performances. At any rate, the performance gave me the impression of making the intolerable tolerable. It was a taming down of anguish.

I am therefore no lover of the theatre, and even less am I a man of the theatre. I really hated the theatre. It bored me. And yet, no. I can still remember that as a child my mother could not get me away from the puppet shows in the Luxembourg Gardens. I could have stayed there spellbound for days on end. I didn't laugh, though. The spectacle of the guignol held me there, stupefied by the sight of these puppets who spoke, who moved, and bludgeoned each other. It was the spectacle of life itself which, strange, improbable, but truer than truth itself, was being presented to me in an infinitely simplified and caricatured form, as though to underline the grotesque and brutal truth. Later too, until I was fifteen, any play enthralled me, and any play gave me the feeling that the world is strange, a feeling whose roots are so deep that it has never left me. Each spectacle awoke in me this sense of the strangeness of the world, which appeared to me nowhere so well as in the theatre. And yet, at the age of thirteen I wrote a play, my first work, which had none of this strangeness in it. It was a patriotic play: youth is an excuse for everything.

When did I stop liking the theatre? From the moment when, becoming somewhat lucid, acquiring a critical spirit, I became aware of the strings, the thick strings of the theatre, that is to say, from the moment when I lost my naïveté. What holy terrors of the theatre could give that back to us? And in the name of what valid magic could the theatre claim the right to cast a spell upon us? There is nothing magic left, nothing awesome: no reason, no justification is sufficient to bring about the rebirth of naïveté in us.

Besides, nothing is more difficult than to write for the theatre. Novels and poems remain. Their efficacy is not blunted even after centuries. We are still interested in reading many minor works of the nineteenth, eighteenth and seventeenth centuries. Many even older works continue to interest us. Painting and music remain. The smallest carved heads on many cathedrals have kept alive their untouched freshness, their moving naïveté, and we shall continue to be sensitive to the architectural rhythms of the monuments of the most ancient civilizations which reveal themselves to us through these monuments, speaking a direct and precise language. But the theatre?

Some people reproach the theatre today with not belonging to its time. In my opinion, it belongs to it far too much. That is its weakness and the cause of its impermanence. I mean the theatre belongs to its time at the same time that it does not belong to it enough. Each epoch requires the introduction of a certain incommunicable "out of time" within time, within the communicable. Everything is a moment circumscribed within history, of course. But in each moment there is all of history: every story is valid when it is trans-historical; in the individual one can read the universal.

The themes which many authors choose depend only upon a certain ideological mode, which is less than the epoch itself. Or else these themes express some particular political thought, and the plays which illustrate them will die with the ideology of which they are tributaries, for ideologies become outdated. Any Christian tomb, any Greek or Etruscan stele touches us more, tells us more about the destiny of man than so many laboriously "committed" plays, which make themselves the instrument of disciplines, of systems of expression, of languages other than those which are their own.

It is true that all authors have wanted to propagandize. The great ones are those who failed, who, consciously or not, arrived at more profound and general truths. Nothing is more precarious than theatrical works. They endure a short time, wear themselves out quickly, and then reveal nothing but their strings.

Corneille, sincerely, bores me. We love him perhaps (without realizing it) simply because of habit. We are forced to. He was imposed upon us in school. Schiller is intolerable to me. The comedies of Marivaux have for a long time seemed to me but futile games. The comedies of Musset are shallow, those of Vigny unactable. The bloody dramas of Victor Hugo make us laugh aloud; on the other hand, whatever one may say, we find it rather difficult to laugh at most of the comedies of Labiche. Dumas *fils*, with his *Lady of the Camellias*, is ridiculously sentimental. And the others! Oscar Wilde? Facile. Ibsen? Boorish. Strindberg? Clumsy. A contemporary author whose tomb is still fresh,

Giraudoux, no longer always comes across, as is the case with the theatre of Cocteau; it seems too artificial to us, too superficial. Its brilliance is tarnished: theatrical methods which are too theatrical in the case of Cocteau; linguistic methods and strings, distinguished ones to be sure, but strings all the same in the case of Giraudoux.

Pirandello himself is bypassed, since his theatre is founded upon theories of personality or of many-faceted truth, theories which since psychoanalysis and depth psychology seem clear as day. By confirming the correctness of Pirandello's theories, modern psychology, necessarily going further in the exploration of the human psyche, gives him a certain validity, but at the same time renders him insufficient and useless: since it says more completely and more scientifically that which Pirandello said. The value of his theatre has nothing to do with its contribution to psychology, but with its theatrical quality which is, of course, elsewhere. It is no longer the discovery of the antagonisms of personality which interests us in Pirandello, but what he does with it, dramatically speaking. Its purely theatrical interest is extra-scientific; it is beyond his ideology. What remains of Pirandello is the mechanism of his theatre, its movement (*jeu*): proof again that the theatre which is built only on ideology, or philosophy, and which owes all its value to that ideology or that philosophy, is built on sand, and must disappear. It is his theatrical language, his purely theatrical instinct which keeps Pirandello alive today.

Likewise, it is not the psychological truth of the passions in Racine's theatre which sustains it, but what Racine, as a poet and as a man of the theatre, did with those truths.

If one counted the dramatists who can still move the public, one would find through the centuries about twenty, or thirty at the most. But the pictures, the poems and the novels which still speak to us can be counted by the thousands. The naïveté necessary for a work of art is lacking in the theatre. I do not say that a dramatic poet cannot appear, a great naïve poet; but, for the moment, I do not see him on the horizon. I mean a lucid naïveté, springing from the profound sources of being, revealing them, revealing them to ourselves, restoring to us our naïveté, our secret being. For the moment, there are no naïve ones, either among the spectators or among the authors.

For what must we reproach the dramatists and the plays? Their strings, I have said, that is to say, their too obvious methods. The theatre may seem to be an inferior literary genre, a minor genre. It is always somewhat approximate. It is doubtless a claptrap art, one which likes to create an effect. It cannot do without it, and that is what people reproach it for. The effects can only be gross. One gets the impression that things become coarse. The nuances of a literary text disappear. A theatre of literary subtleties is soon worn out. The half shades become dark or disappear in the bright light. No penumbra, no refinement is possible. Demonstrations, thesis plays are rough, everything is only approximate. The theatre is not the language of ideas. When it tries to become the vehicle of ideologies, it can only become their popularizer. It simplifies them dangerously. It makes them primary, diminishes them. It becomes naïve, but in the bad sense. Every ideological theatre risks being only a theatre of patronage. What would be, not only its usefulness, but its proper function, if the theatre were condemned to do the work of philosophy, or theology, or politics, or pedagogy? A psychological theatre is insufficiently psychological. It is better to read a treatise on psychology. An ideological theatre is insufficiently philosophical. Instead of going to see the dramatic illustration of such and such a political theory, I prefer to read my usual daily, or listen to a speech by the candidate of my party.

Dissatisfied with the gross naïveté, the rudimentary character of the theatre, philosophers, men of letters, ideologists, refined poets, intelligent people, attempt to make the theatre intelligent. They write with intelligence, with taste, with talent. They put into it what they think. They express their ideas of life, of the world, believing that the play should be a sort of presentation of a thesis, whose solution appears upon the stage. They sometimes give to their works the structure of a syllogism of which the premises are the first two acts, and of which the third act is the conclusion.

It cannot be denied that their construction is sometimes excellent. Yet, it does not correspond to our theatrical needs, since it does not escape from that intermediary zone which is neither entirely art (and to which discursive thought can only give a kind of nourishment), nor entirely the superior level of thought.

*   *   *

Should one renounce the theatre if one refuses to assign it a role of patronage, or to enslave it to other manifestations of the mind, to other systems of expression? Can it have its autonomy like painting or music?

Theatre is one of the most ancient arts. I think that we cannot do without it. We cannot help giving in to the desire to place upon the stage living characters which are at once both real and invented. We cannot resist this need to make them speak and live before us. To incarnate phantoms, to give life is a prodigious and irreplaceable adventure, so much so that I was fascinated when, at the rehearsals of my first play, I saw suddenly moving about the stage of the Noctambules characters which had come out of me. I was frightened. By what right had I done that? Was it permitted? And Nicolas Bataille, my interpreter, how had he been able to become M. Martin? . . . It was almost diabolical. Thus, it is only when I wrote for the theatre entirely by chance and with the intention of ridiculing it, that I began to love it, to rediscover it in myself, to understand it and to be fascinated by it; and I understood what my role would be.

I told myself that the too intelligent dramatists were yet not intelligent enough, that thinkers in the theatre could not find the language of philosophical treatises; that, when they wished to bring to the theatre too many subtleties and nuances, it was at once both too much and not enough; that, if the theatre was only deplorable enlarging of nuances, which disturbed me, it was simply that the magnification was insufficient. The too great was not great enough, the too slightly nuanced, was too nuanced.

If then the essence of the theatre was in this enlarging of effects, it was necessary to exaggerate even more, to underline and accentuate them to the maximum. To push the theatre beyond that intermediate zone which is neither theatre nor literature, is to restore it to its proper frame, to its natural limits. It was necessary not to hide the strings, but to make them even more visible, deliberately evident, to go all the way in the grotesque, in caricature, beyond the pale irony of witty drawing room comedies. Not drawing room comedies, but farce, an extreme burlesque exaggeration. Humor, yes, but with the methods of burlesque. A hard comedy, without finesse, excessive. No dramatic comedies either. But a return to the intolerable. Push everything to a state of paroxysm, there where the sources of tragedy lie. Create a theatre of violence: violently comic, violently dramatic.

Avoid psychology, or rather give it a metaphysical dimension. Theatre is an extreme exaggeration of feelings, an exaggeration which disjoints the real. It is also the dislocation and disarticulation of language.

If on the other hand, the actors bothered me because they appeared too unnatural, it is perhaps because they also wanted to be too natural: by renouncing this, they become natural perhaps in another way. They must not be afraid of being unnatural.

To tear ourselves away from the everyday, from habit, from mental laziness which hides from us the strangeness of reality, we must receive something like a real bludgeon blow. Without a new virginity of spirit, without a purified outlook on existential reality, there is no theatre; there is no art either; we must effect a dislocation of the real, which must precede its reintegration.

To achieve this effect one can sometimes use one method: play against the text. Onto a senseless, absurd, comical text one can graft a *mise en scène* and an interpretation which are grave, solemn, and ceremonious. On the other hand, in order to avoid the ridiculousness of easy tears, of sentimentality, one can graft upon a dramatic text a clownesque interpretation, underline by farce the tragic sense of a play. Light makes shadow deeper, shade accentuates the light. Personally, I have never understood the distinctions that are made between the comic and the tragic. Since the comic is the intuition of the absurd, it seems to me more hopeless than the tragic. The comic offers no escape. I say: hopeless; but in reality it either falls this side of despair or hope, or it goes beyond it.

For some people, the tragic may appear, in one way, comforting, for, if it expresses the impotence of vanquished man, broken by fatality for example, tragedy recognizes by that very fact the reality of a fatality, of a destiny, of laws ruling the universe, incomprehensible sometimes, but objective. And that human impuissance, that uselessness of our efforts can also, in a sense, appear comic.

I have called my comedies "anti-plays," "comical dramas," and my dramas "pseudo-dramas" or "tragical farces," for, it seems to me, the comical is tragic, and the tragedy of man, derisory. For the modern critical spirit nothing can be taken entirely seriously, nor entirely lightly. I have tried in *Victims of Duty* to drown the comic in the tragic; in *The Chairs,* the tragic in the comic, or if you wish, to oppose the comic to the tragic in order to join them in a new theatrical synthesis. But it is not a true synthesis, for these two elements do not mix completely with each other, they coexist, they repulse one another constantly, each setting the other into relief; they criticize each other, mutually deny each other, constituting through this opposition a dynamic balance, a tension. *Victims of Duty* and *The New Tenant* are, I think, my plays which best answer this need.

Similarly, one can oppose the prosaic to the poetic, the banal to the surreal. That is what I have tried to do in *Jack or the Submission,* which I have also called a "naturalist comedy," because, taking my departure from a naturalistic tone, I tried to go beyond naturalism.

Likewise, *Amédée or How to Get Rid of It,* whose action takes place in the apartment of a petty bourgeois family, is a realistic play into which I introduced fantastic elements, which served both to destroy the "realism" and to underline it.

In my first play, *The Bald Soprano,* which was intended at first as a parody of the theatre, and hence a parody of certain human behavior, it was by sinking myself in the banal, by pushing to their utmost limits the most outworn clichés of everyday language, that I tried to achieve the expression of the strangeness in which all human existence seems to be bathed. Tragedy and farce, prosaism and poetry, realism and fantasy, banality and strangeness, these perhaps are the contradictory principles (there is no theatre without antagonisms) which constitute the bases of possible theatrical construction. In this way perhaps the non-natural may appear in its violence to be natural, and the too natural appear non-naturalistic.

Should I add that a primitive theatre is not an elementary theatre; that to refuse to "round off the edges" means to give clear contours, more powerful shapes, and that a theatre which uses simple means is not necessarily a simple theatre?

If one believes that the theatre is only a theatre of words, it is difficult to admit that it can have its own language. It can only be dependent upon other forms of thought which are expressed by words: philosophy or ethics. Things are different if one considers that words constitute only one of the elements of theatrical shock. In the first place, the theatre has a special way of using words: dialogue, words of combat, of conflict. If dialogue is nothing but discussion in the plays of some authors, that is a great fault of theirs. There are other ways of making words theatrical: by using them with ferocious exaggeration in order to give to the theatre its true measure, which is lack of measure, the Word itself should be strained to its limits, language should almost explode, or destroy itself, in its impossibility to contain meanings.

But there is more than words: the theatre is a tale which is lived, beginning again at each performance, and it is also a tale which one sees being lived. The theatre is visual as much as it is auditory. It is not a series of images, like the cinema, but a construction, a moving architecture of scenic images.

Everything is permitted in the theatre: to incarnate characters, but also to materialize anguish, inner presences. It is therefore not only permitted, but it is recommended, to make props act, and objects live, to breathe life into the settings, to make the symbols concrete.

Just as the words are supplemented by the gestures, movement and pantomime which, when words become insufficient, are substituted for them, the physical elements of the décor can act as a supplement also. The use of props is yet another problem. (Artaud has discussed it.)

*　　*　　*

When people say that the theatre should be only social, isn't it really a question of political theatre, and of course with one emphasis or another? To be social is one thing; to be "socialist" or "Marxist" or "fascist" is quite another—it is the expression of an insufficient awareness: the more I see the plays of Brecht, the more I have the impression that time, and his own time, escape him: his man has one dimension less, his epoch is falsified by his very ideology which narrows his field; this is a fault common to ideologists and to people diminished by their fanaticism.

But one can be social in spite of himself, since we are all caught in a sort of historical complex, and we belong to a certain moment in history—which, however, is far from absorbing us entirely and which, on the contrary, expresses and contains only the least essential part of ourselves.

I have spoken especially of a certain technique, of the language of the theatre, the language which is its own. Social material or themes can very well constitute, within this language, the material and themes of the theatre. One is perhaps objective through being subjective. The particular rejoins the general and society is evidently an objective fact: yet, I see the social, that is to say the historical expression of the time to which we belong, even if only through language (and all language is also historical, circumscribed in its time; this is undeniable); I see that historical expression implied quite naturally in the work of art, whether one wishes it to be or not, conscious or not, but spontaneous, not explicit or forced, deliberate or ideological.

Besides, the temporal does not go against the intemporal and the universal: it submits to it.

There are states of mind, intuitions, which are absolutely extra-temporal, extra-historical. When some morning, touched by grace, I wake not only from my nocturnal slumber but also from my accustomed mental slumber, and become suddenly aware of my existence, and of the universal presence, when all appears strange to me and yet familiar, when the wonder of being overcomes me; this feeling, this intuition belongs to any man, to any time. This state of mind, one can find expressed in almost the same words by poets, mystics, philosophers, who feel it exactly as I feel it, and as all men have certainly felt it, if they are not spiritually dead or blinded by the business of politics. One can find this state of mind, clearly expressed, absolutely the same, in the Middle Ages as well as in Antiquity, or at any "historical" period. In that eternal moment, shoemaker and philosopher, "slave" and "master," priest and layman meet, and become identified with each other.

The historical and the ahistorical are joined equally in poetry and painting. The image of the woman arranging her hair is identical in certain Persian miniatures and in the Greek and Etruscan steles, in Egyptian frescos; Renoir, Manet, painters of the seventeenth and eighteenth centuries, did not need to know the paintings of other periods in order to find and express the same attitude, to feel the same emotion before that attitude filled with the same eternal sensual grace. It is a question here, as in the first example, of eternal human emotions. The pictorial style in which this image is rendered is different (often almost imperceptibly) according to the periods. But this "difference" which is revealed as secondary, is only a luminous support for the permanent. Here is evidence of how the temporal, or "historicity" to use a word now in style, is joined to, and identifies itself with, the intemporal, the universal, the sur-historical, and how they sustain one another.

To choose a great example in our field: in the theatre, when Richard II, fallen from power, is alone imprisoned in his cell, it is not Richard II that I see, but all the fallen kings of the earth; and not only all the fallen kings, but also our beliefs, our values, our desacralized truths, corrupted, worn out, our civilizations which disappear, our destiny. When Richard II dies, it is what I hold most dear that I see die; it is I who die with Richard II. Richard II makes me acutely aware of the eternal truth which we forget in history, that truth of which we do not think, and which is simple and infinitely banal: I die, you die, he dies. Thus, in the final analysis it is not history that Shakespeare is writing, although he is using history; it is not a history that he presents me, but *my* history, *our* history, *my* truth beyond time, through showing me a time which goes beyond time and joins universal philosophic truth. In fact, the theatrical masterpiece has an uncommonly exemplary character: it reflects my image; it is a mirror, an awareness, history oriented beyond history toward the most profound truth. One may think that the reasons given by an author—wars, civil strife, rivalry for power— are just or not, one can agree or not with these explanations. But one cannot deny that all kings have disappeared, that they have died, and the realization of this reality, this persistent truth of the impermanence of man, joined together with his need of eternity, is experienced with the profoundest emotion, with the keenest tragic consciousness, with passion. Art is the realm of passion, not that of didactic teaching; it is a question—in this tragedy of tragedies—of the revelation of the most painful reality; I learn, or relearn, what I no longer remembered, and I learn it in the only poetic manner possible, by participating in it with an emotion that is not manufactured or perverted, and which has broken down the paper barriers of ideologies and of the frugal critical or "scientific" spirit. I risk being fooled only when I attend a play which presents a thesis and not reality itself: an ideological, "engaged," deceptive play which is not poetically and profoundly true as only poetry and tragedy can be true. All men die in solitude; all values disintegrate into an ultimate contempt: that is what Shakespeare tells me. The cell of Richard is indeed the cell of all our solitudes. Perhaps Shakespeare wished to tell the story of Richard II: if he had told only that *story of another person,* he would not touch me. But the prison of Richard II is a truth which has not disappeared with history: its invisible walls still stand, after so many philosophies and ideologies have disappeared forever. And all this remains standing because the language is that of living truth, not that of demonstrative reason; the prison of Richard is there, before me, beyond all demonstration; the theatre is that eternal living presence; it answers, without doubt, to the essential structures of tragic truth, and of theatrical reality; its truth has nothing to do with the precarious truths of ideologies, nor with the so-called theatre of ideas: in this play we see theatrical archetypes, the essence of theatre, and theatrical language. A language lost for us today, when allegory and academic explanation seem to have taken the place of the living truth which we must find again. All language evolves, but to evolve, to renew oneself is not to abandon oneself and become something else; it is rather to find oneself at each instant, within each historical moment. One develops in harmony with what one already is. Theatre language can never be anything but theatre language.

The language of painting, and the language of music have developed, and have always fitted themselves into the cultural style of their period, but without ever losing their pictorial or musical style. And that evolution of painting, for example, has never been anything but the rediscovery of painting, of its language and its essence. The course of modern painting shows this clearly. Since Picasso, painting has been trying to free itself from all that is not painting: literature, anecdotes, history, photography. Since Picasso, therefore, painters have been trying to rediscover the fundamental schemas of painting, pure forms, color used as color. And here it is not a question of aestheticism or of what today is called, somewhat incorrectly, formalism, but rather of reality expressed pictorially, *in a language as revealing as that of words or sounds.* If we thought at first that there was a certain disintegration of pictorial language, we have discovered since that basically it was a question of an asepsis, a purification, the rejection of a parasitic language. Similarly, it is after having disarticulated theatrical elements, after having rejected false theatre language, that we must try, as the painters have done, to rearticulate them, purified and reduced to their essences.

The theatre can only be theatre, even though for certain contemporary doctors of "theatrology" this identity with itself is charged with tautology, or considered false, an attitude which strikes me as the most incredible and amazing of paradoxes.

For these doctors, the theatre, being something other than theatre, is ideology, allegory, politics, lectures, essays or literature. This is as aberrant as if one were to claim that music should be archeology, or painting, physics and mathematics.

*   *   *

It may be said that I have expressed nothing new here. I may even be accused of presenting only the most elementary truths. If this were so, I should be extremely happy, for nothing is more difficult than returning to elementary truths, fundamental principles, certitudes. Philosophers themselves seek nothing more than principles which are certain. Primary truths are precisely what we lose sight of, what we forget. That is why we become confused and can no longer understand each other.

However, what I have just said does not constitute a preconceived theory of dramatic art. It has not preceded, but rather followed my very personal experience in the theatre. These few ideas have come from my reflections about my own creations, good or bad. They are afterthoughts. I have no ideas before I write a play. I have them after I have written a play, or when I am not writing at all. I believe that artistic creation is spontaneous. At least it is for me. I repeat, all this is valid especially for me; but if I could believe that I have discovered in myself the instinctive and permanent schemas of the objective reality of the theatre, that I have found at least a part of the essence of theatre, I should be very happy. Only spontaneity can guarantee a direct knowledge of reality. All ideology ends up with indirect knowledge which is only secondary, oblique and falsified. Nothing is true for the artist except what he does not borrow from others.

For a so-called "avant-garde" writer I am going to incur the reproach of having invented nothing. I think one discovers more than one invents, and that invention is really discovery or rediscovery; and if I am considered an "avant-garde" writer, it is not my fault. It is the critics who consider me thus. It has no importance. That definition is as good as another. It means nothing. It is a tag.

Neither is surrealism new. That is to say, it is not an "invention." It only discovered and brought to light a certain way of knowledge, or certain tendencies of the human being which centuries of rationalism had persecuted and suppressed. What does surrealism attempt to liberate? Love and dreams. How could we have forgotten that man is animated by love? How could we fail to see that man dreams? The surrealist revolution was, like all revolutions, a return, a restoration, an expression of indispensable vital and spiritual needs. If it has now solidified, if we can speak of a surrealistic academicism, it is simply that every language finally wears out; from traditional and living it becomes traditionalist and hardened; it is "imitated": it also, in turn, must be rediscovered. (Besides, as we know, surrealism is itself a revival of romanticism; it has its sources, among others, in the power of dream of the German Romantics.) By starting out from a rediscovered method, and a rejuvenated language, one can enlarge the frontiers of the known real world. If there is an avant-garde, it can be valid only if it is not a vogue. It can be only an instinctive discovery, and a new awareness of forgotten models which require, at each moment, to be discovered anew and rejuvenated.

I think people have begun to forget lately what theatre is. I was the first to have forgotten; I think I have discovered it again, for myself, step by step, and I have just described simply my experience with the theatre.

Obviously, I have not touched on a great many problems. One wonders, for example, why a writer like Feydeau, whose technique and mechanical control of the play are perfect, is much less great than other dramatists who also have a perfect technique, or sometimes a less perfect one. It is just that, in a certain sense, everyone is a philosopher; that is to say, that everyone discovers a part of reality, that part which he can discover by himself. When I say philosopher, I do not mean the philosophical technician who only exploits the world views of others. In this sense, since the artist apprehends reality directly, he is a true philosopher. And it is the broadness, the depth, the sharpness of his philosophical vision, his living philosophy, which determine his greatness. The fine quality of works of art comes from the fact that this philosophy is "living," that it is life and not abstract thought. One philosophy perishes when a new philosophy, a new system, surpasses it. The living philosophies of works of art, on the contrary, do not invalidate one another. That is why they can coexist. The great masterpieces, the great poets, seem to justify one another, complete each other, confirm each other; Aeschylus is not cancelled out by Calderón, nor Shakespeare by Chekhov, nor Kleist by Japanese Noh Drama. One scientific theory can nullify another, but the truths of works of art sustain each other. It is art which seems to justify hope in a metaphysical liberalism.

Translated by LEONARD C. PRONKO

On the Experimental
Theatre

BY BERTOLT BRECHT

FOR AT LEAST TWO GENERATIONS now the serious-minded European theatre has existed in an era of experimentation. The diverse experiments have not as yet produced any unequivocal, clearly discernible results, but the era is by no means at an end. It is my opinion that the experiments followed two separate courses, which, though they occasionally intersected, can, when separated, be individually pursued. These two courses of development are distinguished from one another by means of their individual functions: *entertainment* and *instruction*, that is to say, the theatre organized experiments which were to increase its powers of entertaining, and experiments which were to increase its powers of instruction.

In a world as fast-moving and dynamic as ours the enticements of entertainment are quick to wear out. We must always be prepared to meet the desire for progressive public stupefaction with new effects. In order to distract its already distracted spectator the theatre must first of all make him concentrate. It must lure him with its spell out of his noisy environment. The theatre must deal with a spectator who is tired, exhausted with his rationalized day-labor, and vexed with social frictions of all sorts. He has fled his own small world, he sits here a fugitive. He is a fugitive, but he is a customer as well. His escape can be here or elsewhere. The competition of one form of theatre with another form, and of the theatre in general with the cinema, occasions

---

This essay is based on the manuscript of a lecture which Brecht delivered to the Stockholm Students' Theatre and then in a revised version in Helsinki in October, 1940.

continuously new struggles, struggles which will always exist anew.

In reviewing the experiments of Antoine, Brahm, Stanislavsky, Gordon Graig, Reinhardt, Jessner, Meyerhold, Vachtangov, and Piscator, we discover that they quite remarkably enlarged the possibilities of expression in the theatre. Its capacity to entertain has grown unquestionably. The art of ensemble-playing has created an uncommonly sensitive and elastic stage-being. A social milieu may be depicted in its most subtle detail. Vachtangov and Meyerhold drew certain dancelike forms from the Asiatic theatre and created a complete choreography for the drama. Meyerhold realized a radical Constructivism, and Reinhardt transformed natural, would-be showplaces into stages: he performed *Everyman* and *Faust* in public places. Open-air theatres saw productions of *A Midsummer Night's Dream* in the midst of a forest, and in the Soviet Union an attempt was made to repeat the storming of the Winter Palace with the use of the battleship "Aurora." The barriers between stage and spectator were demolished. At Reinhardt's production of *Danton's Death* in the Grosses Schauspielhaus actors sat in the auditorium, and in Moscow Ochlopkov seated spectators on the stage. Reinhardt utilized the "flower way" of the Chinese theatre and borrowed from the circus-arena the technique of playing in the midst of the audience. The direction of crowds was perfected by Stanislavsky, Reinhardt, and Jessner, and the latter won a third dimension for the stage with his stair constructions. Revolving stages and domed cycloramas were invented, and lighting was discovered. The reflector made possible illumination on a large scale. A complete light-board permitted us to conjure up the atmosphere of a Rembrandt painting. We might just as easily in the history of theatre name certain lighting effects Reinhardtian, as in the history of medicine we have named a certain heart operation after Trendelenburg. There are new methods of using the projector, and there is a new way of managing sound. As far as the art of the theatre was concerned, the boundaries between the cabaret and the theatre and between the revue and the theatre were demolished. There were experiments with masks, buskins, and pantomime. Far-reaching experiments were undertaken with the ancient classical repertoire. Time and again Shakespeare was refashioned and changed. We have extracted so many faces from the classical authors that they have scarcely any more in reserve. We have lived to see *Hamlet* in dinner-jackets and *Julius Caesar* in uniforms, and at least dinner-jackets and uniforms have profited by it and won their way to respectability. Experiments, as you can see, are very unequal in their worth, and the most noteworthy are not always the most valuable, though even the most worthless are scarcely ever completely worthless. As far as *Hamlet* in dinner-jackets is concerned, it is scarcely any more of a sacrilege to Shakespeare than the conventional *Hamlet* in silk tights. One is always kept within the framework of a costume play.

One can generally say that the experiments to improve the theatre's powers of entertaining have not been lacking in results. They have in particular led to the development of theatre machinery. They are, however, by no means at an end. In fact, they have never yet been put into general usage, as have the experimental results of other institutions. A new medical operation performed in New York can within a very short time be performed in Tokyo. That, however, is not the case with our modern stage technology. The artist is continuously hindered by an evident reticence in taking over unbiasedly the experimental results of another artist and improving on them. Forgery in art is considered a disgrace. This is one of the reasons why technological progress has for a long while not been so great as it might be. The theatre in general has not for a long while been brought up to the standards of modern technology. It amuses itself with the generally awkward utilization of a primitive turning-mechanism for the stage, with a microphone, and with the installation of a few automobile light-reflectors. Even the experiments in the province of acting techniques are seldom made use of. It is only recently that this or that actor in New York is becoming interested in the methods of the Stanislavsky school.

What are we to say of the other, the second function, which aesthetics have bestowed on the theatre: instruction? Here, too, we find experiments and the results of experiments. The drama of Ibsen, Tolstoy, Strindberg, Gorky, Chekhov, Hauptmann, Shaw, Kaiser, and O'Neill is an experimental drama. It is an important experiment which reshapes the problems of our time into theatrical terms.[1]

We have the social-critical drama of environment from Ibsen to Nordahl Grieg, and the Symbolist drama from Strindberg to Pär Lagerkvist. We have a drama typified, perhaps, by my *Three Penny*

---

[1] The important theatres are naturally prominent for the share they had in the experiments along this line. Chekhov had his Stanislavsky, Ibsen his Brahm, et cetera. However, the initiative along the line of increasing the powers of instruction proceeded next most significantly from the drama itself.

Opera, a parable type of drama which is destructive of ideologies, and we have original dramatic forms, developed by such poets as Auden and Kjeld Abell, and which, seen from a purely technical standpoint, contain elements of the revue. At times the theatre did well in endowing social movements (the emancipation of women perhaps, the administration of justice, hygiene, even, in fact, the movement for the emancipation of the proletariat) with definite impulses. Still it cannot be denied that the theatre's insights into the social situation have not been particularly profound. For the most part, as many of its detractors have pointed out, the theatre has been content to deal with society in only the most superficial ways. Because of the theatre's failure to express man's intrinsic social contexts, all attempts at creating a social drama have resulted in the complete destruction of both the *plot* and the *characters.* The theatre, by placing itself in the service of social reform, suffered as art. Not unjustly, though often with rather dubious arguments, do we lament the prostitution of artistic taste and the blunting of the stylistic sense. In fact, there prevails over our theatre today, as a consequence of the many diverse kinds of experiments, a virtual Babylonian confusion of styles. On one and the same stage, in one and the same play, actors perform with utterly dissimilar techniques, and naturalistic acting is done within fanciful scenic designs. The techniques of speech have fallen into a lamentable state, iambics are spoken as if they were common speech, the parlance of the markets is made rhythmical, et cetera, et cetera. The modern actor finds himself just as helpless when faced with the techniques of movement. It is meant to be individual but is only arbitrary, it is meant to be natural but is only accidental. One and the same actor utilizes an action which is suitable for the circus-arena, and the next moment a piece of mime which is discernible only from the first rows of the orchestra, and at that only with a pair of opera glasses. Let us have a clearance sale of all the styles of all the ages, a totally unfair competition between all possible and impossible effects! One certainly cannot say that successes have been lacking, nor can one say that they have cost nothing.

I come now to that phase of the experimental theatre in which all the hitherto described efforts achieved their highest standard and with it their various turning-points or crises. It is in this phase that all the manifestations of the important process, positive as well as negative, appeared at their most prominent: thus the increase of the powers of entertainment along with the development of the techniques of stage illusion, and the increase of the powers of instruction along with the fall of artistic taste.

The most radical attempt to endow the theatre with an instructive character was undertaken by Piscator. I took part in each of his experiments, and there was none of them which did not have as its objective the heightening of the stage's powers of instruction. It was a question, then, of mastering the important contemporary subjects for the stage: the struggle for petroleum, the War, the Revolution, justice, race problems, et cetera. It seemed necessary to rebuild the theatre completely. It is impossible for me to enumerate here all the inventions and innovations which Piscator utilized together with virtually all of the newer technological advances in order to bring to the stage important modern subjects. You undoubtedly know of some of them, such as the use of film, which transformed the rigid backdrop of the stage into a new co-player, analogous to the Greek chorus, and the conveyor-belt which enabled the stage floor to move so that epic scenes could roll past, as in the march of the good soldier Schweik to the wars. Hitherto these inventions have not been adopted by the international theatre, their manners of lighting the stage have been all but forgotten, their utterly ingenious machinery is rusted, and grass grows over all.

Why is it?

It is necessary in order to discontinue this eminent political theatre to reveal its political origins. The increase of the political powers of learning collided with the approaching political reaction. Today, however, we want to confine ourselves to pursuing the development of the turning-point of the theatre in the province of aesthetics.

The experiments of Piscator caused, above all, complete chaos in the theatre. If the stage was transformed into a machine shop, then the auditorium was transformed into an assembly hall. For Piscator the theatre was a parliament, the public a legislative body. To this parliament was presented in plastic terms important, decision-demanding, public affairs. In place of an address by a member of parliament concerning certain untenable social conditions there appeared an artistic reproduction of the situation. The theatre had the ambition to prepare its parliament, the public, to come to political decisions on the basis of the illustrations, statistics, and slogans shown on the stage. While Piscator's theatre did not waive applause, it desired discussion even more. It did not want merely to provide its spectators with an experience, but in addition to wrest from them a practical resolve to take an active hold on life. All means were justified to achieve this end. The technical aspects of the theatre became inordinately complicated. Piscator's stage manager had in front of him a prompt book which was as different from the prompt book of Reinhardt's stage manager as the orchestral score of a Stravinsky opera is from the manuscript of a lute singer. The machinery on the stage was so heavy that it became necessary to support the stage floor of the Nollendorf Theater with iron and cement struts; so much machinery was hung from the dome that it once collapsed. Aesthetic aspects were completely subordinated in the political theatre. Away with painted sets when one could show a film which was shot at the very place of the action, and which possessed a documentary, certifying worth about it. And welcome the cartoon when the artist, for example George Grosz, had something to say to the parliament-public. When the German Kaiser filed a protest through five attorneys that Piscator intended to personify him on the stage by means of an actor, Piscator merely asked whether the Kaiser himself would like to make an appearance; one might say that Piscator offered him an engagement. In short: the objective was of such significance and importance that all means seemed justified. The preparation of the production accorded with the preparation of the play. A whole staff of playwrights worked together on the play, and their work was aided and controlled by a staff of experts, historians, economists, and statisticians.

The experiments of Piscator were the source of virtually all conventions. They took hold of and changed the creative process of the playwright, the style of production, and the work of the theatre architect. *Altogether they strove for a completely new social function for the theatre.*

The revolutionary bourgeois aesthetic, founded by those great enlighteners, Diderot and Lessing, defined the theatre as a place of entertainment and instruction. The Age of Enlightenment, which ushered in a powerful upsurge of European theatre, recognized no opposition between entertainment and instruction. Pure amusement, even in regard to tragic subjects, seemed to Diderot to be quite empty and discreditable when it failed to add to the knowledge of the spectator, and elements of instruction, naturally in artistic forms, seemed in no way to disturb the aspect of amusement; it was after this that amusement was given more substance.

If we observe the theatre of our time we shall find that the two constituent elements of drama and the theatre, entertainment and instruction, have come more and more into sharp conflict. This opposition exists today.

Naturalism, with its "intellectualization of the arts," which provided it with social bearing, had doubtless paralyzed significant aesthetic forces, particularly that of fantasy, the aesthetic sense, and the genuinely poetic. The instructive elements plainly harmed the artistic elements.

The Expressionism of the postwar era had described the world as will and representation and brought a characteristic solipsism. It was the theatre's answer to the great social crisis, just as the philosophical *Machismus* was philosophy's answer to it. It was a revolt of art against life, and the world existed for it only as vision, strangely shattered, the offspring of frightened minds. Expressionism, which greatly enriched the theatre's means of expression and brought about a hitherto unexploited aesthetic gain, showed itself in no position to interpret the world as an object of human usage. The theatre's powers of instruction shriveled away.

The instructional elements of a Piscator production or of a production like my *Three Penny Opera* were, so to speak, installed; they did not result organically from the whole, they stood in opposition to the whole; they interrupted the flow of the play and its events, they thwarted sympathetic understanding, they were cold showers for those who wanted to sympathize. I hope that the moralizing parts of the *Three Penny Opera* and its didactic songs are to some extent entertaining, but surely there can be no doubt that this entertainment is different from that which one experiences from the scenes of the play proper. The character of this play is two-pronged, instruction and entertainment stand together in open hostility.

We perceive from the fact that through entertainment the public is split into at least two hostile social camps, so that the common art experience falls to pieces; it is a political fact. The enjoyment of learning is subject to social position. The artistic treat is subject to political attitude, so that it can be challenged and become accepted. But even if we consider only the one part of the public that is in political agreement, we are able to see how the conflict between the powers of entertainment and the powers of instruction becomes critical. It is a quite definite, new kind of learning which cannot reconcile itself to a definite, old kind of self-entertainment. In one of the (later) phases of the experiments every new increase in the powers of instruction led to an immediate decrease in the powers of entertainment. ("This isn't theatre any more, it's an adult education class.") Conversely, the effect upon the nervous system, which is the result of emotional acting, consistently threatened the performance's powers of instruction. (Bad actors were often interested in utilizing the instructional aspect of the theatre.) In other words: the more the public was emotionally affected the less capable it was of learning. That is, the more we brought the public to where it agreed, experienced, sympathized, just that much less was it capable of seeing the ins and outs of the matter, that much less did it learn, and the more there was to learn, just that much less was the artistic treat brought to realization.

The crisis was this: the experiments of half a century, brought about in almost all civilized countries, had won for the theatre an utterly new range of subjects, a new sphere of problems, and thereby made it a factor of eminent social significance. But they had brought the theatre to the place where any further development of the verdict-finding, social (political) experience must necessarily destroy the artistic experience. On the other side, however, the artistic experience always came about less often without the further development of the verdict-finding experience. A technical apparatus and a style of production were developed which were able to produce illusion rather than practicality, intoxication rather than elevation, and deception rather than enlightenment.

Of what profit was a Constructivist stage when it was not socially constructive, what profit was there in the finest lighting plant when it illuminated false and childish representations of the world, and what profit was there in a Suggestivist art of the theatre when it served only to convince us that an X was a U? Of what use was the whole box of magic tricks when it could only offer us artificial substitutes for actual experiences? What purpose was there in this constant illumination of problems which always remained unresolved? Was all this meant to gratify not only the nerves but the understanding as well? One could not possibly have ended here.

The development pressed for a fusion of the two functions, entertainment and instruction.

If these endeavors are to attain a social consciousness, then they must finally prepare the theatre to develop a view of life through artistic means, to develop models of the social life of human beings, in order to help the spectator to understand his social surroundings and to help him control them rationally and emotionally.

Man today knows little about the legalities which control his life. As a social being his general reaction is emotional, but these emotional reactions are vague, inexact, ineffective. The sources of his emotions and passions are just as bogged up and polluted as the sources of his knowledge. Man today, living in a rapidly changing world and himself rapidly changing, lacks an image of the world which agrees with him and on the basis of which he can act with a view to success. His conceptions of the social life of human beings are false, inaccurate, and contradictory, his image is what one might call impracticable, that is, with his image of the world, the world of human beings, he cannot control the world. He does not know on what he is dependent, he lacks a grasp on social machinery which is necessary to cause the desired effect. A knowledge of the nature of things, so greatly and so ingeniously increased and expanded, is incapable, without a knowledge of the nature of man, human society in its totality, of making this control of nature a source of happiness for mankind. It will far sooner become a source of unhappiness. So it happens that our great discoveries and inventions have become an ever increasing threat to mankind, so that today nearly every invention is received with a cry of triumph which soon turns into a cry of fear.

Before the war I experienced a genuinely historic scene on the radio: the institute of the physicist Niels Bohr in Copenhagen was being interviewed concerning a revolutionary discovery in the field of nuclear fission. The physicists reported that a new, tremendous source of energy had been discovered. When the interviewer asked whether a practical utilization of the experiment was yet possible, he received the answer: "No, not yet." In a tone of great relief the interviewer replied: "Thank God for that! I firmly believe that mankind is not yet mature enough to take possession of such a source of energy!" It was clear that he had only the war industries in mind. The physicist Albert Einstein does not go quite so far, but he goes far enough, when in a few short sentences, which are to be buried in a capsule at the

New York World's Fair, as a report on our time to future generations, he writes the following:

> Our time is a mine of inventive intellects whose inventions could ease our lives considerably. We cross the seas by means of mechanical power, and we also use that power to free mankind from all fatiguing physical labor. We have learned to fly and are able by means of electric waves to disseminate news and information throughout the entire world. Yet production and distribution of merchandise is far from organized, so that each of us must live in fear of being forced from the economic sphere. Moreover, people living in different lands murder one another at irregular periodic intervals, so that all who ponder the future must live in fear. This comes from the fact that the intelligence and character of the masses are incomparably lower than the intelligence and character of the few, those who produce things of worth for the common good.

Einstein thus proves the fact that the control of nature, insofar as we have control of it, contributes little to a happy life for man, and further that man in general is lacking in knowledge how to turn these discoveries and inventions to his own use.[2] They know too little about their own nature. The fact that man knows so little about himself is the reason why his knowledge of nature is of so little help to him. In point of fact, the monstrous oppression and exploitation of man by man, the warlike butcheries and peaceable degradations of all kinds across the entire planet have almost become natural by now, but man, faced with these natural manifestations, is unfortunately not so ingenious and qualified as when faced with other natural manifestations. The great wars, for example, seem as innumerable as earth tremors, and therefore as seemingly inevitable as the power of nature itself, but whereas earth tremors come to an end, man's inhumanity to man seems never to reach an end. It is clear how much would be gained, if, for example, the theatre, if not art itself, were capable of providing us with a practicable view of life. An art capable of this would be able to take firm hold on social development, it would not merely radiate more or

---

[2] We need not here enter into a painstaking critique of the technocratic point of view of the highly educated. Normally that which is of use to society will proceed completely from the masses, and the few inventive intellects are very helpless where the sphere of economics is concerned. We are satisfied here with the fact that Einstein confirms the ignorance concerning cooperative interests, directly and indirectly.

less apathetic impulses but deliver its findings to sensitive and intelligent men of the world, the world of human beings, for their use.

But the problem is not at all simple. The very first experiments showed that art, in order to perform its duty, had to stimulate certain emotions, provide certain experiences, but by no means correct views of life or genuine illustrations of happenings between men. It achieved its effects with incomplete, deceitful, or obsolete views of life. Through artistic suggestion, which it knows how to exercise, it invests the most absurd assertions concerning human relations with the appearance of truth. The more powerful it is, the more unverifiable its productions. In place of logic we have flights of fancy, in place of argument we have rhetoric. Aesthetics demand a particular plausibility for all happenings, otherwise effects will either not occur or else be impaired. At the same time, however, there is also the question of a purely aesthetic plausibility, a so-called aesthetic logic. The poet is granted his own world, it has its own legality. If this or that set of elements is specified, then all other elements must be similarly specified and the principle of specification must be in some degree uniform in order to save the whole.

Art achieves this privilege of being able to construct its own world, which need not conform to any other, through a particular phenomenon which, on the basis of the Suggestivist technique, asserts that within the artist there exists the established sympathetic understanding of the spectator, and which passes from the artist into the characters and events on the stage. It is this principle of sympathetic understanding which we have now to consider.

Sympathetic understanding is a main support of the prevailing aesthetic. In the imposing *Poetics* of Aristotle we have a description of how catharsis, that is, the spiritual purification of the spectator, was brought about through *mimesis*. The actor imitates the hero (Oedipus or Prometheus), and he does so with such suggestion and power of conversion that the spectator imitates him in the role and thus possesses himself of the hero's experience. Hegel, who, to my knowledge, drew up the last of the important systems of aesthetics, refers to the ability of man to experience the same emotions when faced with simulated reality as he does when faced with reality itself. What I want to acquaint you with now is that a series of experiments to establish a practicable view of life by means of the theatre's resources has led to the staggering question whether to achieve this end it is necessary, more or less, to surrender sympathetic understanding. Unless one perceives humanity, with all its conditions, proceedings, manners of behavior, and institutions, as something stable and unchangeable, and unless one accepts the attitudes of humanity, as one has accepted them about nature with such success for several centuries, those critical attitudes concerning change and the mastery of nature, then one is unable to utilize the technique of sympathetic understanding. Sympathetic understanding of changeable human beings, of avoidable acts, and of superfluous pain, et cetera, is not possible. As long as the stars of his fate hang over King Lear, as long as we consider him as being unchangeable, his deeds subject to nature without restriction, even presented as being fated, so long can we be sympathetically understanding toward him. To discuss his behavior is as impossible as a discussion of the splitting of the atom would have been in the tenth century.

If the intercourse between stage and public were to occur on the basis of sympathetic understanding, then at any given moment the spectator could have seen only as much as the hero saw with whom he was joined in sympathetic understanding. And toward particular situations on the stage opposite him he could only have such emotional responses as the "mood" on stage permitted. The observations, emotions, and perceptions of the spectators were the same as those which brought the characters on stage into line. The stage could scarcely generate emotions, permit observations, and facilitate understanding, which are not suggestively represented on it. Lear's wrath over his daughters infects the spectator, that is, the spectator, watching him, could only experience wrath, not perhaps amazement or uneasiness, and the same holds for other possible emotions. The wrath of Lear, therefore, could not be tested against its justification nor could it be provided with a prophecy of its possible consequences. It was not to be discussed, only to be shared in. In this way social phenomena appeared eternal, natural, unchangeable, unhistorical, and did not hold for discussion. My use of the term "discussion" here does not imply a dispassionate treatment of a theme, a purely intellectual process. We are not concerned with simply making the spectator immune to the wrath of Lear. It is only that the direct transplantation of this wrath must be stopped. An example: The wrath of Lear is shared in by his faithful servant Kent. Kent soundly thrashes a servant of the thankless daughters, who is instructed to disobey one of Lear's wishes. Shall the spectator of our time share Lear's wrath and approve of it, while in essence sympathizing with the thrashing of the servant, carried out on Lear's orders? The question is this: how can this scene be played so that the spectator, on the contrary, flies into a passion because of Lear's wrath? Only an emotion of this kind which can deny the spectator sympathetic understanding, which generally only he can experience, and which generally could occur only to him, and then only if he breaks through the theatre's power of suggestion, can be socially justified. Tolstoy had excellent things to say on this very matter.

Sympathetic understanding is the important artificial means of an age in which man is the variable and his surroundings the constant. One can be sympathetically understanding only toward a person who, unlike ourselves, bears the stars of his destiny within him.

Human beings go to the theatre in order to be swept away, captivated, impressed, uplifted, horrified, moved, kept in suspense, released, diverted, set free, set going, transplanted from their own time, and supplied with illusions. All of this goes so much without saying that the art of the theatre is candidly defined as having the power to release, sweep away, uplift, et cetera. It is not an art at all unless it does so.

The question, then, is this: is the artistic treat at all possible without sympathetic understanding, or, in any case, is it possible on a basis other than sympathetic understanding?

What could a new basis such as this offer us?

What can be substituted for *pity* and *terror,* the twin-yoked classical cause of Aristotle's catharsis? When one renounces hypnosis to what can one appeal? What attitude should a spectator partake of in this new theatre, when he is denied the illusionary, passive, resigned-to-fate attitude? He should no longer be abducted from his own world into the world of art, no longer be kidnapped; on the contrary, he should be ushered into his own real world, with attentive faculties. Would it be possible, perhaps, to substitute for pity, helpful collaboration? Is it possible therewith to create a new contact between the stage and the spectator, might this offer a new basis for the artistic treat? I cannot describe here the new technology of playwriting, of theatre construction, and of acting techniques, through which our experiments were carried out. The principle consists in introducing in place of sympathetic understanding what we will call *alienation.*

What is alienation?

To alienate an event or a character is simply to take what to the event or character is obvious, known, evident, and produce surprise and curiosity out of it. Let us consider again the wrath of Lear over the thanklessness of his daughters. Through the technique of sympathetic understanding the actor is able to present this wrath in such a way that the spectator sees it as the most natural thing in the world, so that he cannot imagine how Lear could not become wrathful, so that he is in complete agreement with Lear, sympathizing with him completely, having himself fallen into the same wrath. Through the technique of alienation, on the other hand, the actor presents the wrath of Lear in such a way that the spectator can be surprised at it, so that he can conceive of still other reactions from Lear as well as that of wrath. The attitude of Lear is alienated, that is, it is presented as belonging specifically to Lear, as something shocking, remarkable, as a social phenomenon which is not self-evident. This emotion of wrath is human, but it is not universally applicable, there are human beings who do not experience it. The experiences of Lear need not produce in all people of all times the emotion of wrath. Wrath may be an eternally possible reaction of the human being, but this kind of wrath, the kind of wrath which manifests itself in this way and which has such origins as those of Lear, is an ephemeral thing. The process of alienation, then, is the process of historifying, of presenting events and persons as historical, and therefore as ephemeral. The same, of course, may happen with contemporaries, their attitudes may also be presented as ephemeral, historical, and evanescent.

What do we achieve by this? We achieve the fact that the spectator need no longer see the human beings presented on the stage as being unchangeable, unadaptable, and handed over helpless to fate. What he sees is that this human being is thus and so because conditions are thus and so. And conditions are thus and so because human beings are thus and so. This human being, however, is capable of being presented not only in this way, as he is, but in other ways also, as he might be; conditions, too, are capable of being presented in other ways than as they are. As a result of this the spectator has a new attitude in the theatre. He has the same attitude toward the images of the human world opposite him on the stage which he, as a human being, has had toward nature during this century. He is also welcomed into the theatre as the great reformer, one who is capable of coming to grips with the natural and social processes, one who no longer merely accepts the world passively but who masters it. The theatre no longer seeks to intoxicate him, supply him with illusions, make him forget the world, to reconcile him with his fate. The theatre now spreads the world in front of him to take hold of and use for his own good.

The technique of alienation was developed in Germany through a new series of experiments. At the Theater am Schiffbauerdamm in Berlin we attempted to develop a new style of production. The most gifted of the younger generation of actors worked with us. There were Helene Weigel, Peter Lorre, Oskar Homolka, Neher and Busch. Our experiments could not be carried through so methodically as those of the foreign schools of Stanislavsky, Meyerhold, and Vachtangov because we had no state support, but our experiments were, therefore, pursued more widely and not merely in the professional theatre. Artists participated in experiments of schools, workers' choruses, amateur groups, et cetera. From the beginning amateur groups were developed along with the professional. The experiments led to a vast simplification of apparatus, style of production, and subject matter.

It was a question throughout of continuing the earlier experiments, and those of Piscator's theatre in particular. Even in Piscator's last experiments the consequent development of the technical apparatus led to the realization that the machinery which then dominated everything might also permit a beautiful simplicity of production. The so-called *epic* style of production, which we developed at the Theater am Schiffbauerdamm, revealed its artistic qualities relatively quickly and the *non-Aristotelian technique of drama* set about working importantly with important social subjects. Possibilities appeared for transforming the dancelike elements and the elements of group composition of Meyerhold's school from something artificial into something artistic, and the naturalistic elements of Stanislavsky's into realistic elements. The art of speech was joined with the art of movement, while workaday speech and the recitation of verse were thoroughly fashioned from the so-called *movement principle*. Theatre construction was completely revolutionized. Piscator's principles, freely employed, permitted not only an instructive theatre but a beautiful one as well. Symbolism and Illusionism might be liquidated in like manner, and the *Neher principle* for the development of scenic design permitted the scenic designer, according to the needs determined in rehearsal, to gain profit from the acting of the performers and to influence the acting in his own way. The playwright was able to propose his play to the actors and the scenic designer in uninterrupted collaboration, to influence as well as be influenced. Painters and musicians at once regained their independence and were able through their own artificial means to make their presence felt on the subject matter: the collective art project appeared before the spectator as a series of dissociated elements.

From the start the classical repertoire organized itself on the basis of many such experiments. The artificial means of alienation opened a broad path of approach to the vital importance of the dramatic works of other ages. Through alienation it became possible to produce entertainingly and instructively the worthwhile old plays without disturbing elements of over-actualization and museum-like treatment.

Liberation from the compulsion to practice hypnosis is noted to be particularly advantageous to the contemporary amateur theatre (worker-, student- and child-actors). It is becoming conceivable to draw boundaries between the performances of amateur and professional actors without the need to relinquish one of the basic functions of the theatre.

On the basis of the new foundation, for example, such divergent acting techniques as perhaps those of the Vachtangov or the Ochlopkov troops and the Workers' troop could be joined. The heterogeneous experiments of half a century appear to have found a basis for their utilization.

Nevertheless, these experiments are not so easily described, and I have simply to assert here that what we intend is to make the real artistic treat possible on the basis of alienation. This is not too terribly surprising since, seen from a purely technical point of view, even the theatres of past ages produced results through the use of alienation effects, the Chinese theatre, for example, the classical Spanish theatre, the popular theatre of Breughel's time, and the Elizabethan theatre.

Is this new style of production *the* new style, is it a technique which is complete and which can be surveyed as such, the definitive result of all the experiments? The answer is: No. It is *one* way, the way which *we* have gone. Experiments must continue. The same problem exists for all art, and it is a gigantic one. The solution which we are striving toward is only *one* of the perhaps possible solutions to the problem which is this: how can the theatre be both entertaining and instructive at the same time? How can it be drawn away from this intellectual narcotics-traffic and be changed from a place of illusion to a place of practical experience? How can the shackled, ignorant, freedom- and knowledge-seeking human being of our century, the tormented and heroic, abused and ingenious, the changeable and the world-changing human being of this frightful and important century achieve his own theatre which will help him to master not only himself but also the world?

Translated by CARL MUELLER

Comedy

BY CHRISTOPHER FRY

A FRIEND ONCE TOLD ME that when he was under the influence of ether he dreamed he was turning over the pages of a great book, in which he knew he would find, on the last page, the meaning of life. The pages of the book were alternately tragic and comic, and he turned page after page, his excitement growing, not only because he was approaching the answer but because he couldn't know, until he arrived, on which side of the book the final page would be. At last it came: the universe opened up to him in a hundred words: and they were uproariously funny. He came back to consciousness crying with laughter, remembering everything. He opened his lips to speak. It was then that the great and comic answer plunged back out of his reach.

If I had to draw a picture of the person of Comedy it is so I should like to draw it: the tears of laughter running down the face, one hand still lying on the tragic page which so nearly contained the answer, the lips about to frame the great revelation, only to find it had gone as disconcertingly as a chair twitched away when we went to sit down. Comedy is an escape, not from truth but from despair: a narrow escape into faith. It believes in a universal cause for delight, even though knowledge of the cause is always twitched away from under us, which leaves us to rest on our own buoyancy. In tragedy every moment is eternity; in comedy eternity is a moment. In tragedy we suffer pain; in comedy pain is a fool, suffered gladly.

Charles Williams once said to me—indeed it was the last thing he said to me: he died not long after: and it was shouted from the tail-board of a moving bus, over the heads of pedestrians and bicyclists outside the Midland Station, Oxford—"When we're dead we shall have the sensation of having enjoyed life altogether, whatever has happened to us." The distance between us widened, and he leaned out into the space so that his voice should reach me: "Even if we've been murdered, what a pleasure to have been capable of it!"; and, having spoken the words for comedy, away he went like the revelation which almost came out of the ether.

He was not at all saying that everything is for the best in the best of all possible worlds. He was saying—or so it seems to me—that there is an angle of experience where the dark is distilled into light: either here or hereafter, in or out of time: where our tragic fate finds itself with perfect pitch, and goes straight to the key which creation was composed in. And comedy senses and reaches out to this experience. It says, in effect, that, groaning as we may be, we move in the figure of a dance, and, so moving, we trace the outline of the mystery.

Laughter did not come by chance, but how or why it came is beyond comprehension, unless we think of it as a kind of perception. The human animal, beginning to feel his spiritual inches, broke in onto an unfamiliar tension of life, where laughter became inevitable. But how? Could he, in his first unlaughing condition, have contrived a comic view of life and then developed the strange rib-shaking response? Or is it not more likely that when he was able to grasp the tragic nature of time he was of a stature to sense its comic nature also; and, by the experience of tragedy and the intuition of comedy, to make his difficult way? The difference between tragedy and comedy is the difference between experience and intuition. In the experience we strive against every condition of our animal life: against death, against the frustration of ambition, against the instability of human love. In the intuition we trust the arduous eccentricities we're born to, and see the oddness of a creature who has never got acclimatized to being created. Laughter inclines me to know that man is essential spirit; his body, with its functions and accidents and frustrations, is endlessly quaint and remarkable to him; and though comedy accepts our position in time, it barely accepts our posture in space.

The bridge by which we cross from tragedy to comedy and back again is precarious and narrow. We find ourselves in one or the other by the turn of a thought; a turn such as we make when we turn from speaking to listening. I know that when I set about writing a comedy the idea presents itself to me first of all as tragedy. The characters press on to the theme with all their divisions and perplexities heavy about them; they are already entered for the race to doom, and good and evil are an infernal tangle skinning the fingers that try to unravel them. If the characters were not qualified for tragedy there would be no comedy, and to some extent I have to cross the one before I can light on the other. In a century less flayed and quivering we might reach it more directly; but not now, unless every word we write is going to mock us. A bridge has to be crossed, a thought has to be turned. Somehow the characters have to unmortify themselves: to affirm life and assimilate death and persevere in joy. Their hearts must be as determined as the phoenix; what burns must also light and renew: not by a vulnerable optimism but by a hard-won maturity of delight, by the intuition of comedy, an active patience declaring the solvency of good. The Book of Job is the great reservoir of comedy. "But there is a spirit in man . . . Fair weather cometh out of the north . . . The blessing of him that was ready to perish came upon me: And I caused the widow's heart to sing for joy."

I have come, you may think, to the verge of saying that comedy is greater than tragedy. On the verge I stand and go no further. Tragedy's experience hammers against the mystery to make a breach which would admit the whole triumphant answer. Intuition has no such potential. But there are times in the state of man when comedy has a special worth, and the present is one of them: a time when the loudest faith has been faith in a trampling materialism, when literature has been thought unrealistic which did not mark and remark our poverty and doom. Joy (of a kind) has been all on the devil's side, and one of the necessities of our time is to redeem it. If not, we are in poor sort to meet the circumstances, the circumstances being the contention of death with life, which is to say evil with good, which is to say desolation with delight. Laughter may seem to be only like an exhalation of air, but out of that air we came; in the beginning we inhaled it; it is a truth, not a fantasy, a truth voluble of good which comedy stoutly maintains.

Religion and the Theatre

BY UGO BETTI

TO APPROACH A SUBJECT LIKE this in a truly meaningful way, it seems to me that it is necessary first to force oneself to a humble objectivity and even to a certain detachment. This subject is too important and we are bound to it by too jealous a commitment to allow ourselves to dismiss it with pat solutions or lyrical effusions. It is necessary to examine it with a dispassionate eye instead of imagining what we would like it to be. The point is to understand to what extent the movement which is drawing the theatre toward religious, Christian themes is authentic.

I am speaking, of course, of the theatre of today, which is history in the making, a phenomenon still in the process of taking shape. In my opinion, only the theatre of today is in every respect truly theatre, that is, actual collaboration between speakers and listeners in the common effort to formulate the dialogue of our epoch and to give expression to its aspirations.

In the meantime, there is indeed one point worthy of consideration: that such a subject—Christ and the theatre, and even more generally, religion and the theatre—has assumed, in the conscience of many, a new importance precisely at a time when large areas of disbelief, or at least indifference, seem to spread both in the individual soul and in the world.

At least, such is the appearance. Nonetheless, it is precisely now that a confused instinct leads many playwrights and many audiences to converge on themes, problems, figures, and events which, consciously or not, revolve like the wheels of a mill, spun by the visible or hidden current of the same stream: Religion.

This may be religion viewed as a good already attained, which must now be exalted and asserted; or as a good yet to be attained, toward which one is moved by an indistinct desire if not by a precise aim; or as the inner re-elaboration of certain principles in order to make them alive and integral; or even religion viewed as an enemy to be attacked, but not without a wealth of distress and remorse.

Many contemporary plays are indeed religious in an obvious way, and since they represent edifying episodes and settings which are peculiarly sacred, they could, in fact, be performed just as well in a church square as on the stage of a theatre. In general, these works are so well known that I find it unnecessary to name them. Their titles are frequently displayed on the billboards, and audiences, even in the most sophisticated cities, and perhaps especially here, flock to see them.

But if we wish to interpret this religious character in broader terms, the field is considerably widened. One may go so far as to say that it is above all the theatre which corroborates an observation that is only surprising at first sight: if our epoch has affinities with any other, it is more with the passionate Middle Ages than with the brilliant and tolerant Renaissance. In some respects, our epoch, too, is eager for universal systems, and it is not so much preoccupied with living and prospering in them, as in fighting for them, in asserting that they *are* universal and absolute: in a word, religious. This need for universal systems often demands to be heard in the theatre, although through very different and frequently incongruous voices. But, if considered as an indication, perhaps the more these voices appear incongruous—incongruous because they are unconscious: a spontaneous movement and not a pre-established plan—the more their importance as a symptom must be recognized. We are concerned with the theatre, that is, with an art. This is not an area where a rigorous, logical consistency—critical, political, or philosophical—is essential; here, what is often alive and positive is precisely that which, on the plane of logic and orthodoxy, may seem unclear.

That part of the contemporary theatre which is insensitive to this need may be said to consist of plays which are little above the level of entertainment and, if listened to attentively, sound to us a little out of tune with the times, and basically antiquated. What truly sets these plays in motion, perhaps under the pretense of real problems, is a basic indifference to any problem whatever, an air of routine which is at times good-natured, at times impertinent, and fundamentally nihilistic even though gay on the surface. It is, in short, the survivor of the facile, post-romantic hedonism of the nineteenth century under a different guise, scarcely modernized by a certain irony. They are anachronistic plays; although numerous, they are not part of the picture. The true picture, surveyed in its entirety, induces us to conclude that all, or almost all of the contemporary theatre that counts draws its life from needs which, although variously expressed, are essentially religious.

The basic authenticity of these needs seems to me unquestionable. They are born, ultimately, of the ineradicable need of modern man to feel reassured by certain hopes. But it is equally unquestionable that such a deep authenticity is combined with countless other heterogeneous motives which contaminate it and at times end by overwhelming it.

The first of these contaminations is that of "religiosity," I mean a religion which is no longer a precise issue and necessity—and maybe even a painful error—but a benign substitute, a flexible fall-back, a comfortable *flou* which evades precisely the dilemmas that are well defined (the "either-or," the clear-cut boundaries between good and evil, the responsibility toward others and toward ourselves), a poetic way of making us always right and never wrong. Closely related to this is the vague humanitarianism with which the modern age pads every edge a little, and, pushing them toward a meaningless philanthropy, has diluted all principles and relationships of politics, family, justice, and, naturally, religion. It is used to make us all feel good and at peace with our conscience, without any great effort. How much shrewdness, even if unconscious, under this sugar-coating! In the theatre we can taste its flavor toward the third act, in the reconciliations and effusions which resolve everything, and perhaps a grand finale accompanied by organ music. Not that I am disturbed by the sound of organs or by the effusions at the end, quite the contrary. But I think that one has to pay for those results and suffer for them; and when I see them given away free, I become suspicious. This extreme need for love, this great flame —Christ—is, I think, something else.

Another contamination comes from the decadent self-gratification by which an emotion, originally religious, is little by little cherished and nurtured in and for itself, a perturbation savored like a quivering sensation, a rare experience: confessions in which suddenly glow the oozings of I don't know what sexuality; martyrdom, guilelessness, ecstasy, whose cruelty or self-annihilation is pierced (even though very remotely) by some kind of inversion. (I cannot avoid thinking of certain moments in *The Cocktail Party*.)

Next to this there is the trap of the décor. The religious issue often implies, especially for us Latins, an ostentatious background. Gold, music, purples, rays falling from high stained-glass windows, angels' tresses on frescos; one feels, at times, that the poet writing, let's say, *The Martyrdom of San Sebastian,* or the director staging an *auto sacramental,* has ended by being more attracted to all this than to the rest—more to gestures, colors and drapery than to the sentiment.

Another contamination, it seems to me, is the one caused by the intellect: too intently bent on its inner polemics, on its own way of "being Christian," on more and more subtle doubts and hypotheses expressed through self-questioning and increasingly more labyrinthine crises so that these gradually fascinate the intellect, but perhaps more for their complication and subtlety per se than for their substance. Then, once the contact with facts has been weakened, the self-revelations and the polemics come close to resembling an agonizing chess game of words, a dry equation of algebraic signs. In all this, apart from a certain gratification, there is no want of a real ferment which I would also call useful if I didn't see that certain scrupulous self-examinations end, almost without exception, by acknowledging their own inanity and by characteristically returning to the initial propositions, which would indicate a certain lack either of courage at the conclusive moment or of concreteness in the premises.

Not even the theatre seems to me immune from such indulgences, whose real place is in diaries and essays, although the physical weight and near coarseness, peculiar to the theatre, reject by their very nature all that is of little weight, and easily reveal, in the harsh brightness of the footlights, the quasi-arbitrariness of certain arabesques: arabesques that are almost a luxury (whether or not literature, as action, fulfills a commitment of a religious nature); antitheses that are mainly verbal ("he will bear, then, the martyrdom of not having suffered martyrdom"); complications that are refined and, I would say, marginal (martyrs who spend their last vigil in self-contemplation, examining with subtle syllogisms their own spiritual experience—whether it is one of fear, of pride, of forgiveness, or what have you). Inquiries of this kind are certainly not superfluous, but since they deal with exceptional cases, they evade the real, important issues, the central ones, those shared by everybody—the issues of the people we meet on the street, whose conscience, in regard to religion, is not preoccupied with such fine points, but with other problems which are humbler and probably more important and, in the end, more meaningful and universal; with other and far more dangerous doubts which, finally, are also our own doubts and dangers; with other and truer anguishes.

Such an excess of subtlety, such an eagerness to attach importance to the least coils of one's conscience—in short, such a lack of coarseness—probably betrays a certain lack of seriousness, in the moral sense of that word—a nursing of one's own perturbation, which, from the beginning, carries within it the punishment of sterility. Nevertheless, in spite of all its errors and lack of concreteness, there is something positive in all this. Undoubtedly, there is the need to discuss certain situations anew, to react to passive resignation, to live one's faith and not to accept it as a free gift, to enrich it with a suffering and an effort of one's own. Indeed, there is in all this a rich possibility, and an important one, which can be understood especially by comparing it with another of the dangers which threaten the authenticity—let us say it: even the usefulness—of the religious issue in art, and specifically in the theatre: the opposite danger, which I will call habitual complacency.

But at this point I must honestly admit that these pages (I realize it as I go on) cannot avoid being, above all, a confession. In the long run, all the issues inevitably confront me already conditioned by my pre-occupations as a writer. The confusions and misrepresentations to which the originally religious impulse of a play is subject, the contaminations of which I have spoken so far, are contaminations which beguile me too; they are the traps that I should like to avoid and to which, when I have finished writing, I suspect, once again, I have succumbed. Religiosity without rigor; the extreme need to love and be loved which, however, remains so indolent; an accommodating and soft humanitarianism; the sensation more alluring than feeling; the frame which enamors more than the picture; the condescension in showing or believing one's own intelligence and in putting oneself on display; certainly, all these faults are mine too, for it would be strange if I were immune to the malaise affecting practically all the literature of our age. On the other hand, precisely the fact that I am tainted with these faults (and the fact that I am involved, as an old craftsman, in such difficulties), precisely this gives me the right, my only right, to have my say, although a crude and unqualified theoretician, in the tremendous subject of this essay.

It is in this spirit of making a confession that, coming now to speak of the danger represented by habitual complacency, I will begin with a humble disclosure: rarely, after seeing a religious play, especially if explicitly and programatically religious, rarely, I say, have I returned home and gone over it in my mind without experiencing a certain dissatisfaction—but not because I had been irked by the "contaminations" of which I have already spoken. In general they were works without faults, works entirely dedicated to the humble—and lofty and ancient—task of being religious and nothing else; interpretations of glorious miracles; representations of edifying sacrifices; viscissitudes of Carmelite nuns led to the scaffold or of Jesuits put to the test; by and large excellent works, and unobjectionable in every respect. And yet I experienced a sense of disappointment.

This disappointment was due first of all, if I may say so, to reasons of pure dramatics. From the first scene it was altogether too obvious how the whole thing was going to end. No matter how cleverly or ingenuously the author had shuffled his cards, everything happened exactly as it had been arranged and also, unfortunately, as it had been foreseen. Battles were won and lost at the very outset—won, naturally, by the good cause and lost by the evil, won by the spiritual and lost by the material, won by faith and lost by disbelief. But, in a religious work, what other solution can conflicts of such a nature have? The posing of such conflicts is enough to give us their solution. Perhaps the fault (I am still speaking from a dramatic point of view) of the plays which disappointed me consisted precisely in this: from the very beginning every passion and every character appeared already labeled and defined, or (if the author had ably managed to deceive us) they had been labeled and defined in the author's own mind. They entered into the plays, then, already judged and without hope, judged *a priori* and not brought in to struggle with real alternatives of victory and defeat, but to run through a fixed (and, therefore, habitual) trajectory, measured by a yardstick which allows no error. (I repeat once more that I am speaking from a dramatic point of view.) That's why plays which had Freedom as their goal seemed to the man of the theatre somewhat lacking in freedom, why plays having Life as their subject matter seemed in want of life. Don't misunderstand me: those plays did not lack emotive power. The great crosses shedding their light on the darkness, the sacred chants rising above Error, those immolations, those miracles, those heroic deeds—sublime flowers of a sincere, and severely tried, faith—had the power of making the lady next to me wipe away her tears and even of filling my heart with palpitations. I do not wish to sound irreverent, but such an emotive power seemed to me somewhat automatic and physical. If you will forgive me the analogy, it recalled to my mind the emotion by which, undoubtedly, both young and old are assailed when they watch the flag go by from a crowded sidewalk, and behind the flag the marching step of an heroic troop amidst the sounding of trumpets and the roll of drums. A slight shiver runs automatically through the crowd, but it is a slight shiver that remains such: not one of those who experience it would dream, a moment later, of leaving his own business to join the army, heaven forbid, or of immolating himself. Thus the tears that flowed down the cheeks of the lady at my side left me with the suspicion that they would have very little influence on what she would do once she was back home. Those tears did not change that woman. The sacrifice of the Carmelite nuns had certainly moved her, but, nonetheless, it would not occur to her the next day, or six months hence, to refrain from certain actions and habits. In sum, that emotive power and those plays fell short. The conventional targets they reached no longer amount to much. The true targets, the dangerous targets of today—that is, certain objections widespread in the world, certain disbeliefs, certain discouragements—are probably beyond the range of fire, and the sacrifices of the Carmelites or of Thomas à Beckett cannot even scratch them.

That contrast between good and evil, then, had a very mediocre effect on a world whose characteristic is precisely this: to believe very little in the real existence of good and evil. For some time the world has suspected that vice and virtue are only products like vitriol and sugar, that certain moral conflicts are mere conventions sanctioned by smart people to keep the fools in check. Above all, I fear that several of the ladies in the audience, or several of their friends, are rather skeptical about what Someone said to each and every one of them: "Verily I say unto thee, Today shalt thou be with me in paradise." I am of the opinion that today many people are scarcely convinced that they will be resurrected after death in order that they may be judged. At any rate, they don't believe in it strongly enough to conform their actions to such a conviction. That is all. It is very simple: one must try to convince them again.

In regard to such a situation, what is the thinking of many Catholics, particularly writers and critics? Their thinking strikes me as curiously rosy. I say "curiously" because the reality of today, on the crust of the world, from the big atheisms to the small indifferences, from the apocalyptic thundering in the far away horizon to the most trivial episodes.

of everyday exchange and intercourse, the reality of today does not seem to me to encourage a great optimism, but rather, it appears such that persons in a position of high responsibility solemnly avow their concern over it, and even speak of crusades. The optimism of a complacent conscience, however, does not allow concern. What strikes one and causes one to envy them is a kind of soft, quiescent contentment, always repeating that "all is well"—the words of those who live off the fat of the land, and know it. The frame of mind that is at the bottom of this acquiescence seems to me the same as that of the critic who concluded that "tragedy" ended the very moment in which Christ spoke, because wars stop when victory begins. That critic was speaking only of the theatre, but his words leave us nonetheless perplexed. Then wars would be over for mankind; which would mean, to remain in the field of art and the theatre, that Art and Theatre are over too, if it is true that art is always tragedy. With Art and Theatre finished, we are left with only an elegant delight with which to garland our leisure. Leisure, nothing but leisure, if everything were said and done; and our efforts and conflicts would be, to a great extent, superfluous since we have been given the Truth which resolves them once and forever.

I am speaking with the timidity of one who is groping through a maze of problems that are too big for him, and who, at this point, sees himself reduced to the modest resource of a hesitant common sense. We were indeed given a final victory and truth. This is sure. But why these landslides around us, then? And still others announce their coming with far-off thundering. Why these defeats here and there? And why, today and perhaps again tomorrow, this flood of cruelty and hatred, greater than ever before in history? What is the dam that gave way? And, on the other hand, this giving way—was it useless? Is this vast perturbation which is in us and in many others, useless too?

Is error useless—totally useless—and is this effort in our time to fight against it, but at the same time to know it and therefore to love it and extract from it a beneficial suffering, useless too? Should the fact that we have already arrived make our journey useless? We have arrived, but are we surrounded by the everlasting calmness of a haven, by the still waters of a harbor? Why, then, should Bernanos' abbess say to her novice, "Our rules are not a refuge. It isn't the rules that guard us, but we who guard the rules"? Has the danger ceased to exist; is vigilance useless; is doubt itself forbidden, even though it was allowed Christ when He said, "Remove this cup from me," or when He cried with a loud voice at the ninth hour, "Eli, Eli, lama, sabachthani"? Is it a lie, then, this hope we have that Man's life is useful, that it is an ascending, even though difficult, path toward the ever fuller, more intimate, and enlightened discovery of that Truth? Granted the stability and perfection of that Truth, how is it possible not to think that our humble ways, the ways in which we, frail men, gradually become convinced of it and prove to ourselves its eternal validity, may change with time, just as, with time, they lose their efficacy? And don't we see around us so much weakness and bewilderment, and, indeed, a pressing need to be convinced on a new basis in the face of certain new objections, thus more firmly reassuring ourselves of those certainties without which we cannot live? Happy are they who are calm, sure, strong, and no longer need anything, or at least think they don't. But how can we avoid thinking, also, of those who are weak, without faith, and without hope? Is it not true that we must think of them before all?

When I think of men without hope an image often comes to my mind. I imagine them as inhabitants of an arid planet, without water or earth. Since these two elements—the source of life and the place where it exists—are totally unknown to the senses of these men, they are also totally unknown to their minds. But one day, having split, by chance, the rock on which they live, they discover some strange objects that are embedded in it. These objects are also rocks, but different from the others. These men cannot even fathom what a grain of wheat or a fish is, but what they now have before their eyes is a petrified grain and a petrified fish, and they do not know it. Their wise men carefully examine and re-examine those curious scales, those peculiar shapes, those inexplicable formations. And finally these very same shapes and formations, irreconcilable with all other hypotheses, will necessarily and of themselves create an hypothesis which is almost unbelievable, and yet the only one possible. Each one of these two fossils cannot but presuppose a certain unknown element. One will call forth the sea, the other, the earth. Bent over those scales, these men will finally behold what they never have and never will see in their mortal lives, but which, somewhere, if those scales exist, must certainly exist as well—the blue, infinite ocean, the green, marvelous pastures: Life.

No other way could have convinced them: not even an oath. It would have been an inane declaration, words of an unknown language. Only now are they convinced, since they themselves have discovered those scales.

I fear that it is not always possible or useful to speak of faith to those who despair, or to describe that fresh water, that earth in flower, to them. They do not know, and perhaps they do not want to know, what freshness and gardens are. They do not live in such a world, or they do not believe they do.

However, it can be demonstrated that they do belong to it. But demonstrated, perhaps, in one way only. One must enter their refuge and dig into it and know it. In order to do this, we must go to that rocky land and accept it as it is. The proofs must be found there, for it would be of no use to bring them from outside. I believe that by studying man carefully one will undoubtedly discover that, just as the grain of wheat presupposes the earth and the fish, the water, man presupposes God.

I realize that, even at this point, these are nothing but justifications. The means whose validity I am supporting are none but the means which, in writing for the theatre, I, myself, have tried to follow, although in part, unconsciously. But what else should I uphold if not these confused efforts—more than ideas—which have impelled me for so many years? All I can do is try clumsily to prove again certain things to someone, starting from zero. I believe, truly believe, that if we search untiringly at the bottom of all human abdications we will always end by finding, under so many "no's," a small "yes" which will outweigh every objection and will be sufficient to rebuild everything. One must not be afraid of that desert. On the contrary, everything must actually be razed to the ground first, one must find himself on that arid planet, and must have gone there without panaceas in his pocket. When we have truly suffered and understood human baseness, we will find at the bottom (since in error not all is error) several illogical and, I would say, strange needs: "illogical" because they cannot be measured by the yardstick of human reason, "strange" because unknown or, rather, opposed to the mechanism and the advantage of the world in which we live and in which we have discovered them. They deny this world and paint a different one, revealing a "bewildering incongruity between our existence and what it ought to be according to the aspirations of our soul." (I wrote these words twenty-five years ago as an introduction to my first play.)

They are inexplicable needs. But in the soul of the unjust man, and even in the soul of the judge who betrays justice, we will discover that, in the end, he, himself, cannot breathe or survive without justice. Underneath the most hardened bitterness we will, at a certain point, discover in the cruel, selfish, lost souls, a need for mercy, harmony, solidarity, immortality, trust, forgiveness, and, above all, for love: a mercy and a love which are far greater than the pale imitations offered by this world. This is a thirst which all the fountains of the earth cannot quench. Each of these mysterious needs is one side of a perimeter whose complete figure, when we finally perceive it, has one name: GOD.

Translated by GINO RIZZO
and WILLIAM MERIWETHER

Eugene O'Neill

BY HUGO VON HOFMANNSTHAL

IT WAS AT THE SALZBURG FESTIVAL last summer that I first heard the name of Eugene O'Neill. Max Reinhardt was producing one of my plays there; a sort of mystery, a synthetic or symbolic handling of allegorical material, mounted in a church. There were a few Americans in our audience, who aroused my curiosity by relating merely the plots of *The Emperor Jones* and *The Hairy Ape*.

Some time after, I read both these plays; also *Anna Christie* and *The First Man*. These plays and a few others, I am told, have placed Eugene O'Neill in the position of the foremost living American playwright. Judging from those of his plays with which I am familiar, his work is throughout essentially of the theatre. Each play is clear-cut and sharp in outline, solidly constructed from beginning to end; *Anna Christie* and *The First Man* as well as the more original and striking *Emperor Jones* and *The Hairy Ape*. The structural power and pre-eminent simplicity of these works are intensified by the use of certain technical expedients and processes which seem dear to the heart of this dramatist and, I may presume, to the heart of the American theatregoer as well; for instance, the oft-used device of the repetition of a word, a situation, or a motive. In *The Hairy Ape*, the motive of repetition progresses uninterruptedly from scene to scene; the effect becomes more and more tense as the action hurries on to the end. Mr. O'Neill appears to have a decided predilection for striking contrasts, like that, for instance, between the life of the sea and the life of the land, in *Anna Christie*, or between the dull narrowness of middle-class existence and unhampered morality, in *The First Man*. The essential dramatic plot—the "fable," that is—is invariably linked to and revealed by that visual element which the theatre, and above all, I believe, the modern theatre, de-

125

mands. The dialogue is powerful, often direct, and frequently endowed with a brutal though picturesque lyricism.

In an American weekly publication I find the following judgment on Mr. O'Neill, written by an intelligent and very able native critic: "He has a current of thought and feeling that is essentially theatrical. Taken off the stage it might often seem exaggerated, out of taste or monotonous." To this just praise—for it is intended as praise—I can heartily subscribe. But the same writer goes on to say, however, that in this dramatist's best scenes there is a power in the dialogue that is found in only one work among thousands. Granting that this is true, it seems to me that the manner in which Mr. O'Neill handles his dialogue offers an opportunity for some interesting speculations of a general character on the whole question of dramatic dialogue.

In my opinion, granting the primary importance of the dramatic fable, or plot, the creative dramatist is revealed through his handling of dialogue. By this, be it understood, I do not mean the lyrical quality or rhetorical power; these elements are in themselves of little importance in determining the value of dialogue. Let us assume a distinction between literature and drama, and say that the best dialogue is that which, including the purely stylistic or literary qualities, possesses at the same time what is perhaps the most important of all: the quality of movement, of suggestive mimetic action. The best dramatic dialogue reveals not only the motives that determine what a character is to do—as well as what he tries to conceal—but suggests his very appearance, his metaphysical being as well as the grosser material figure. How this is done remains one of the unanswerable riddles of artistic creation. This suggestion of the "metaphysical" enables us to determine in an instant, the moment a person enters the room, whether he is sympathetic or abhorrent, whether he brings agitation or peace; he affects the atmosphere about us, making it solemn or trivial, as the case may be.

The best dialogue is that which charges the atmosphere with this sort of tension; the more powerful it is the less dependent does it become upon the mechanical details of stage presentation.

We ought not too often invoke the name of Shakespeare—in whose presence we all become pygmies—but for a moment let us call to mind that Shakespeare has given us practically no stage-directions; everything he has to say is said in the dialogue; and yet we receive pure visual impressions of persons and movement; we *know* that King Lear is tall and old, that Falstaff is fat.

Masterly dialogue resembles the movements of a high-spirited horse: there is not a single unnecessary movement, everything tends toward a predetermined goal; but at the same time each movement unconsciously betrays a richness and variety of vital energy that seems directed to no special end; it appears rather like the prodigality of an inexhaustible abundance.

In the best works of Strindberg we find dialogue of this sort, occasionally in Ibsen, and always in Shakespeare; as fecund and strong in the low comedy give-and-take scenes with clown and fools as in the horror-stricken words of Macbeth.

Measured by this high ideal, the characters in Mr. O'Neill's plays seem to me a little too direct: they utter the precise words demanded of them by the logic of the situation; they seem to stand rooted in the situation where for the time being they happen to be placed; they are not sufficiently drenched in the atmosphere of their own individual past. Paradoxically, Mr. O'Neill's characters are not sufficiently fixed in the present because they are not sufficiently fixed in the past. Much of what they say seems too openly and frankly sincere, and consequently lacking in the element of wonder or surprise: for the ultimate sincerity that comes from the lips of man is always surprising. Their silence, too, does not always convince me; often it falls short of eloquence, and the way in which the characters go from one theme to another and return to the central theme is lacking in that seemingly inevitable abandon that creates vitality. Besides, they are too prodigal with their shouting and cursing, and the result is that they leave me a little cold toward the other things they have to say. The habit of repetition, which is given free rein in the plot itself as well as in the dialogue, becomes so insistent as to overstep the border of the dramatically effective and actually to become a dramatic weakness.

The essence of drama is movement, but that movement must be held in check, firmly controlled.

I shall not venture to decide which is the more important in drama, the driving motive-element of action, or the retarding or "static" element; at any rate, it is the combination, the interpenetration of the two that makes great drama. In Shakespeare's plays there is not a line that does not serve the ultimate end, but when one goes through the text to discover this for oneself, one perceives that the relation between means and end is by no means evident: the means seem tortuously indirect, often diametrically opposed to the end. Nineteen lines out of twenty in a comedy or tragedy of Shakespeare are (seemingly) a digression, an inter-polative obstruction thrown across the path of the direct rays; retarding motives of every sort impede the onward march of events. But it is precisely these obstacles that reveal the plasticity, the vitality, of the story and characters; it is these that cause the necessary atmosphere about the central idea of the work. As a matter of fact, the unity of the play lies in these diversified and apparently aimless "digressions."

If one goes through *Antony and Cleopatra* looking only for the chain of physical events, the hard outlines of the plot, and neglects the indescribable atmosphere of pomp and circumstance, the spectacle of the downfall of pride and the fulfillment of destiny, the contrasting colors of Orient and Occident, all of which is made manifest through the dialogue, what is left? Nothing more than the confusion and incoherence of nine out of every ten motion picture dramas. Or if one considers the best pieces of Gerhart Hauptmann merely as samples of superficial naturalism, one would find them pedantic and weak in char-acterization. Or again, take the productions of the doctrinaire natural-ists: a good example is the dramatizations of the Goncourt novels. Thirty years ago these played a role of considerable importance, so far as theatrical history is concerned; but there is no life in them, nor was there when they were first produced; they suffer from lack of fresh air. Hauptmann's best plays, on the other hand, are bathed in it; it unifies and breathes vitality into them because it is the breath of life itself, transfused by that secret process which makes all great art, be it drama or canvas, giving it richness, variety and contrast. This is what the painters call *"le rapport des valeurs."* The plays of Strindberg are unified in this wise, not because of the bare plot on which they are built, but through the medium of an indescribable atmosphere that hovers some-where between the realm of the actual and the dream-world.

The European drama is an old institution, laden with the experience of years, but as suspicious and watchful as a venerable though not yet impotent human being.

We know that the dynamic element in drama is a vigorous element, eternally striving for ascendancy. But we also know that great drama is and always has been—from the time of Aeschylus down to the present —an amalgamation of the dynamic and (shall we say?) "static" ele-ments, and we are therefore a trifle suspicious of every effort toward the predominance of one element over another. The nineteenth century witnessed many such efforts, and each time great drama disappeared during the process. There is a constant danger that action—whether it masquerade as thesis-play or play of ideas, problem-play or drama of intrigue, or simply as the vehicle of a virtuoso playing with an anecdote —may prevail over the subtle and difficult but indispensable combination of dynamic and "static," the inseparable oneness of plastic form and action.

Sardou, the heir of Scribe, created a type of play the ingredients of which were entirely dynamic; action took the place of all else, and for twenty years Sardou dominated the stages of Europe, while his followers —the Sudermanns, the Bernsteins, the Pineros—have continued to dominate it to the admiration of the middle classes of all nations and the abomination of the artists! This was the type of play in which the personages were never guilty of any "irrational" exhibition of character: they were the fixed units in a sharply outlined plot, manipulated by the skilled hand of the playwright; and they passed their lives in rooms hermetically sealed against the breath of mortals.

Sardou coined an expression for his style of play: "Life through movement," which was turned against him by his critics, who retorted: "Movement through life." The critics were all true artists: Zola, Villiers de l'Isle-Adam and their followers, among whom was the young Strindberg; but the most influential was Antoine, a man of the theatre.

But the pendulum swung back, and for the time being, perhaps, the European drama has gone too far in the opposite direction. It may be that this is the reason why the plays of so powerful a dramatist as Hauptmann are not popular outside Germany; for a large part of the German public is ready and able to listen to plays in which the "static" element is predominant, dramas in which psychological characterization and lyricism are of more importance than plot. Possibly this tendency is even a little overdeveloped.

Judged from this point of view, Hauptmann's plays are the exact antithesis of the plays of Eugene O'Neill. Where Mr. O'Neill reveals the first burst of his emotions in powerful, clean-cut pictures that seem almost like simple ballads in our complex world, Hauptmann applies himself to making his characters plastic; he does this by throwing a half-light over his men and women and allowing the values to appear slowly, to emerge in new and true and wonderful aspects, gradually shown through an accumulation of tiny and seemingly unimportant incidents of everyday life. As a result, Hauptmann's plots do not progress with directness or force; and at first sight his scenes appear to possess neither dynamic nor even truly "static" elements; they seem somewhat confused. But what ultimately strengthens these scenes and gives them the rhythm of life is a steady and unremitting infusion of the essence of life, which is soul. Hauptmann's method is that of Rembrandt the etcher, who works with a fine steel needle. Since Hauptmann continues to work in this fashion, he must necessarily give little thought to his audience; and indeed he is in actual danger of losing sight of them altogether. Meantime, he manages to accumulate so much of the spiritual life of his characters that his last acts are filled with an almost explosive force, so that there is no need for the introduction of any mechanical tension. Ibsen has done the same sort of thing in the last act of *The Wild Duck,* and Ibsen is the master from whom Hauptmann has learned most.

In the case of Mr. O'Neill, however, his first acts impress me as being the strongest; while the last, I shall not say go to pieces but, undoubtedly, are very much weaker than the others. The close of *The Hairy Ape,* as well as that of *The Emperor Jones,* seems to me to be too direct, too simple, too expected; it is a little disappointing to a European with his complex background, to see the arrow strike the target toward which he has watched it speeding all the while. The last acts of *Anna Christie* and *The First Man* seem somewhat evasive, undecided. The reason for this general weakness is, I think, that the dramatist, unable to make his dialogue a complete expression of human motives, is forced at the end simply to squeeze it out like a wet sponge.

I have no intention of giving advice to a man of Mr. O'Neill's achievements; what I have said is not said by way of adverse criticism; it is rather the putting together of dramaturgical reflections inspired by a consideration of his plays. His qualities as a dramatist are already very great, and I have no doubt that he will make progress when, in the course of time, which is necessary to each man who creates, he shall have acquired better control over his materials, and above all over his own considerable talents.

Translated by BARRETT H. CLARK

Beyond Bourgeois Theatre

BY JEAN-PAUL SARTRE

THE BOURGEOISIE HAS BEEN IN control of the theatre for about 150 years now. First of all, it controls it by the price of land, which rose so sharply in the nineteenth century that, as you know, the workers left the city, resulting in buildings and entire quarters belonging to the bourgeois; the theatres are almost all located in the center of the city. The bourgeoisie controls the theatre by the price of tickets which rose steadily in order to make the theatre a profit-making enterprise. In France it also controls it by centralization, so that in just those cities where contact with a varied audience would be possible, plays do not come or come much later, on tour. Finally, it controls it through the critics. It is an error to contrast the newspaper critic with the public. The critic is the mirror of his public. If he writes nonsense, it is because the public which reads the newspaper will speak nonsense too; therefore, it would be futile to oppose one to the other . . .

. . . One deals here with an absolute control, the more because this same bourgeoisie, to scuttle a play, has merely to do one thing—namely, not to come. It is evident then that the dictatorship of the bourgeoisie has created a bourgeois theatre. Is this simply dangerous, this introduction of a too particular content, or has this dictatorship destroyed the very foundations of what the theatre should be? This is what we shall attempt to discover.

. . . A question immediately arises: why do men live surrounded by their own images? After all, they could very well not have any images. You remember that Baudelaire used to speak of the "tyranny of human passion." Sometimes it is so tiring to submit to this tyranny all day. My God, why must we also have portraits in our room, why must we see representations of ourselves in the theatre, why must we walk in the

131

midst of statues which represent us, why must we go to the movies and always see ourselves again? There is a kind of endless repetition of oneself by people, all of you and by myself, which is rather surprising. If one reflects on it, however, it is not so difficult to explain. I think that people live in the midst of their own images because they do not succeed in being real objects for themselves. Men are objects for others but they are not completely objects for themselves. Take an individual example, be it in the form of the experiment of the mirror which is so important in all of early childhood, be it in the errors of an animal who looks into a mirror, be it in the mistake of an adult who, in a dark room, suddenly sees someone in a mirror and does not notice that it is he. One comes to oneself as to an object, because one comes to oneself as to another. That is objectivity. As soon as you recognize yourself, you are no longer an object. In fact, one does not see one's own face as one sees that of others. One sees it with privileged elements because one has a profound interest in the one who is there; it is impossible to seize him with this absolutely cold and formal bond which is simple sight. One seizes him by a kind of participation.

. . . What I say about the individual is valid for any social group as well. Men cannot see themselves from the outside, and the real reason for this is that in order truly to seize a man as object, one would have, at the same time and contradictorily, both to understand and not to understand his actions. For you evidently cannot consider that you have before you a truly objectified man, someone of whom you can say, he's really someone I know, if you don't know him through an understanding of what he seeks, what he wants, beginning with his future, with his most personal efforts to attain his ends. But if you know him by understanding him, this also means that, whatever disapprobations you may feel with regard to his conduct on other levels, you share his aims, you are in a completely closed world or rather, if you wish, not closed but limited, limited by itself and from which you can never escape . . . If, on the other hand, you cease to understand his aims and if he becomes, at that moment, a being who is uniquely comprehensible, or at least explicable by the order of things, at that very moment you have lost the man, you have the insect. So that between this understanding of man in which man is never wholly an object but rather a quasi-object for other men, and this refusal to understand, there is no place for men to know one another completely, as objects. One might be a total object for the ants or for the angels, but not as a man for men.

. . . The theatre being an image, gestures are the image of action, and (here is something never said since the advent of bourgeois theatre and which must nevertheless be said) dramatic action is the action of characters. People always think that dramatic action means great gestures, bustle. No, that's not action, that's noise and tumult. Action, in the true sense of the word, is that of the character; there are no images in the theatre but the image of the act, and if one seeks the definition of theatre, one must ask what an act is, because the theatre can represent nothing but the act. Sculpture represents the form of the body, the theatre the act of this body. Consequently, what we want to recover when we go to the theatre is evidently ourselves, but ourselves not as we are, more or less poor, more or less proud of our youth and our beauty; rather to recover ourselves as we act, as we work, as we meet difficulties, as we are men who have rules and who establish rules for these actions. Unfortunately, as you see, we are very far at this moment from the bourgeois theatre; if what I say to you in no way resembles what has been playing on the stage for the last 150 years, except, of course, for a few exceptions, it is because the bourgeois theatre does not want any dramatic action. It desires, more precisely, neo-dramatic action; but it does not want the action of man to be represented, it wants the action of the author constructing events. In truth the bourgeoisie wants to have an image of itself represented, but—and here one understands why Brecht created his epic theatre, why he went completely in the other direction—an image which is pure participation; it absolutely does not want to be represented as a quasi-object. When it is totally object, that's not very agreeable . . . The bourgeois theatre is therefore subjective, not because it shows what is going on inside the head of the character (often one does not see this at all), but because the bourgeoisie wants a representation of itself which is subjective. That is to say, it wants produced in the theatre an image of man according to its own ideology and not man seeking through this sort of world of individuals who see one another, of groups which form judgments about one another, because then, the bourgeoisie would be contested.

One recognizes what is human in the bourgeoisie by what is bad, since the reasoning usually is: it's human when someone has just committed a knavery, a cowardice; therefore, it is necessary that this nature be bad and it is necessary that it be immutable. I don't insist on that point, and you can see why: if man is bad, then that which counts is order, any order at all . . . Besides, if human nature is bad and eternal, isn't it evident that no effort is necessary to achieve some progress . . . But, to act, which is precisely the object of the theatre, is to change the world and in changing it, of necessity to change oneself. Fine. The bourgeoisie has changed the world profoundly, and now it no longer has any desire to be changed itself, above all from without. If it changes, it is in order to adapt itself, to keep what it has, and in this position what it asks of the theatre is not to be disturbed by the idea of action . . . There can be no action, because in these plays the moving element, as in the philosophy of Aristotle, must be a rapid disturbance between two moments of calm . . . In effect, in its plays the bourgeois theatre has replaced action with passion, and action such as it is known today in the theatre simply means a practical construction.

. . . Brecht felt that the distance between actors and audience was not great enough, that one tried much too much to *move* the audience, to touch them, and not enough to *show* them; in other words, too many participational relationships, too many images, not enough objectivity. In my opinion the bourgeois public is foolish not because it participates, but because it participates in an image which is the image of a fool.

. . . We have a number of plays today which, in good faith, use the expressionist themes again without realizing it. For example, the theme of Beckett, in *Waiting for Godot,* is a very remarkable thing. I find it the best play since 1945, but one must admit that it is expressionist and that it is at the same time pessimist . . . But it is a play which, at bottom, has a content pleasing to the bourgeois. In the same way, another recent play, Ionesco's *Rhinoceros,* is an expressionist play, since you have a man who becomes "a rhinoceros. . . ." What does it mean to become a rhinoceros? Is it to become a fascist or a communist, or both? It is evident that if the bourgeois public is delighted with it, it must be both. Do you follow me? It is absolutely impossible to derive any meaning from Ionesco's play except that a great misfortune, a great peril of annihilation menaces the world and that, good heavens, the danger of contagion is very grave . . . And why is there one man who resists? At least we could learn why, but no, we learn not even that. He resists because he is there. He resists because he is *Ionesco:* he represents Ionesco, he says I resist, and there he remains in the midst of the rhinoceroses, the only one to defend man without our being very sure if it might not be better to be a rhinoceros. Nothing has been proved to the contrary . . .

. . . I only mean to say that you always have the right to speak ill of the bourgeois as a man, but not as a bourgeois. That's the heart of the matter. The pessimism must be a total pessimism, a pessimism of inaction, it must be a pessimism which condemns all possibilities, all hopes, individuals. But if it is a moderate pessimism which simply says: the situation is not good, our ruling classes could do better than they do, etc. . . . Then that's no longer theatre, is it? That's subversion. I don't want you to think that pessimistic theatre is not bourgeois theatre. All the theatre I have just mentioned, of passivity, of permissiveness, of dead end and of evil, is bourgeois theatre . . . If, on the contrary, we want to know what true theatre is, we must look in the opposite direction. This means that dramatic action is the narration of an action, is the staging of an action, one or several, of a few individuals or of a whole group—some people find themselves at the point of wanting something and they try to realize this desire. It makes no difference whether they succeed or fail; what is clear is that they must realize an attempt on the stage and that this is what we demand to see.

. . . From this arises a problem: the accessories are of no use. The settings are never of any use. One can never illuminate a place by some thing. That is not the director's role; these are merely bits of bravura. The only manner in which objects are born, is in the gestures: the gesture of stabbing gives birth to the knife.

. . . The real problem is to know how to create real contradictions and a real dialectic of the object, the act and the man in the theatre. This is one of the most difficult things, precisely because the object comes after the action. In the films the object engenders the action, in the theatre it comes after, is engendered by it. Thus the whole problem of the dialectic of work is a real problem. In a film you can very easily recount the life of a mechanic in a documentary without boring anyone. Can you imagine this in the theatre? With a cardboard locomotive! With fireworks to move it! This is impossible, and yet what is the theatre to speak of if not of work, for in the final analysis action and work are the same thing. Here is the true inner contradiction of the theatre, and here is why it has not yet been resolved; because it is not enough, as the epic theatre shows us, to show contradictions which engender actions, actions which are not quite action because they bear too strongly the mark of their former maledictions. What we must find out is how to convey work in the theatre without having someone say, "Ah! You have worked hard, my friend." This has never been resolved . . . There is a language particular to the theatre: it must be as irreversible as action; that is to say, not in a single sentence nor a single piece of dramatic prose spoken by an actor, must one be able to change the order of sentences at will . . . The meaning of action is that it always radicalizes itself, unless the person acting dies or there is some brusque interference . . . The action itself always goes to the end, it is irreversible, and if it is irreversible, the story too must be irreversible. But then you will ask me, "Is there nothing but action? Aren't there passions? Don't people love, and don't they hate? The theatre you describe is indeed hard and cold!" My answer is that, on the contrary, we will have only characters who are passionate, but only in the good sense of the word and not in the bad. The bad sense of the word passion means: blindly sufficient unto yourself and to others, so that you accomplish only foolishness and finally you wander away from your interests by massacring everyone around you; but you have understood nothing of what is happening to you: a fit of passion, people say, meaning a fit of foolishness. I have never met people who were like that. I have met people who were foolish, but foolishness and passion didn't necessarily go together and usually, when they were passionate, they were less foolish.

. . . Today it is impossible to distinguish in a general way the individual man from the social man in us, and the social man is, of necessity, at the base of all of our passions. Envy is an exigency, an extremely unfortunate passion but at the same time a feeling of right . . . Passion is a way of sensing that one is right, of relating oneself to a social world of exigencies and values. To justify wanting to keep something, to take, destroy, construct something, passionate men do nothing but reason . . . They are frequently very tiresome and Pirandello saw this: in Pirandello, every time a man comes to grips with a passion, he speaks endlessly, because the passion expresses itself through words, through calculations, through researches . . . Vaillant has said, "Italians are jurists," and I think passionate men are also jurists. In these conditions, passion appears when a right is infringed; the passion is a reciprocal phenomenon, in the sense that it is a social claim an individual makes when he decides to go to any length to realize it. From that moment, he must judge himself wronged by another and the other must judge himself wronged by this right. In effect, passion exists only in the form of contradictory demands.

. . . There is no need for psychology in the theatre. Psychology is a waste of time, because plays are long, the public has only a brief span of attention, and nuances have absolutely no interest. A play is something which hurls people into an undertaking. There is no need for psychology. Instead, there is need of delimiting very precisely what position, what situation each character can take, as a function of the causes and the anterior contradictions produced with respect to the principal action. In this way we will have a certain number of secondary or primary characters who will define themselves in the course of the action itself, and this action must be a common enterprise containing the contradictions of each and of all. For example, the very contradictions of war are marked by the contradictions of *Mother Courage* by Brecht, for she is a woman who detests war and who thrives on it. War hurts her in every possible way but she cannot live without it, she is happy when it begins again and she is miserable when it continues— an admirable choice, to have taken the contradictions of war in order to see war . . . Up to that point all goes smoothly. We all agree; the real problem arises in a different way, it arises the moment we ask ourselves: is it necessary that the object created thus, which is the play, be represented before the audience *qua* object or *qua* image? I mean: is it really necessary, under the pretext that the bourgeoisie used it as a weapon, to reject participation, which is the profound essence of the theatre? And if one does not suppress, must one at least reduce it so as to give a greater place to application and to understanding? Or must one consider the whole problem from a different angle, by refusing precisely to suppress this participation? The epic theatre aims to show us the individual adventure in the measure that it expresses the social adventure, and it aims at the same time, in a non-didactic way but based on didactic plays, to show us the implications and the reciprocal corrections beginning with a larger system, for example, modern capitalistic society.

There is a choice in Brecht. The proof is that in *The Caucasian Chalk Circle* he distinguishes levels of reality and levels of characters. One may debate whether there are political or moral judgments (or whatever you wish) made about these, but why declare *a priori* that certain characters, namely the bad ones, for example the brutes who are palace guards and who play cards all day and kill people as if they were nothing, why declare that they are to wear masks while the two or three characters from the people are not to wear any? At that moment, therefore, in the name of social contradictions we establish people who are actually empty bodies, who are eaten away inside and whom we need only represent with masks. Then another category which will be further away from the mask but still not quite human, and finally the servant girl and her fiancé who are a true woman and a true man almost without make-up and acting in a natural manner because they have a kind of plenitude. But what gives them more dimension, under the pretext that they do things in the direction of social utility, in the direction of their nature and their reality, than these guards? The latter are people no more or less dimensional, they are men. This way of conceiving things is too simple. It consists in saying that man is transformed into an abstract—it is a way of understanding Marxism which is not the good way. To put various realities into perspective indicates an extremely dubious ideological position. Such a thing must not be accepted. Reality cannot be put into perspective because it is not *in* perspective. It *is*, on the other levels, but a man is a man, whatever he be, and there are no men who must be conceived more or less fully. If this is an esthetic point of view, it must be based on something and there it is founded on nothing. In my opinion, therefore, hierarchies are constructed and perspectives established which are not suitable. Besides, who proves to us that this way of suppressing the participation we seek is staked on a true philosophy? That Marx is the great philosopher of the nineteenth century, there is no doubt. But there is also no doubt that there are five hundred interpretations of Marx. Therefore, why declare that the theatre will be demonstrative if it is uncertain what is to be demonstrated? And if the theatre must limit itself to a few reflections, to carrying out certain very rudimentary thoughts found in Marx, the simplest, I see no need to create estrangement for this. If the theatre should go further, let it be revealed how, and what is to be shown us . . . Which proves that there will not be a great number of epic theatres which will have varying meanings, for the difference between the epic and the dramatic theatre is that the author who creates dramatic theatre speaks in his own name, tells a story with his own interpretation, while the other is demonstrative and does not speak in his own words. He effaces himself at the same time that he effaces the audience before the play he presents. At this level, that's fine when it concerns a society which is in the process of disappearing and when one takes the point of view of one of the classes, for example the class which is rising or which wants to rise, and which is doing so on the shoulders of the others. It's fine in a period when, for example, Brecht can consider himself the spokesman of the oppressed classes and "judge-explicator" of the bourgeoisie to those classes. But now let us suppose that in East Germany, for example, Brecht had had the opportunity of speaking of East Germany as well . . . Let us suppose that Brecht had wanted to explain, for himself or for his public, in what ways there are also con-tradictions in socialist society. Would he have used the same method? Would one have seen functionaries guilty of a little negligence or of a total lack of imagination, would they have worn masks? Would one have seen them from outside and in the absurdity of their contradictions or, on the contrary, at that moment *with* their contradictions—for Brecht was honest, but from the inside, in sympathy with them. To explain another way, if we imagine the history of a functionary who has committed faults, errors which manifest the contradictions of socialism, I am convinced that this character would have been treated by Brecht taking his aims into consideration, considering that he is a man who was defined from the outset by aims which must be understood, the same aims as Brecht, to accomplish the revolution. When one does not share the aims of estrangement and, as a result, show people from the outside, but when one is in a society whose principles one shares, this becomes more difficult and therefore one must say, "Yes, he is guilty, but the poor boy, you don't realize the problems there are . . . Here are the contradictions . . . ," etc. At that moment we are dealing with another theatre, a theatre which tries to understand. This is pre-cisely the difference between the epic and the dramatic theatre: that in the dramatic one can try to understand, and in the epic as it now exists, one explains what one doesn't understand. I am not speaking of Brecht himself, but in a general way. Thus, if you wish, we shall say that if there is a clear insufficiency in the epic theatre, this is due to the fact that Brecht never resolved (and he never had any reason to do so), in the framework of Marxism, the problem of subjectivity and objectivity. And therefore he was never able to make a meaningful place in his work for subjectivity as it should be.

. . . The serious flaw in dramatic theatre is that it has sprung, all the same, from the bourgeois theatre, that it has sprung from means created by its individualism and is still poorly adapted to speaking of work. The other cannot do this either, but it is quite evident that it would be a pity to renounce one or the other of these branches and say that each author may not seek, if he wishes, to create an epic or a truly dramatic drama. In these conditions it seems that all the forces which the young theatre can marshal against the bourgeois plays which we have now, must be united, and that there is, in short, no true antagonism between the dramatic form and the epic form, except that one of them draws toward the quasi-objectivity of the object, which is man. The error here lies in believing that one can present a society-object to the audience, while the other form, if uncorrected, would go too far in the direction of sympathy with the aim of objectivity, and thus would risk falling to the bourgeois side. Therefore, I believe that today the problem can be pinpointed between these two forms of theatre.

Translated by RIMA DRELL RECK

2. The Artist:
Acting and Directing

Murder of the Director

BY JEAN VILAR

Some artisan's arguments—Rehearsals à l'italienne—The actor—Blocking—Necessary humility of set, music, lighting—Being able to summarize the play—Being able to detach oneself from it—Knowing each actor—Suggestion, not imposition.

1

THE FOLLOWING NOTES CONCERN ONLY a particular technique of theatrical art, that of transposing a written work from the imaginary realm of reading to the concrete realm of the stage. To look for anything more than "means of interpretation" in these often deliberately cryptic lines would be vain.

When so many theories, *ars poetica* and metaphysics have been made up about this art, it is perhaps necessary that one advance, as a preliminary, a few artisan's considerations.

2

One can never read the play often enough. Actors never read it often enough. They think they understand the play when they follow the plot more or less clearly—a fundamental error.

Sticking my neck out, I would point out that in general, directors underrate the professional intelligence of actors. They are asked to be bodies only, animated pawns on the director's chessboard. The play once read by the director, read a second time à *l'italienne*, the actors are thrust onto the stage. What is the result?

Subjected too early to the demands of physical presence and action, the actors fall back on their habitual, conventional reactions, and develop their characters conventionally and arbitrarily, before their professional intelligence and their sensibilities can grasp the director's intention. Whence, so many hack performances!

For there are hack performances in the most sensitive actor, just as a writer will produce hack work when he hurries, or is hurried. How many actors, including some of the best, have murmured to us for twenty years in the same voice, with the same bearing and gestures, with the same emotional quality, in the most diametrically opposed roles!

Hence the necessity for many reading rehearsals: about a third of the total number. At least. Manuscript in hand, seat firmly planted on a chair, body in repose. Thus the deepest sensibilities will gradually pitch themselves to the desired note, as the actor comes to understand, or feel, the new character that is to become himself.

3

All characters must be *composed*. All good actors are necessarily *composers*. All roles are the result of *composition*.

4

The composition of a character is the work of creation which, alone, assimilates the actor's craft to the artist's; for composing a character implies selection, observation, research, inspiration, and discipline.

5

The actor selects within and around himself.

Around himself, because nature presents to his eyes the most various and distinct models, for his observation; one might almost say, for his contemplation.

Within himself, because if, on the one hand, the actor cannot sufficiently observe the life teeming around him, neither can he sufficiently expose his sensibilities to contact with it.

In short, the actor must be able to retain in his visual memory the human types that strike his attention, as also the sympathetic (or sensory) memory of his own wounds and moral suffering. He must know how to use this memory and, better yet, cultivate it.

6

In blocking, the point is to simplify and pare down. Contrary to the usual practice, the idea is not to *exploit* space, but to forget or ignore it.

For a production to have its full power of suggestion, it is not necessary that a so-called scene of action should be "busy" (with acrobatics, fisticuffs, brawling and other "realistic" or "symbolic" activity). One or two gestures, and the text, suffice; provided both are "right."

7

The work of blocking and physical characterization should be fairly quickly completed by good professional actors: say fifteen rehearsals out of forty.

8

An actor's—or a director's—talent does not necessarily lie in the variety and strength of his powers (which are a relatively unimportant gift of Providence), but above all in the refining of his powers, the severity of his selectivity, in his voluntary self-impoverishment.

9

Music-hall theatre: a great actor, a splendid costume, a striking décor, music brimming with genius, strong-colored lighting.

10

No actor worthy of the name imposes himself on the text; he serves it. Humbly. Let the electrician, musician, and designer, accordingly, be even more humble than this "right interpreter."

11

Character and Actor

The script carefully studied and the characters "felt" in all their ramifications, in the course of the fifteen or twenty reading rehearsals, the director begins the bland work of blocking, completes it, and finds himself at once in a renewed struggle with those slippery monsters, the characters. The actors know it well, for character and actor are two separate entities. For long days, the first eludes the second with infernal ease. The worst thing to do at this stage is to try to fight the demon, to force him to your will. If you wish him to come and meekly enter into your body and soul, forget him. The director's role, as expert observer of this pursuit by osmosis, is to inspire the actor with confidence, to convince him that he has, in the very expressive phrase, "found" or "rediscovered" his character. It is by no means naïve to state that at a certain point in the development of a character, the confidence is all. It is by non-violence, by confidence in his ultimate conquest of the elusive monster, that the actor finally triumphs.

12

The scenic artist must realize the designer's sketches. Alternatively, there should be a designer-carpenter, right hand of the director, with full powers over the stage: a man of taste, devoted to his work, cultured. A hard trade.

13

Of Costume

In theatre, the hood sometimes makes the monk.

14

What Must Be Done?

The work of production must include a written analysis of the play. The director must write it, and not despise the thankless job. The drafting of such an analysis compels the director to a clear and exhaustive knowledge of the play.

15

Question: Can one interpret something one doesn't understand?

16

Coda to "What Must Be Done?"

How many playwrights would be incapable of giving you a precise analysis of their play! of its plot, even!

17

A director who cannot detach himself from his work during the final rehearsals is only a mediocre craftsman, however much it might seem that this is the very point at which he should be most intensely

involved in it. Failing this detachment, the director blinds himself—
the worst possible error. Such poor fools forget that the theatre is play,
in which inspiration and child-like wonder are more important than
sweat and tantrums.

It is true that such detachment is so difficult to achieve at the right
time that it is not surprising to find that few directors either desire or
achieve it.

18

A quality fully as important to the actor in the right practice of his
art as sensitivity and instinct, is the spirit of *finesse* (for a definition,
see Pascal, who opposes it to the spirit of geometry). Without this
quality, his work will only present a riot of anarchic expressions.

19

The actor is not a machine. This is a truism that needs to be shouted
in people's ears. The actor is neither pawn nor robot. The director
must assume from the start that his players have all the necessary talent.

20

Intermission

"The idleness of an artist is work, and his work, repose." Signed,
Balzac.

21

There is no technique of interpretation, but only practices, *techniques* (plural). Personal experience is all, and personal empiricism.

22

For the director, every actor is a special case. From this follows the
requirement that he know every member of his cast well. Know his
work, of course, but even more his *person,* up to the threshold of his
inner life, and perhaps even beyond.

23

Director and Actor

Where the actor is concerned, the director's art is one of suggestion.
He does not impose, he suggests. Above all, he must not be brutal. The

"soul of an actor" is not an idle phrase: even more than the "soul of a poet," it is a continuing necessity. One does not win a creature's soul by brutalizing it, and the actor's soul is more necessary to the work of theatre than his sensitivity.

24

Of Simplicity

Three references:

a. Shakespeare-Hamlet: "Speak the speech, I pray you, as I pronounced it to you, trippingly on the tongue; but if you mouth it . . . I had as lief the town-crier spoke my lines . . . Be not too tame neither, but let your own discretion be your tutor . . . etc," and all the rest of this famous passage.

b. Moliere: *The Versailles Impromptu.*

c. Talmá-Lekain: "Lekain guarded against that hunger for applause that torments most actors and leads them into frequent error; he wished to please only the discriminating members of the audience. He rejected all theatrical fakery, aiming to produce a genuine effect by avoiding all 'effects' . . . He *practiced a right economy of movement and gesture, deeming this an essential part of the art, since their multiplication detracts from dignity of bearing.*" (Talmá)

25

A production must be reduced to its simplest—and most difficult —expression: the stage action or, more precisely, the acting. Hence, the stage must not be turned into a crossroads of all the arts, major and minor (painting, architecture, electromania, musicomania, mechanics, etc.).

The designer must be put in his place, which is to solve the sight-line problems of masking and teasers and to see to the construction of such set and hand properties as are strictly necessary to the action on stage.[1]

The immoderate use of projectors, floodlights and arc lamps should be left to the music-hall and the circus.

Music should be used only for overtures and scene bridges, and

---

[1] His chief task being to find the single *keynote of the set,* if set there must be. (J.V.)

otherwise only when the script explicitly calls for music off, a song, or a musical interlude.

In short, all effects should be eliminated which are extraneous to the pure and Spartan laws of the stage, and the production reduced to the physical and moral action of the players.

Translated by CHRISTOPHER KOTSCHNIS

Design for Acting:
The Quest of Technique

BY MORRIS CARNOVSKY

I'M GLAD THAT THE NAME and purpose of these conferences define my function here along lines that happen to be congenial to myself. The Factor of Acting in the Working Theatre—the subject is organic in my life to an overwhelming degree. I think I've gone beyond the point where it would be possible for anyone to ask me, as a woman put it to me bluntly years ago, "What's uppermost in you, the actor or the man?" The answer, I hope, is now, "Both." For I've learned that if you endeavor to express your life without some form to receive it, you're apt to produce a chaotic mess—and on the other hand, if you play-act at life, well, there you'll certainly come a cropper.

Though what's implied in the question above is one of the fundamental challenges of the creative life. Form and content. The style—and the man himself. Stanislavsky chose his title "My Life in Art" and meant it quite literally, for he literally immolated himself in the search for the methods and materials of his craft. I don't know whether in the sum of things he emerged as a great Actor, but as a searcher, he was a very great Man.

For myself, I say I only hope that I've somewhat narrowed the gap between what I am and what I do. If that sounds deliberately modest, let it stand. I don't aim to practice modesty for its own sake, that would be inartistic. The modesty I feel is a "technical" thing, and stems from a healthy respect for the lifelong difficulties of the task every true craftsman sets himself. It is a *key*, to objectivity, if you will, a kind of objectivity which it is necessary to assume, by an act of will, before you can say: What am I up against? What is my relation to my medium? What does it want of me? How do we effect the bridge? By what means do we arrive at a common conclusion? In what sign shall I conquer? And also: How shall I know my enemies?—my difficulties and my limitations?

A moment ago I referred to modesty as a *technical* matter. The word "technique" has to be explained especially in regard to my own craft, since for many it still retains the atmosphere of a bright and glossy competence, something machine-made, inevitable in the way it functions—"you put it in here and it comes out there"—particularly adapted to sparkling dialogue and sophisticated effects, "timing," creased trousers and secure décolletage, smart deaths and entrances. Measured sobs and gusts of professional laughter to account for the anguish of loss and the joy of living. An actor of my acquaintance has made a tidy career for himself out of something called "footwork"—this, he solemnly assured me, was the underlying secret of all good acting. Malvolio might have said it: " 'Tis but footwork—all is but footwork." My friend neglected to tell me what happened when he was sitting down! However—

In the Twenties, when I first came to New York and to the service of the theatre, the stage was the stamping ground of many an attitude and fixed persuasion such as the above. It was a field day for every sort of exhibitionism, dominated by "stars" who were expected to be the exhibitionists par excellence. It was a competition not so much of living or cultural values as of showmanship. The lily of truth was often unrecognizable for the gilding that weighed it down. Among these stars there were some, of course, that burned with a purer light; it was as if they didn't know how to conceal the thing they *were*. David Warfield, with one shoe on the rich soil of the Ghetto, the other getting a shine up in the Lambs' Club. Otis Skinner, using every trick in the bag to convey the juiciest romanticism I have ever seen. Mrs. Fiske, Mistress of the Theatrical Inn, barely disguising a warm heart beneath her devastating and witty rhythms. "Whizzing exhalations" like Emily Stevens and Jeanne Eagels burning in their comets' flight with an alcoholic blue flame, giving themselves to the fires with obstinate grandeur—what else was there to do?

If the student of acting took these as his models, he was more likely to absorb their foibles and eccentricities than the magnificence of their *Idea*. To talk and walk brightly with crisp "stylish" diction in the hectic manner of the day, this was what they'd learned in "School"—

that is, by observation, by Stock, and the threat of losing their job. They were often pathetically self-conscious about this "technique" of theirs. A very good actor I knew and admired had a singular trick of elongating vowel sounds in the most unlikely places—monosyllables like "if," "as," "but," particularly "but." "Bu-u-ut," he would say, "Bu-u-ut screw your courage to the sticking point a-a-and we'll not fail." Or "I—i-if you be-e-e." Etc. I asked him about it once and he answered promptly and with pride, "Why, that's my sostenuto *but!*"

Now, you must not think because I describe these interesting phenomena as quirks that I dismiss them entirely as unworthy of the craft of acting. Or that I regard a pleasant, fastidious, and crisp manner of speech and presence as a sign of decadence. In our last decade poor Marlon Brando has precipitated upon his head the reputation and credit for having restored the Yahoo to his rightful place in society, but we need not admire him the less for that. All innovators must take their chances. And there is generally a deeper reason for odd behavior, stemming from something that is striving to be said.

For myself, I learned as much as I could, largely by imitation, from the "technique" of these older actors. I even think I now understand what they were driving at. For example, my friend of the "footwork." I now believe that he had discovered for himself a useful and comfortable arcanum in the area of physical rhythm, a very important thing for actors. He had found through experience that it was blissfully reassuring to be in the right place at the right time! His dukes and his butlers were never caught flatfooted, as they say in boxing. Out of the balance between his words and his movements, he had perfected a kind of personal dance. This pleased him and gave him ultimate confidence. . . . And what of him of the sostenuto "but"? He was a lover of words—*all* words, even those that are customarily neglected. He rescued them from oblivion and gave them dignity. But (bu-u-ut) more importantly, he made them *act!* There was a warning note in that "but" of his, a promise in his "and," a threat in his "if." I find that most interesting, because it betokened an *inner* life and energy that was the mark of this man's talent, his brush-stroke, as it were.

The actors of the Twenties often seemed to be all dressed up with no place to go. Except into the Thirties—which is what they did, eventually. They went pitching down the funnel of the years, practicing all the techniques they knew, believing in their own effectiveness and their own sincerities. And reaching out, too, for a better language of craft, more expanse to their horizons, greater satisfaction for their spirits. They had no leadership. It was each man for himself. The murmurs that reached them from foreign shores, murmurs of vibrant new names—Craig, Appia, Jessner, Reinhardt, Stanislavsky, Copeau—these seemed to promise a new kind of showmanship, but there was no one around—with the exception of a few scene designers who began to sit up and take notice—to interpret the swelling theme of a *New Theatre* to them. Theatre possibly for the first time understood as a profound organic experience shared by *all* its elements, audience, designers, lighting experts, producers, directors—and, of course, actors.

I say there was no one around to utter a warning or to say: "Be of good cheer! At last you are about to receive a vessel for your talents. Not a knighthood nor an empty citation, nor a cigar banded with your name. No champagne banquets with speeches to inflate your vanity and encourage you in your worst professional habits. No fan clubs milling about the stage door and shouting your name in the worn, ironic streets. Not these things, but a place—a place where your actors' nature will be understood and used, through work, through discipline, through struggle, through proper organization, to the end that you will inherit the only thing worth having—namely, your Self."

In the clarion tones of this annunciation, I realize that I am anticipating history in the shape of such possible headlines as "American Theatre Finds Its Way Out!" or "Actors Break Their Chains As Dead Hand Shrivels" (or at least "When The Saints Come Marching In"). But history, as we know, is never that easy, even in its best conclusions. Because the struggle continues. "That's for sure," as we say in our pungent idiom. The American Theatre hasn't found its way out, nor has the dead hand entirely relaxed its grip. But there have been tremendous advances. An interchange of movements, bloods, languages, nationalities; an intermingling of ideas. The Depression jolted us back on our heels; when our eyes cleared, their expression was simpler, more modest, more compassionate. The war made us reach out our hands to our friends in all places.

I was part of this transformation as far as it applied to theatre, since I lived through it. It was in a very real sense a revolution. Like all such changes, it cast its shadow before as well as after. There was this leaderless, troubled floundering as through swamps in the dark; the dawn when it came was yet uncertain and it is still working its strength up toward the full light of day. As far as acting technique was concerned, there was much honest striving in the Twenties. I came in contact with some of the best of it in six years of the Theatre Guild. In the Guild, the specialité de la maison was the good play. Its directors gambled on the intelligent, fretting public, suffering the indigestion of so much questionable food in the theatre; they gambled and won. They found themselves with the responsibility of serving up their good plays—Shaw, O'Neill, Behrman, Molnar—with the assistance of actors who were not only competent and worldly, but intelligent. The demand created a supply. And eventually the Guild (pushed to it, no doubt, by economic as well as artistic necessity) took the truly noble step of supporting their program of plays with a hand-picked "permanent" acting company. The idea was abandoned as unworkable after a few rather glorious years. Many successes, happy, well-fed actors, radiant box offices. The Bible records that "Jeshurun waxed fat and he kicked." Hollywood slithered around the corner and stepped up the volume of her siren-song: Oh come, all ye unfaithful; and some of the actors disappeared, not without a sheepish backward glance. But I'm not sure that that was the reason for the failure of the company idea. The Guild had become, by repetition and success, a show-shop on a higher plane. They no longer *needed* an acting company, preferring the freedom and variety of the open market.

However, this particular emphasis need not detain us. Speaking for myself, I had every obvious reason to be satisfied during this period. I played a succession of good parts, my colleagues were some of the finest actors of the day—Dudley Digges, Henry Travers, the Lunts, Edward G. Robinson, many others. We all came together most amiably to perform the play, but few among us had any real connection with their fellows, either socially or in the matter of a common understanding of what they had to say or of how they said it. If we had absorbed any basic life-values, you could not read our minds' construction in our faces, or in our behavior at rehearsals or on the stage. It was curious, but none of these good craftsmen seemed able or willing to discuss their craft. They were undoubtedly passionate about their work, but the passion produced no babies, as it were. The Guild survivors would probably interrupt at this point to exclaim: Oh yeah? what about your beloved Group Theatre? But that birth was not exactly organic. It's true that many of the expenses of the accouchement were borne by Guild funds, and for this we must be eternally grateful—I say it without irony. Nevertheless, the Group was regarded for years (probably still is) as a kind of biological sport, a hag-whelp, a Caliban spawned by some obscure Sycorax, worshipping strangely at the altars of Setebos Sergeitch Stanislavsky!

But the "Drang" toward the Group Idea was far from inorganic. It was rooted in the poignant needs of real people who were ready to strike hands and say, in the British phrase, "Come on, mates, let's have a bash at it!" Separation and loneliness, they felt, were not good for the soul, even though the body was well-fed. "What *is* this thing we love, the theatre?" they seemed to say. "And if you love a thing, you *do* something about it, *for* it. We know that this medium to which we have committed our lives is a collective one. The unit of it is the living actor. Because he is unashamedly alive, he turns his eyes outward to behold his brother-actor, lost in the same human predicament. When their eyes meet, the scene begins. When their ideas collide, they move forward in the service of the play, and possibly to a commonly shared point of view about life and art. What else is it to be what Hamlet calls 'the abstract and brief chronicles of the time'?"

To be or not to be—a moment of choice. Our elders would have judged that we were expressing ourselves rather flamboyantly. "Youth, youth." And not all the young actors felt as I have described, precious few, in fact. Despite the gathering clouds of the Depression, many actors were comfortably entrenched, and any change seemed ominous, irrational. Why look a gift-horse in the teeth? they would complain irritably. And as for learning, it's experientia that docets the stultos, not blind experiment! One of these younger actors, a dear, good fellow, very witty and explosive, called me all kinds of a damn fool when I told him I was thinking of leaving the Guild and joining the Group, then later, when we got talking about calmer subjects, he confided to me that (dammit!) acting presented him with one curious problem— in the middle of a scene, he would lift his hand in an impulsive gesture to about here (shoulder high), and then for the life of him he didn't know how to get it down! I wasn't able to help him at the time. A simple case of hypertension.

Certainly in those days I wasn't very articulate about my own notions of craft—I hadn't earned the right to be. It was a case of no foundation all along the line. I was acquainted with my friend's tensions, since I recognized them full well in myself. Tension of the body, mirrored by inner tension, leading inevitably to forced, mechanical, exhibitionistic action (Get that laugh! Nail down that effect!) with here and there a saving grace of truthful feeling that would disentangle itself and float upward like a wisp of smoke into the flies. When it didn't happen, squeeze as I might, I was unhappy. I was considered a good actor, too, and *that* made me ashamed. I was fed up with fumbling. I was undoubtedly learning many valuable lessons along the way, but I didn't know them by name. I see now that the effort to depict the character led me too far from its proper roots in my own individuality. I had misplaced my Self, which was far worse than a hand left dangling in the air. I yearned for my own return and I didn't know how to get it back. I think it could be said of me then as now that I was *seeking my Image*. Call it a wholeness, integrity; *my* life in Art, if you will.

I was not alone, as I discovered more and more when the Group Theatre got underway. My fellow-workers all aspired to earn the name of Actor. The smell of grease paint was but one element in the confused aroma that drifted our way from the gardens of this brave new world. We set sail into the Thirties on the good ship Nonconformity. The isle as we approached it was full of noises, and we aimed at making sense of it all. We were eager to get down to First Causes, even if it meant making fools of ourselves—which history records we often did. We were at once exploring for the lost Adam and the gold of Peru. If the memory of our endeavors vibrates somewhat with a fuzzy romanticism, I'm not too concerned. Shakespeare may have had his fellow-actors in mind when he put it down: We are such stuff as dreams are made on. (I seem to be quoting *Tempest* quite a lot.) We *were* romantic, from necessity—and necessity for whatever reason is very real. We needed, as I said, a Place for our exercises; we needed peace, in which to learn the grammar of struggle.

Please bear in mind, in spite of appearances, that I am still getting around to Actors' Technique—that property of any art which (as Michael Chekhov quotes it) "is sometimes apt to dampen, as it were, the spark of inspiration in a *mediocre* artist; but the same technique in the hands of a master can fan that spark into an unquenchable flame." . . . Consummation devoutly to be wished. And that's how we wanted it —devoutly, passionately. Not everyone in the same way; some of us were monks by temperament, some were sybarites, others opportunists, a crank or two—for it takes all kinds to make a Group. At our best, though, there was a glow about us; we had been chosen, and in a sense had chosen each other. We respected our three directors who had taken us for better or worse and were far ahead of us in their separate intuitions about the difficulties of this childlike safari in an inimical world.

The glow came, I think, from the sharing of the common task. The age around us was a discombobulated one; our relationship to it was not clear to us. We experienced a kind of sanity in the very act of concentrating on the problems of acting. It forced us to look inside ourselves. We scrutinized ourselves minutely, ourselves through each other; we anatomized ourselves; we taught ourselves to become intensely aware; we stalked our own weaknesses remorselessly. We built on our momentary successes and discoveries with the satisfaction of Egyptians piling up a pyramid stone by stone. We were each others' guinea pigs, and from observation and criticism of our experiments we learned to describe the actor's equipment in terms that became a new Esperanto. The poet Francis Thompson has an image somewhere of Science: "Science, old noser, that with anatomizing scalpel tents its three-inch of thy skin and brags 'All's bare!'" Our tendency to probe and break things down became a nuisance and good friends warned us of the fate of Humpty-Dumpty. But we have spent the rest of our lives putting ourselves together again. The proof of this particular synthesis lies in the eating, if I may mix puddings and rainbows, in the practical kitchen of the Theatre.

If our sight had remained so fanatically focussed only on the dark and private world of our actors' organism, we might really have emerged as "old nosers," with new "footworks" and "sostenuto buts." But—aside from the fact that we were mindful of our bodies and took normal delight in them, the more so as we sensed the organic interflow of mind and body, and the sovereignty of Will and Imagination to arouse and control them—aside from this fact, the new-found concentration on our functions as actors, forced us also to turn our eyes outward upon the nature of the *objective* world. Our citizenship in this world was acquiring a gravity and an inter-connection and even a responsibility that we hadn't dreamed of in that other time before we'd crossed the Jordan. The world of music and plastic movement, the world of painting and photography, of current history and politics, of the many cultures that made our American culture, the consequences of the Depression and the grim incredible prevalence of the shivering breadline and the apple-seller. That new awareness of ours expanded in all directions; according to temperament and capacity, each person drank of the world around him, even though sometimes it ran like a bitter liquor through his veins. Sympathy or repulsion—they were bred of objective circumstances, a look at the world. "Watchman, what of the night!" When we returned to our exercises we had something to say about it.

Plus ça change; but *plus* not altogether *la même chose.* The interpenetration of the two longings I have described—intense consciousness of Self combined with an insatiable thirst to understand our contemporaries and their times—produced a "new" type of actor. Shall we label him actor-philosopher, or actor-citizen? Or, socially conscious actor? One hesitates to encase this fly in umber; better to call him—just—Actor. "Abstract and brief chronicle of the time"—that word "abstract," though Shakespeare didn't altogether intend it so, permits me to say this: as one of these creatures, I am not willing to see the wild flutter of its wings nailed down upon a ticketed board. The important point lies in the fact that the amalgamation I speak of provided an enormous quickening of the imagination, and when that happens, laws and labels are apt to fly out of the window. The creative impulse —like Ariel—is essentially wild and homeless, chafing against limitations. Somewhere in the heart of this impatient shimmering movement is a spirit, heedless of normal lets and hindrances. It craves to release itself, in a burst of music. All the more, therefore, unless it is to be allowed to attain freedom beyond all recognition, does it need the bondage imposed upon it by some master-force and will. The name of Setebos will have to yield to Prospero—Prospero Sergeitch.

Stanislavsky . . . Adam in the Garden of Eden apparently had no difficulty at all about the names he chose for all created things. He was divinely inspired! Even in translation from Edenese, they come across magnificently: tiger, lamb, elephant, hyena, cat—most satisfactory. But if you want to know what really was happening, and how the struggle for concrete forms takes place without supernatural prompting —then consider *My Life in Art* by Stanislavsky.

On reading this book recently, I was struck again and again by the quantity of things that we already take for granted these days about ourselves as actors. "But of course," we say, "how obvious!" It is the case again of Columbus' egg—very clear, once it's been demonstrated. The touching quality in Stanislavsky's book is the first one he confesses in himself, his obstinacy. To the very last page, for all his majesty of presence and overwhelming knowledge and sophistication, he remains a child, with the concentrated purposefulness of a child learning to walk. "Strange," he seems always to be muttering to himself, "Strange, very strange. I fell. But—let's try again." Like a good Captain, he shares every hardship of his men; he bivouacs on the bare cold ground. He loves them for every glimmer of progress they show; he growls at their laziness, their complacency, their vanities. He presides over his province with farsighted roving eyes, with the look of a skeptical lion. "Know your enemies," he seems to rumble in his throat, "False pathos, cheap tricks, artificiality, disrespect, timidity, tension, fashionableness. And again, laziness!" . . . "I don't believe you!"—his actors flinched and quailed before that dreaded battle cry of his, roared out of the depths of the auditorium. And yet, on opening nights, when Stanislavsky, being often ill was obliged to stay home from the theatre, they would call him on the telephone to be reassured and steadied by the sound of his voice.

Toward the end of the book (it is 1914—Stanislavsky is almost 60 and the seagull on the curtain of the Moscow Art Theatre has come to rest permanently in the imagination of the world) there is a moving section called simply "The Voice." It might also have been called "Let's Face It!" Stanislavsky has faced this matter of the voice thousands of times in his life, and yet there he faces it again with a kind of wistful and defiant finality. Nowhere does the beacon of art that draws him on burn more purely than in this chapter. It is there for you to read, but I would like to quote only this:

> As for me, some people praised me, others (and there were more of them) criticized me. In this book, both before and now, I judge myself not by press reviews and public opinions, but by my own feelings and thoughts. I would not exchange my failure for any success in the world, for it taught me a great deal. . . . Music helped me to solve many problems that had been racking my brain and it convinced me that an actor should know how to speak. . . . Isn't it strange I had to live almost sixty years *before I felt with all my being* this simple and well-known truth, a truth that most actors do not know?

The target, the summary of his beliefs and teachings, is stated in his last chapter. This is no "Ave atque vale," for Prospero is just buckling down to work and continual quest, and there are many years before him. He quotes the painter Dégas as saying: "If you have a hundred thousand francs' worth of skill, spend another five sous to buy more." Then he goes on to speak of "The torch of living tradition and the conscious road to the gates of the unconscious, the true foundation of theatrical art."

This is a torch which can be passed only from hand to hand, and not from the stage; through instruction, through the revelation of mysteries, on the one hand, and through exercises and stubborn and inspired effort to grasp these mysteries, on the other.

The main difference between the art of the actor and all other arts is that other artists may create whenever they are inspired. The stage artist, however, must be the master of his own inspiration and must know how to call it forth at the time announced on the theatre's posters. This is the chief secret of our art. Without this, the most perfect technique, the greatest gifts, are powerless. . . . The inability to find a conscious path to unconscious creativeness led actors to disastrous prejudices which deny inner, spiritual technique. They became stagnant and mistook theatrical self-consciousness for true inspiration.

What will my rôle be in this future task? (i.e., the sphere of the actor's inner and outer technique) In my last years of life, I would like to be what I am in reality, what I must be on the strength of the laws of nature according to which I have lived and worked in art.

. . . Fundamentally, the processes of stage creation remain the same for the younger generation as they were for the older. It is precisely in this sphere that young actors distort and maim their nature. We can help them, we can warn them in time.

. . . The result of my life-long search is my so-called "system," the method of acting that I have discovered and that allows the actor to create images, reveal the life of the human spirit, and naturally incarnate it in a beautiful artistic form on the stage. . . .

Stanislavsky did not dread change. He welcomed it. It was with joy that he saw younger actors and directors, in his lifetime, absorb what he had taught and give it forth in new forms. Michael Chekhov, Vakhtangov, many others. Though he referred to it as "my system," he was never "Sir Oracle" about it. He gloried in the fact that the Voices to which he listened were but promptings from the greatest technicians of the Past, and confirmed by the most stirring practice of his own youthful observation—Salvini, Rossi, Chaliapin, Yermolova, Duse. The "system" was for those that needed it. To Harold Clurman he once said: "One only asks, is it truthful, is it beautiful. And if I see much beautiful acting anywhere, shall I say, 'Just a moment there! It's true, you act marvellously, I am deeply moved, nevertheless I must reject it because you've never been to my School!'?" He may have talked of "mysteries," but he was much more concerned with the "revelation" that might make them clear as day. For the actor there is only one "mystery" and it lies in the interrelationship of the refractory body with the wayward soul. The particular solution may determine *anyone's* life in art. The key that Stanislavsky placed in the hands of the actor was —the actor's own consciousness.

What does this include? Everything. Everything that comes within the grasp of his five senses and is subject to his will. The use of his body, his voice; his inner gifts, sense of rhythm, response to imagery, his sympathies, even his moral point of view. Always, his *conscious recognition* of these things. As he grows in their service, he will grow to love himself, but not with self-love, only as a vessel of craft. If it's Shakespeare he's playing, or Aeschylus, or Molière, or Shaw, he will love their words because they have been chosen and arranged with deep craft, almost with guile—a camouflage to deceive mortality. The wonder and simplicity of "Tu l'as voulu, Dandin!" Or . . . "She never told her love, but let concealment like a worm i' the bud feed on her damask cheek. She pined in thought, and with a green and yellow melancholy she sat like patience on a monument, smiling at grief." Or the sheer rippling delight of exclaiming: "Cry to it, nuncle, as the cockney did to the eels when she put 'em i' the paste alive! She knapped 'em o' the coxcombs with a stick and cried, 'Down, wantons, down!' It was her brother who in pure kindness to his horse, buttered his hay." . . . Or the despair of ever coming within a mile of: "Light thickens; and the crow Makes wing to th' rooky wood: Good things of day begin to droop and drowse; Whiles night's black agents to their preys do rouse. . . ."

Such are the splendors and the miseries of the actor's world. But one thing is certain, mere thinking won't make it come to pass. It's not a general matter of "work to be done," but of concrete tasks, consciously undertaken and mastered by repetition. They are the irreducible minimum of our business. Specific things done, moment to moment. Grasp this, and at once there's a clearing of the decks—all reliance on so-called actors' instinct, inspiration, divine fire, and such-like dangerous fantasies must go. Not that these things don't matter in their place; there will be a time for such a word, to misquote Macbeth. But for the actor they are the consequence, not the shapers of action. One must not be in a hurry to dismiss divine fire when it happens. But it *is* a matter of *when* it occurs. Perhaps this "Gott-sach," as the Germans call it, has to do with our ingrained memories. We are the sum of what we have experienced, yes, but more deeply, we are what we remember in our bones. The poet Rilke says:

> For the sake of a few lines one must see many cities, men and things. One must know the animals, one must feel how the birds fly and know the gesture with which the small flowers open in the morning. One must be able to think back to roads . . . meetings . . . partings . . . days of childhood . . . parents . . . nights of travel . . . many nights of love . . . screams of women in labor . . . the dying . . . the dead . . . And still it is not enough to have memories. One must be able to forget them when they are many, and one must have the great patience to wait until they come again. For it is not yet the memories themselves. Not until they have turned to blood within us, to glance, to gesture, nameless and no longer to be distinguished from ourselves—not until then can it happen that in a most rare hour the first word of a verse arises in their midst and goes forth from them.

Here, at the threshold of the unconscious, as Stanislavsky called it, is the continental divide of our discussion. It is time we climbed down to the flatlands. Since I have hinted at some of the rapt possibilities, I expect you to ask: But how?—just how do you go about achieving them? Even now, I have an impulse to shirk the answer—to say merely: go to the ant, thou sluggard!—in this case, the mighty ant Konstantin Sergeitch. For it is all there, in his books and in the evidence of his practical collected works.

Not always were his followers capable of seizing upon the full meaning of his work, or enlarging upon it. The exception was Eugene Vakhtangov, the brilliant young director, or better still, the partnership of Vakhtangov-Michael Chekhov, since it was the latter who has left us (in a single smallish volume—*To the Actor*) the conclusions that followed from their flint-and-steel collaboration. I knew Chekhov. He was an immensely complicated man, an Ariel, a great teacher. Simplicity is a very complicated thing, and Michael Chekhov set out to simplify the vast implications of his Master's artistic struggles. The basic discoveries having already been made, he took them into his body, so to speak, filtered them through his own powerful individuality and imagination, and gave them an even more elementary character. It is interesting to set some of their terminology side by side. Where Stanislavsky spoke of "Relaxation of Muscles," Chekhov did not hesitate to call it "Feeling of Ease." Where Stanislavsky broke off his brilliant

observations on Action and Objective, Chekhov combined them with
Character in his marvelous intuition of the Psychological Gesture.
Most of all, he understood the harmony of "Body and Psychology," as
he put it. "Listen to your bodies," he would say, "and they will interpret the movement of your *inner* impulses." Great intellect though he
was, he scorned its usefulness for the actor, preferring to obey what one
might call the "muscularity" of the Imagination.

But to return to your question of "How?" . . . Perhaps it will be useful to imagine, to visualize exactly what is happening, in a play we
are looking at. Not so much *in*, as *behind* it, *through* it. As an audience,
let us say we are fortunate; we are witnessing a realistic play of stature
performed by a company of highly trained craftsmen, sensitive and experienced men and women. We are familiar with their work; we like
them even before the curtain rises, but this only sharpens our sense of
responsibility. It is they who have taught us what to expect of them;
it is for us to be alert and fully attentive. In this way we will be able to
give the play back to them; by seeing the point, we will confirm them in
their power to *make* us see the point. We want them to be what they
have always been—the beautiful, expressive voices, the subtle, sinewy
bodies, their lightness and resiliency of spirit, their moody transforma-
tions, their seeming worship of the ultimate good in life. We want all
of these things all over again, yet offered to us somehow in a new light,
as these fine technicians know how to turn them.

The curtain rises. Within the music of the playwright's words we
begin to perceive an issue that embodies a basic struggle. The decision
lies in the hands of a group of characters who battle it out to the final
curtain, and even beyond, in the aroused responses of the spectators.
That much could be the summary of almost any play in the doing. But
we are here for a special pleasure—to observe our actors, to tent them
to the quick. The first five or ten minutes seem to pass in a kind of
sparring, easy yet tentative, as if they hadn't quite made up their
minds. And then, here it comes, as so often before, stealing upon us
before we are aware, the realization that these people are in the highest
degree in *connection* with each other. And this they are without
strain, by no overt means. Not offhand; if these actors *wanted* to be
offhand, they would *be* offhand. But as if they were saying with simple
deliberation: I am here—you are there—we are here—we are in this
together. We sense again the peculiar and reassuring pleasure there is in
watching our actors *look*, simply look; their eyes are full of vision, when

they look, they *see*. They see not only what they want to see by an act of special concentration which explores the significance of the moment, they also prepare for future looks, future significances. Already this is life, but it is above life. It is the same with their listening. They not only listen, they hear. And so with their other senses, of which perhaps touching is the most obvious. But one sense cannot be divided from the others. These actors come alive all in one piece; they can touch with their eyes, taste and smell with their ears. And what's more, they *talk*. That is to say, they *truly* communicate by means of words and silences.

The dialogue begins to prepare for a small event—one of the actors has a speech to which the others all listen. You know in advance that he loves this speech, for there's a glow of anticipation in him as it comes near, the mouth of his imagination begins to water—he launches into it, tearing at it with little nips, the speech feeds him with imagery and his eyes light up as he *sees* ever more and more. He enjoys the responses of his fellows—they give him strength and a strange freedom as he goes plunging along to the end. In the chorus of yeses that follows, enters one bearing a gift. He is elderly, self-deprecating, though his heart is full of love. But these qualities are not yet fully established in him; we sense him alternately feeding at some center within himself and reaching out to find some object or person with which or whom he can establish outer connection. Before long he has it; eye meets eye, an intangible circle is defined, he snuggles into his character as into a warm coat; life in the form of the ensuing action radiates from him without effort, with infectious reality . . . There is another, who has been brooding to one side of the stage. We know him as the Bear. He seems apart from the others, objective, critical. But his inner attitude, not yet revealed, scorns any obvious indications, bodily or facial; it simply radiates out of some energy he has known how to store up in himself. The speech of the previous young actor has apparently stayed with him; now, strolling lazily toward the group, he harks back to it with challenge and contempt. He cuts through the scene like a hot ploughshare; challenge and contempt become welded into a private grief—his face becomes ironed out into a moving simplicity, strangely classical. He remains connected with some image within himself, tears stand in his eyes, he disdains them with an angry lift of his head, you can see they have come unbidden and we divine in this moment that actor and man have found an intense union. They too, are connected.

. . . A woman has wandered in during this last outburst; she is the one we call Greensleeves. We know about her. Life has dealt her many a hard blow, but she has found in herself the strength to resist bitterness. Now her lovely face is molded into an expression past suffering, compassionate and pure. *There* is one of her characteristic gestures, head on the side, a quizzical fleeting smile, the partly open hand raised and let fall. She hears the man's words, her face becomes grave; she wants to stay out of it, she turns away and describes little circles with her finger on the table, then she hears a strange tone in the man's voice, she turns to see the tears glistening—a flash of sullen resistance crosses her face, "What have I to do with you?" followed by a sigh. She is connected with him through understanding—her face is a mask of compassion. She folds her arms and waits, filled with some special grace for which there is no name but her own, and which is yet not static, but suspended, in conflict. Two powers seem to fill the stage with dramatic potential—the power of masculine integrity and the power of love.

In the performance of these four or five little "pictures" that I have pilfered from various places and strung together at random, I want to point out that there is nothing *calculated*—not the man's tears, nor the woman's sigh, nor the old man's radiations, nor the young man's abandonment. These actors do what they have to do—it is second nature by now—out of obedience to certain fundamental stimulations which make everything else come to pass. They are too wise to fall into the error of copying themselves. Nevertheless, night after night they are capable of conveying the content of the play without superficial indication or studied effectiveness, simply by safeguarding the truth. One notices that 1) they accept themselves; they open themselves, too: they know how to leave themselves free to receive all impressions. 2) They accept and relate to each other. 3) They adapt to the circumstances of the play with intelligence and sensitiveness. 4) They give and take through their senses; also through action and reaction. 5) They have rhythm in speech and action. 6) They are constantly in contact with something, whether it be an inanimate object, their partners, a thought, an image, or a memory. 7) As a result of all these, their emotions simply occur, easily, abundantly.

There are larger vistas beyond—the completion of the Main Action, the grades and climaxes, the whole composition of the play. But I deliberately set these aside in order to examine the intimate condition of the actor at work. One is rightly suspicious of readers' digests as substitutes for a man's lifelong labor. But I think we can agree that the unit of what happens when that curtain goes up is the Moment. The Moment is the responsibility of the actor at work. And if I had to reduce the great gold vein of Stanislavsky's mine to a single practical nugget, I would say—that for the actor there is no moment on the stage that cannot be examined and accounted for in terms of three basic elements—the Self, the Object, and the Action.

The actor, like all craftsmen, brings himSelf to the work. He also finds himSelf *in* the work, and he brings back this perpetually renewed Self time after time, *to* the work. Technically, this is what I understand by Stanislavsky's Relaxation, Chekhov's Feeling of Ease. You may take it as relaxation and leave it at that if you prefer. But for me, it is a more central and intimate way of feeling at home on the stage. More than that, it is a source of power, and inexhaustible. The Self is all we have—it is well to realize it, to accept it, and most importantly, to use it. Does this seem obvious?—then why is our stage still afflicted with tensions of all kinds, tensions of the body and the mind, contortions of the spirit? When the curtain rose on those little "pictures" of ours it was the first thing we sensed—these actors were not Self-conscious, they were Self-possessed. We will return, in the end, to Self.

Michael Chekhov prefaces one of his chapters with this remark by Leonardo da Vinci: "The soul desires to dwell with the body because without the members of the body it can neither act nor feel." In much the same way, the Self needs the objective world—otherwise it has no meaning, it is like a motor idling, it is not connected. May we not think of our waking day (and according to the Freudians much more importantly our sleeping time!) as an uninterrupted succession of pictures, ideas, thoughts, fantasies, actualities. We are constantly seeing, even when our eyes are closed. The actor's Self utilizes this fact significantly; collaborating with the Author's lines, and between the lines as well, he weaves a continuous tissue of these Objects, these "lies like truth," amusing fiction, coruscating images, grim deeds and memories. He is on intimate terms with them, unbidden as they frequently are when they come. In return they "give" him something, as we say—a focus of concentration, a storehouse of reassurance. As long as they are alive, he is alive. That actor of ours, brooding off there on the side was drinking deep of this flow of objects; the woman Green-sleeves, drawn in almost against her will, the victim of memories and faiths of which she herself has become the sacrifice—then, when they could contain themselves no more, they overflowed in action.

Which is the third of our three ingredients. Action, considered thus, may be thought of as an expression of the *energy* which is set up between the Self and the Object. As such it has an "oscillating" character—back and forth, back and forth. Is this to consider it too curiously? And are we discarding Stanislavsky's orthodox dictum of desire: I want, therefore I act? Well—have we actors not found in practice that often and often even the word, desire, killeth? But isn't desiring the electrical continuum of looking and seeing? "And the eyes of them both were opened and they knew that they were naked." (Genesis 3:7) The Bible comes to the support of Prospero Alexeitch. And once we have set that energy *going*, will it be so difficult to know what we *want*? Again, I must warn you, as I warn myself, that these things must not be taken mechanically, lest we fall again into the error of the "old noser." They are neither a formula nor a recipe. They are the shorthand, as it were, of a long experience. Symbols. All symbols have to be earned, and paid for with the usual legal tender—blood, sweat, and tears.

I hope that you will let me share with you a private experience which properly falls outside the limits of this discussion. And yet, not so, since it stemmed organically from what I was thinking about all these subjects. It is not accidental, that from time to time, as you noticed, I have been referring in one way or another to Shakespeare's *Tempest*. It happens to be one of the plays we will do this summer at Stratford. I stand in awe, as all of us do, before the work of this man. I think that as men change and progress, their understanding of him will progress and change. Each age will evaluate him in its own terms, for "others abide our question, thou art free." Now, as for *Tempest*, I had long ago caught its "message" of ultimate reconciliation of man with man, in the form of an allegory that seemed to measure the relative goodness and spirituality of created things in a series of contrasts. Wisdom and brute stupidity. Disembodied beauty and earthbound carnality. Unworldliness and malevolence. Innocence and bitter knowledge. True, these things are there, and we may arrange them in a gorgeous bouquet of moralities, if we wish (enclosing a card from W.S.). But I don't think so. Not now. It was not only for these things that Prospero broke his staff. The inner event had to do with Shakespeare's resignation from the kingdom of poesy. This has been remarked before, as we know. But I can only say that for myself I had never felt the special poignancy, the *technical* poignancy, if you will, of this resignation, as I did while I was struggling to put down the ideas of this very technical paper. Beauty is truth —but truth is also beauty. The truth of the lifelong struggle, for the right word, the right cadence, the right pause ("That's my dainty Ariel"), the right storm ("My brave spirit"), the right tranquillity ("Delicate Ariel, I'll set thee free for this"), the right object, the right action, the right sense of Self (sound of staff, breaking).

These are the thoughts I wanted to share with you (I feel they are the "right" thoughts), principally to point out that they came to me as intimations rising out of this whole consideration of actors' technique. It's how a craftsman's mind works—that is how we actors find our correct objectives. It is a matter of many levels, not one.

Postscript on Self. . . . There's a homely American story. It tells of an Indian and a white trapper who went out hunting together. They blundered into some very wild country, farther and farther away from familiar surroundings and the ancestral teepee. Night was falling and the coyotes beginning to howl. The white man stopped and said: "Look here, Eagle Feather, you know what I think? I think we're lost!" To which the noble savage replied: "Me not lost. Teepee lost."

An Audience of Critics
and the Lost Art
of "Seeing" Plays

BY THEODORE HOFFMAN

FOR SOME TIME NOW I have been trying to shrug off the hunch that contemporary audiences and dramatic critics have lost the art of seeing plays. Now this is a disturbing thought to anyone engaged in the practice of theatre. It is hard to work without some faith in the intelligence and appreciation of either critics or audiences. When you don't succeed in maintaining that faith to some degree, you feel anxious and guilty, and begin to get paranoic.

But "paranoia" occurs when imaginary dangers are identified as real; and although I am perfectly willing to regard my feelings as neurotic, I have also found that they seem to be widely shared in the profession. Something has happened to audiences and critics that fills the theatre with irritation. The mere mention of a critic's name in professional circles causes hackles to rise. And it is only in the outer echelons of show business *kitsch*, where "ratings" prevail, that one finds any of the old-fashioned love of audiences. Of course, this situation isn't entirely new. One of the theatre's immutable traditions has been to join Hamlet in regarding true art as "caviar to the general." But as I read theatre history, I get the impression that the theatre's conventional attitude in the past has been one of benign contempt, while today's is more one of defensive antagonism. It is as if we felt threatened with annihilation, and since it is easier to analyze than be analyzed, I feel obliged to weigh the justice of my worries.

Let's take the critics first. There does exist, of course, between the theatre and criticism an unwritten gentleman's agreement whereby the theatre goes on inviting critics to investigate the true nature of drama and critics go on modestly suggesting, or solemnly asserting, that their sole purpose is to educate brave new audiences. But the true state of affairs is perpetual cold, even frozen, warfare. It is easy to understand the theatre's hostility to any group that determines the size of its bread and butter, but those critics who are *not* concerned with contemporary drama are, if possible, subjected to more contumely than those who are. Behind the theatre's touchy resistance to the critics one can sense a gnawing suspicion that the critics are really professional rivals of some sort, that they are out to replace the theatre with something else.

If one then reads the critics, one finds between the lines a smug belief that *they* are the true theatre artists, that *they* bring plays to life, that the theatre isn't really necessary to experience drama. In fact, I sometimes feel that only Coleridge and Lamb have been honest. They, at least, asserted that the qualities they loved in drama could not be presented on the stage and that the proper place to stage plays is in the mind's eye. In short, they openly proclaimed what most drama critics take for granted, that plays are really meant to be read.

Ah, but what about the daily reviewers, who do attend plays constantly and write about productions? The question is: just what do they do at plays? It is common knowledge in the theatre that most reviewers are not only untrained in the theatre arts, but woefully ignorant of them. Reviewers are always praising bad plays actors have saved, damning directors who have been betrayed by actors who refuse to follow direction, ignoring performances of actors who do sound work in being faithful to plays the reviewers dislike, praising actors who use all the vicious tricks of the trade to stand out in a production and violate the ideals of ensemble performance, and so on, down the line of possible combinations of errors. The daily reviewers are rarely capable of describing how an actor has interpreted a part, or a director a play, except, of course, with revivals, and then we get a comparison with an older production, not the text. Compare the reviews of a new play with the script, without seeing the play, and you will be astounded at how incapable the reviewers are of separating the script from the production. Reviewers do review the play, only they seem to operate on the naïve assumption that what they see on the stage is the playwright's play, a habit that perhaps explains some of the hostility between playwrights and theatre practitioners.

One should not, however, get angry at the reviewer for doing his job, which is, after all, to serve as a kind of litmus paper predictor of how his readers are likely to respond. If he is not really concerned with acting, directing, and designing, it is because his readers are not. If his approach is literary, it is not because his training is in literary criticism. The casual techniques of the reviewers appall serious critics and none of the daily reviewers has produced an extended study of the work of any playwright or period. If the reviewers are ignorant of both critical and theatre techniques, it is certainly not for want of models. The weekly reviewers, like Clurman, Bentley, Hewes, Tynan, Hayes, are most of the good things that the reviewers are not, and it is not just the several days of gestation that make them that way, for the daily reviewers are not vastly different in their weekly leaders; just more ruminative and more polished. And, what is more, it is *their* reviews that make a play a hit or failure. In short, they speak for their readers and for the theatre's audiences. They are as bright as the better educated segments of the New York theatre audience. They speak the same intellectual jargon. They parade the same degree of sophistication. They see neither more nor less than their audiences, and we would be wise to regard them not as the shame of the age, but as the habit of the age. The habit, I might say the disease, of the age is to regard theatre as drama and to understand drama in terms of literature. And the only way we shall cure the disease is to cultivate the lost art of *seeing* plays.

That the disease has a strong grip on our society can be proved by looking at our university theatres and drama departments, which like to feel that they uphold the standards lacking in the professional theatre. It is rather shocking to encounter again and again in educational theatre philosophy the proposition that the function of educational theatre is to help the student participants understand "drama." Its cultural purpose, we are told, is "to bring drama" to audiences. "The play's the thing" is a valuable notion, especially for directors who find it easier to use their own concept of the play rather than the playwright's, but in educational theatre it seems to have the meaning that theatre is the sugar on the pill that can lead people to read drama, that the theatre is only a device, a plaything, that leads to more serious occupations, like criticism.

Surely anyone who appreciates good theatre can only be astounded at how seldom it is found in universities, at how little theatre training "drama majors" receive, at how little professional experience drama faculties possess. The universities are regarded as the main source of "experimental" theatre in America, but the experiments usually consist of a scheme—an unusual set, a gimmick approach, a staging trick—which may be clever in conception but is usually impossible to carry out fully because the actors and technicians are deficient in the fundamentals of theatre art. One might claim that almost all experimental theatre in America has been in the hands of people who are incapable of doing respectable work along the lines of the kind of theatre they seek to replace or surpass. What emerges out of experimental university productions is at best a suggestion, which is applauded as an achievement. The giveaway is to be found in the note that invariably appears in university theatre programs. The "note" is either a brief critical analysis of the play or an interpretation of the production. Such notes, of course, are essential, since the production rarely conveys the information contained in the note, even though the cast has been schooled to discuss it *ad nauseum*. Without the note, audiences might not know what they have seen, and if the intention of the production is made known, the audience is more willing to believe that the production has succeeded.

The lessons taught by our "educational" theatre might be less expensively imparted in the classroom, but that would be to emphasize the university's duty to the "humanities" at the expense of its duty to the "community." Fortunately, both the community and students share the commercial audience's strange perversity of accepting theatre as a painless and socially entertaining way of reading plays.

This perhaps explains why the "professional" schools of drama, which are not hindered by illogical commitments to the liberal arts, present plays that are more varied in selection, higher in intellectual quality, and more imaginatively staged, than those of the "educational" theatre. The professional schools are still devoted to training students in the theatre arts. They are not hindered by administrations or faculties that place the theatre arts among manual crafts like cooking and carpentry. As a result, they operate with higher standards and are naturally attracted to plays that are conceived in terms of the imaginative power of the theatre arts. And since the professional schools are primarily concerned with the training of talent, and know that students learn theatre practice better by working in good plays than bad, they need not cater to the demands of the less appreciative members of the community. There is perhaps no greater irony in the theatre today than the fact that so many of the plays professional theatre people appear in for money are put on as art in the "educational" theatre. To meet any of the established artists of the professional theatre is to be impressed by their personal good taste in drama, and by their education and critical perception. It is the audience that sets the standards of American theatre, and it is either incredible, or a noble tribute to our educational system's desire to prepare students for contemporary life, that the plays and the approach to plays that can be called "commercial" are prevalent in "educational" theatre.

One readily understands the situation, of course. Drama departments have often had to begin as offshoots and stepchildren of speech and literature departments merely in order to exist and in the process have surrendered their rights to autonomy. They exist under the aegis of drama as the "spoken word." Their play programs are under the scrutiny of literature professors whose recognitions of drama rarely extend beyond a few English classics and whose hostility to contemporary anything has been notorious. Theatres get built to "serve the community," and this too often means that university drama departments are a branch of public relations, designed to make the university a substitute for the missing local theatre, which would be doing Broadway rehashes if it did exist. Curricula are controlled by committees that want measurable results, techniques that can be mimeographed, courses that involve text books, programs that make it possible for non-majors to dabble and get "wide experience." Faculty members, of course, must have degrees and publish, and however much lip-service is paid to "equivalent achievement" it is a rare occasion when qualification corresponds to competence. Oh, it is a difficult situation, especially when the university theatre must pretend to be something it is not, and the professional theatre should be grateful to the few university teachers who manage against all obstacles to maintain standards and do the occasional brilliant job. Meanwhile the graduates migrate to New York to discover that they know nothing, and talented students leave in their sophomore year, with subterranean feelings of guilt about having spurned "art," to learn their craft the hard way and be amazed at how much more artistic satisfaction they get from submitting to the yoke of professional discipline.

Reviewers, audiences, educators—all victims of the evil side of theatre! Rather a ghastly assertion to make. But I am willing to go even further, and toss in the historians and the serious critics of drama. For further symptoms of the low state of "educational" theatre, one can turn to the learned articles and books of its practitioners. There we find only the most perfunctory mention of the theatre arts (or else non-functional pedantic theory on the same), but lots of theatre "history" and a great deal of play analysis that reflects the techniques and vocabulary of modern literary criticism.

Now, modern literary criticism is a great thing in itself. It ably performs the main functions of criticism. It brings works of literature to life for readers and provides means of fully appreciating them; it has examined the works of the past in such a way as to inspire present day writers. The "new" critics of the twenties created a cultural revolution in our reading habits, and effected such a bond between literary artists and critics that the two groups seem almost interchangeable. One may complain of the labored complexity of its method, the pedantic rococo of its style, and the pomposity of its mien, but it has made available to us many previously neglected works of the past. Donne, Melville, Swift, to name only a few, are worth any annoyance we may feel, and the widespread popular willingness to try "difficult" literature is something all serious artists should rejoice in. But the result has hurt our theatre. The prestige and challenge of the poetic and fictional forms have siphoned most of our writing talent into those fields. One can make a case for O'Neill and Williams but one also has to admit that their imaginative power in the theatre has not equaled that of Hemingway and Faulkner in fiction, nor Eliot and Stevens in poetry. Nor has modern critical talent been attracted to the theatre. Bentley, Fergusson and Gassner are the only critics we have whose ability is commensurate with that of the host of critics who have worked the literary mine. Perhaps, if the drama critics had effected the revolution in drama that the literary critics effected in literature we should have a better theatre today, but the sad truth is that the *literary* revolution has also been effected in drama for the worse.

One proof is to be found in the histories of drama and theatre. They are two different subjects. Drama history takes on the fifth-century Greeks, lingers over the Elizabethans, loiters momentarily among a few neoclassical masterpieces, and skips to 1880. Theatre history struggles through fourth- and third-century Greece and ancient Rome, painfully pushes through pages of the medieval period, runs wild in the Italian Renaissance, and devotes tremendous attention to the nineteenth century. The two histories do not readily combine and one might conclude that the great periods of theatre have inhibited the writing of good plays, except for the fact that buried in the great ages of theatre are numerous interesting plays that our critics and, as a consequence, our theatre, have utterly ignored.

The implications of this strange situation are worth considering. Almost all histories and studies of drama operate on the assumption that the only important form of drama is tragedy (with a few concessions to "high comedy"). Critics have assumed either that the theatre has always been trying to produce tragedy, in which case they "discover" evolutionary trends in this direction, or that the value of plays depends on how well they measure up in form and content to classical tragedy, and then we get personal theories of esthetics or patchwork definitions of the tragic mode and form. In the process, most drama is neglected as insignificant, and we are given the explanation that in the absence of great tragic writers, the pyrotechnics of the theatre take over until genius reappears. This well-intended act of rejection has deprived us of much usable tradition, and also represents an ignorant use of history.

I think one could make a pretty good cultural case out for the comic form as the normal mode of the theatre and classical tragedy as its enemy. Whenever the theatre has been left alone to develop by itself, the plays it produces are comic and it develops techniques of theatre that make comedy a profound, imaginative and perceptive form of art. When the world of literature intervenes, with its efforts to impose a classical tragic mode on drama, as it did in fourth-century Greece, sixteenth-century Italy, eighteenth-century England, and nineteenth-century Europe, the natural dramatic movements of the theatre have quickly faded. One may cite the Greeks and Elizabethans as contrary evidence, but the answer is clear. Classical Greek tragedy is the only pure form of tragedy that ever grew out of theatre, perhaps because it grew out of a theatre of religion, and every attempt to imitate it has failed. Shakespeare was a man of the theatre. What is great in his tragedies is his comic counterpoint, and his masterful violation of the classical elements his contemporaries derived from Seneca. The great comic tradition that runs from the *commedia dell' arte* through Molière, Gozzi, Goldoni, Marivaux, Nestroy and Labiche is almost unknown to us, partly because our theatre has lost the art of playing such works significantly, partly because our critics have ignored them and neglected to encourage their translation.

Perhaps right there, in the matter of translation, we can find the most crippling obstacle to our full appreciation of the theatre. It has always been the duty of critics to foster good translations. In literature, a half-century of excellent translation has expanded our appreciation of the past. But anyone in the theatre who has tried to stage the great European drama of the past, even of the recent past, knows that although most existing translations may be read, they cannot be produced, and the reason is obvious. The critic-translators of drama have been deficient in their knowledge of theatre. In recent years, Eric Bentley has performed the greatest critical service our theatre has known this century, not through his writing, which is brilliant and valuable, but through the series of usable translations he has persuaded competent writers to make and publishing houses to print. But until more translators learn how to translate in terms of theatre, or theatre people take up the financially unprofitable task of decently translating the drama of the past, we shall not be in a position in this country fully to evaluate and use our genuine dramatic heritage.

I suppose, however, that the real theatrical sins of critics have been inflicted on Shakespeare. Shakespeare responds very well to the techniques of modern criticism. He is complex and deep, and any approach to his work, theatrical or critical, has much to unravel. I freely admit that much of modern Shakespearean criticism is marvelous, that it provides the reader with great illumination, and that it convincingly reveals the basic ideas of the plays. My complaint is that it treats the plays as literature and that its methods are of no help to the theatre. The critic lingers over the image, plumbing its implications; the actor can only hold a word so long and suggest so much. The critic can juxtapose passages; the director is bound to a linear presentation. The critic can ignore parts of the play that don't interest him (or suggest, infuriatingly, that what he has found in one scene is infused throughout the play); the director is stuck with them, and they often comprise most of the play.

The ultimate truths which critics discover and directors create may be the same (which I doubt), but the methods of realizing them differ so greatly that Shakespearean criticism has become all but useless. An example here might help. The last act of any play is theatrically important. It is there that the playwright brings his artistic climax to its fullest meaning. Most criticism of *Hamlet* recognizes the importance of Hamlet's "the readiness is all." The play can be found in it. Critics also like "Absent thee from felicity a while." Matthew Arnold defined it as a touchstone of poetry. But no director can put the fifth act into those two lines or into the one page scene in which they occur. He must deal with the difficult and incongruous comedy of the gravediggers, the long, inert, and almost irrelevant story of Hamlet's trip to England, the incredibly complex and implausible dueling-poisoning scene with its resultant four corpses littering the stage, and, finally, the dazzling crowd effect of Fortinbras' entrance and finale. Surely, if *Hamlet* is a great play Shakespeare put its final greatness into that last act, and we can't explain away the parts we don't like by calling them "conventions" (such as Fortinbras being needed to "clear" the stage because the Globe had no curtain). Either they mean something or they don't. And if they don't, *Hamlet* is not such a great "play." I'm willing to maintain that the Elizabethan audience responded to the whole of Act V, and that if *Hamlet* is to be a great play for our audiences we must find ways of staging Act V significantly enough to brush away our audiences' conventional demands for mechanically smooth construction, for symmetrical climaxes, and for plausible plots. When critics place the meaning of *Hamlet* in Act V in such a way that it can be immediately conveyed into theatrical reality, I shall begin to admit that Shakespeare has been studied as a playwright.

But such criticism hardly exists, and audiences have come to appreciate Shakespeare as literature. The productions that attempt to present Shakespeare with the same imaginative depth that goes into other plays are rare, and usually fail. Actually, Shakespeare's plays are easier to produce satisfactorily on our stage than any others. All that is needed is to costume and design the play lavishly, for embellishment, not meaning; and to deliver the lines clearly and beautifully, without any nuance of meaning but infused with generalized emotion. This is the "neutral" way, and it works well. Audiences are free to read their own interpretation into the production if they know the play and to be impressed by the "beauty of the language" if they don't. If interpretation is really demanded, a "gimmick" can be found and the play transferred to another period. This has been called the "Puck on roller skates" approach.

The picture I have tried to present here is that of an audience of critics which, when it goes to theatre, converts what it sees into a series of printed pages. The picture is of a cultural situation at a particular point in history. The question that remains to be asked is: How did we get that way? One need go back only seventy-five years. The critics of the last quarter of the nineteenth century appreciated acting as it has rarely been appreciated. George Henry Lewes, Henry James and George Bernard Shaw had a knack of describing plays as they appeared on the stage that only Stark Young has approached in Anglo-American criticism since. They had reason for it. The nineteenth century was an age of great acting—not just of the technique of acting, but of the art of acting. The actors of that age brought a talent to plays that often elevated them on the stage to a degree of meaning and beauty that the plays did not (and do not) possess on paper.

It is wrong, in a way, for historians to tax Henry Irving with bad taste for having played *The Bells* more than he did Shakespeare. Irving's *The Bells* probably was as much a meaningful and realized work of art as many other actors' Shakespeare. Undoubtedly, his Shakespeare might have been better than his *Bells*, but the point of the matter is that he had audiences which saw the play not in terms of its text, but in terms of what he created on the stage. As the movement we now call "Modern Drama" developed, it faced obstacles like Irving. For one thing, it wanted to deal with experience the star actors and their vehicles did not take to. Secondly, it felt an urge to introduce new styles into the theatre. Sympathetic critics (like Shaw) began to attack the old drama and the failure of the old actors to assimilate the new. Since the new drama was acted by actors who were not stars, the critics' emphasis soon shifted to the play. Since the playwrights began to provide the imaginative material for the actors, the actors themselves came to believe in the need to develop their roles completely out of the play itself. Since modern drama was, at first, naturalistic, the new acting required convincing character portrayal. As a result, the art of free interpretation began to disappear, at least from the Russian and American theatre. Around 1900 a new factor intervened—the theatrical producer, the man who took the playwright's script and staged it. The playwright, partly because he had come to write in such a way that the theatrical realization of his play was based directly on his script, partly because his old direct working contact with the actors had been taken over by the producers and directors, partly because his art had become realistic, came to learn his art by copying society directly, to do his writing at home, and to become separated from the theatre.

The point is important. Our present system of theatre which demands that the playwright write his play without any real knowledge of its final stage form, that he "submit" it to a producer who then assembles staff, theatre, cast, etc., is unique in the history of theatre. Almost all the great playwrights were directly involved in the producing of their plays. (The same is true of five of the six great modern playwrights; Ibsen, Strindberg, Shaw, Pirandello and Brecht were all able to plan the staging of their plays; and Chekhov, the sole exception, complained that Stanislavsky had completely misinterpreted his work.) The traditional method of writing plays has always been to conceive of them as theatrical productions. Shakespeare undoubtedly knew even more about how his plays would look on the stage than a director of contemporary plays, since he probably staged them himself, wrote them for his own theatre, cast them before he wrote them, and even wrote them to fit the talents of particular actors. One might say that the great plays have been created on the stage, that they *exist* as works of art only on the stage, and that when we read them in books we are reading reductions of plays, nothing more than what actors call "sides," dialogue to be learned. The real meaning of the great plays of the past can never be fathomed through examining "texts." One must *add* to the text a knowledge of how the theatre worked when the play was written and a live understanding of the creative techniques which cause a play to exist as a work of art.

Today, however, the play exists in the text and stage productions are regarded only as an attempt to provide a sort of corresponding imitation of the text. We seem to have unconsciously accepted the view that a play can have only one possible authentic production, and it is for this reason that the texts of plays supplied by publishers and agents come equipped with every stage move spelled out in detail, with a fixed ground plan of the set, with photographs of the original production, so that we may be accurate and present the real play to our audiences. Today's theatre obituaries invariably describe an actor as famous for having "created" a particular character—not for having demonstrated his competence by playing a variety of roles, nor for having given brilliant new interpretations to established roles, but for having been the one person who fit one particular part. It is even more disturbing to note the new method of casting according to personality type. The actor is no longer even a "juvenile lead," or a "fat comic," or an "old character man,"—categorizations that at least promised a variety of parts. He is now relegated to playing the same character over and over again, a sad suggestion that the theatre is succumbing to the same disease that has infected critics and audiences.

When shall we stop going to the theatre to read plays? Well, the symptoms of health are present in any disease, except the most malignant, and the theatre really is the "fabulous invalid" who gets up from the death-bed when we least expect it. We can wait for a new kind of play or a new kind of style to medicine us out of our ills. The new kind of play has existed for years in Europe, where playwrights have been able to maintain a working relationship with the theatre and repertory companies, subsidized theatres and actor-managers have kept alive the supremacy of the theatre arts. The "experimental" playwrights of continental Europe have been experimental not because they have imitated modern literature or poetry, but because they have sought to express themselves in theatrical terms, and the great directors, like Jouvet, Barrault, Viertel, and Brecht have been there to make their plays "exist" on the stage. The more the work of playwrights like Giraudoux, Anouilh, Brecht, Lorca and Sartre is done in this country the more our audiences will be forced to look at the stage in order to understand what is going on.

Even in our own theatre, certain sea-changes are taking place. The acting-playwriting situation is coming full circle. Twenty years of bad plays and new acting techniques have resulted in a situation where the acting improves on the play even though the purpose of the improvement is still to convince audiences that the play is good. An actor like Marlon Brando can give a quotidien reality to any cardboard part. He may someday bring his talent to good plays. Elia Kazan can transform any play into something far better than its text. He is, in effect, the best playwright we have. When Kazan, and other leading talents, begin to stop pretending that the theatre only "produces" plays, we may get something new in the way of invigorating style. That such a situation is on the way may perhaps be read in certain misgivings leading figures in the "Method" movement have expressed about its adequacy for tackling Shakespeare. They agree that it needs broadening, that voice techniques and stage movement need to be re-emphasized. (Some schools, of course, never have de-emphasized voice and movement study.) The great mime teacher, Etienne Decroux, worked last year at the Actors' Studio. The great mime, Marcel Marceau, has been royally received in this country. We may yet know again an American theatre that rejoices in the arts of the theatre and knows instinctively that plays can never exist on paper. The signs look very promising in the theatre; and, after all, the critics have always come around in the end. And audiences? Well, how can you expect to work in the theatre without some hope that audiences are intelligent and appreciative, and capable of *seeing* plays.

Stanislavski and
the Playwright

BY ROBERT W. CORRIGAN

No NAME IN ACTING IS revered more in the American theatre than is Stanislavski's. He has been the high priest of American acting since the 1930's when the Group Theatre incorporated his system into their program; and today, a modified Stanislavski system is central to the "Method" of the Actor's Studio. Whether this great regard for Stanislavski has been a good thing for our theatre is much debated, but very little has been said about the effect of Stanislavski's system upon the way the actor approaches the written text of a play. It is time this be considered, for the effects have been insidious and may well have been harmful to the art of our theatre.

I

Stanislavski began as a reformer. Acting in the Russian theatre in the nineteenth century had deteriorated to little more than the presentation of clichés and stereotypes in an operatic manner. In his attempts to improve the level of acting on the Russian stage, Stanislavski was right in his insistence that acting demanded concentration, grace of movement, a sense of environment, and motivated behavior on the stage. But these demands were not the ingredients of his system; they were but the starting point from which he developed it. It is only when we examine his system of acting that we discover it to be a two-edged sword that can do as much harm as good to the theatre. For the Stanislavski system, while it is the "only organic technique of acting

182

in the modern theatre,"[1] has also tended to ignore the playwright and more often than not has transformed the director from one whose purpose is to order the production in such a way as to realize the playwright's intention on the stage, to a coach of a kind of acting that is very often artistically beside the point.

The explanation of Stanislavski's failure to understand the relationship of the actor to the playwright can be found in his definition of acting. In *An Actor Prepares* he states *"in our art you must live the part every moment that you are playing it, and every time."*[2] At the end of the same book he concludes his case by saying *"Our type of creativeness is the conception and birth of a new being—the person in the part. It is a natural act similar to the birth of a human being . . . If you analyze this process you will be convinced that laws regulate organic nature, whether she is creating a new phenomenon biologically or imaginatively . . . Nature's laws are binding on all, without exception, and woe to those who break them."*[3] Or, as Norris Houghton in his book, *Moscow Rehearsals*, describes Stanislavski's system: "When the actor has found the nature and origin of his emotions, then he must say 'I am this person.' There can be no separation between the actor and his part."[4] From these passages it is clear that Stanislavski never perceptively distinguished between nature and art; he even used these concepts interchangeably. As a result, Stanislavski failed to realize that in a work of art, as differentiated from a natural phenomenon, one is always aware of the guiding hand of the artist. Every work of art is the product of the artist's attempt to communicate his emotions and/or his emotionalized experiences; but if these emotions and experiences are to be communicated in any meaningful way they must be arranged and controlled by a governing intention—a thought, an idea, a perception, an attitude. They must be given a communicable form by the artist and it is the governing intention that determines and realizes this form. It is this controlling force of the artist which characterizes the work of art and differentiates it from the phenomena of nature.

In the theatre, the playwright must be the primary creator. His intention *must* be expressed in every aspect of the production. Knowl-

---

[1] Harold Clurman, "Founders of the Modern Theatre," *Theatre Workshop* I, 1937, p. 75.
[2] K. Stanislavski, *An Actor Prepares*, New York, 1936, p. 18.
[3] *Ibid.*, pp. 294–5.
[4] Norris Houghton, *Moscow Rehearsals*, New York, 1936, p. 75.

edge of his intention can only come from the text of the play itself; for the text *is* the form through which the playwright expresses his idea to the other artists of the theatre. (This does not deny the possibility that the text may not always communicate the playwright's idea in the clearest possible way; and, therefore, the director or actor may suggest ways to rewrite the text in order to improve it.) Whether the play is a tragedy or a comedy, whether it is in the style of Greek, Elizabethan, or modern drama, whether at any given moment the emphasis of expression shifts from the actor to the setting or from one actor to another, the chief aim of all the artists of the theatre must always be to realize that attitude toward life expressed by the playwright in his play.

But it is precisely this concern for the playwright's intention that is lacking in Stanislavski's system of acting. For in his insistence that the actor always be true to nature, it is possible for the actor to be true to nature without ever (or at best accidentally) realizing or expressing the playwright's governing intention. Stanislavski teaches actors to *live* on the stage and not to *act* on stage. Over and over again in his demonstrations in *An Actor Prepares* he teaches his students not how to act, not how to express the playwright's ideas, but how to relive as fully and believably as possible a certain experience. In this he fails to recognize that experiencing the events that may occur in a play is not the same thing as perceiving what these events mean in the context of the play as a whole. It is a system which teaches the actor to understand what he does in a given situation, without teaching him the meaning which the playwright intends this situation to express. In short, it is possible to be true to nature without ever being true to the idea of the play.

For example, in the exercises in *An Actor Prepares* designed to evoke those realistic details that are necessary "to convince our physical natures of the truth of what you are doing on the stage," Stanislavski assumes that "feelings, drawn from our actual experience and transferred to our parts, are what give life to the play."[5] It is all well and good for the actor to understand how he behaves in a natural situation, but when that situation appears in two or more plays the feeling of the natural situation may be the right way to act in one play and be totally wrong in the others. The naturalistic fallacy in the Stanislavski system tends to make the actor unaware that making love, for instance, would

---

[5] Stanislavski, *op. cit.,* p. 126.

be done one way in a Shakespearean comedy and another way in a
Shaw comedy (anyone who has directed naturalistically trained actors
in a production of Shaw will know what I mean); that, indeed, making
love in *Twelfth Night* would be done differently than in *Cymbeline;*
or finally, that making love in *As You Like It* when directed by Hugh
Hunt would be done in one way and in quite another when directed
by Elia Kazan.

In his search for psychological motivations that are true to nature
Stanislavski tends to disregard the author's intention. The Stanislavski-
trained actor, who comes to depend only on life, only on honest personal
experiences and the believable representation of these experiences, very
likely will fail to reflect and express that particular vision which the
playwright is striving to communicate in his play. If the actor fails to
perceive how the playwright's intention transforms a natural incident
into something else, then, no matter how truthful his representation of
that incident may be, he will succeed only in giving the audience the
event and not the author's transformation of that event; a transformation which takes the event out of the realm of nature and places it into
the world of the play.

II

Thus far I have been dealing with Stanislavski's attitude toward the
playwright in the general terms of theatre aesthetics. Perhaps I can
further substantiate my point by taking a specific example. Anyone
acquainted with the writings of Chekhov, whose plays assured Stanislavski his place in the shrine of great actors, is aware that the playwright had little respect for Stanislavski either as an actor or a director.
Chekhov continually complained that Stanislavski "ruined" his plays
because of his lack of taste and his failure to understand them. Stanislavski, on his part, was always uncomfortable with Chekhov and
thought Chekhov was joking whenever he responded to the question
"What does this scene mean?" with "Listen, I wrote it down; it is
all there."

We tend to forget that such a wide gulf existed between the two
men for we have identified Stanislavski, Chekhov, and the Moscow
Art Theatre as a single unit for half a century. Furthermore, Stanislavski's productions of Chekhov's plays were so much better than what
was being produced in the Russian theatre at the time that it is easy

to overlook the shortcomings of the Moscow Art Theatre productions. A brief examination of the two artists' writings will show, however, that they rarely agreed about the productions of Chekhov's plays and that the difficulty springs from Stanislavski's faulty understanding of the playwright's art and function in the theatre.

In *My Life in Art*, Stanislavski describes the dominant quality of Chekhov's art as follows:

> Read him in the kitchen of life, and you will find nothing in him but the simple plot, mosquitoes, crickets, boredom, gray little people. But take him where art soars, and you will feel in the everyday plots of his plays the eternal longings of man for happiness, his strivings upwards . . . All the plays of Chekhov are permeated and end in a faith in a better future . . . The men of Chekhov do not bathe in their own sorrow. Just the opposite; they seek life, joy, laughter, courage . . . They are active and surge to overcome the hard and unbearable impasses into which life has plunged them.[6]

Chekhov's opinion on this subject can be found in Magarshack's *Chekhov: A Life* which quotes the following conversation between Chekhov and Alexander Tikhonov:

> I am often reproached with writing about trifles. I'm told I have no positive heroes; revolutionaries, Alexanders of Macedon, or even, as in Leskov's stories, honest police inspectors. But where am I to get them from? Our life is provincial, our towns are unpaved, our villages are poor, our people are shabby. When we are young, we all chirp rapturously like sparrows on a heap of muck, but at the age of forty we are already old and start thinking of death . . . What sort of heroes are we? Then he talked of the way Stanislavski had been misinterpreting his plays. His aim in writing them, he said, was to make people realize how bad and boring their lives were.[7]

That Stanislavski misinterpreted *The Sea Gull* can be seen from excerpts of his discussion of the play.

> This was the open-air theatre of the unsuccessful and unacknowledged Treplev. The tragedy is self-evident. Can the provincial mother understand the complex longings of her talented son? How talented is this Treplev with the soul of Chekhov and a true comprehension of art! Nina

---

6 K. Stanislavski, *My Life in Art*, New York, 1956. pp. 347–8.
7 D. Magarshack, *Chekhov: A Life*, New York, 1952. pp. 371–2.

Zarechnaya is the cause of the failure of Treplev's talented play. She is too young to understand the deep gloom of the soul of Treplev. She has not suffered enough to perceive the eternal tragedy of the world.[8]

In a letter about the production to Gorky, Chekhov wrote:

> I saw a performance of *The Sea Gull* without scenery and I cannot say that I am able to pass an impartial judgment on it because the Seagull herself acted abominably, sobbing all the time, and Trigorin (Stanislavski) walked about the stage and talked as though he were paralyzed; he has "no will of his own," so the actor interpreted it in such a way that it made me sick to look at him.[9]

And Olga Knipper tells us that it was Stanislavski's complete distortion of the ruling idea of the play that made Chekhov "walk on to the stage, looking grave and pale, and declare in a very determined voice that his play should end with the third act as the fourth act was not his at all."[10] Probably most pertinent to our discussion is the following passage in Magarshack:

> But while admiring the new theatre, Chekhov was far from enthusiastic about what he had seen of the production of *The Sea Gull*. When discussing the different realistic touches introduced by Stanislavski, such as the croaking of frogs, the chirring of grasshoppers and the barking of dogs, Chekhov said: "realistic? But the stage is art. Kramskoy has a picture on which the faces are painted beautifully. What would happen if one cut out the nose of one of the faces and substituted a real one for it? The nose would be realistic but the picture would be ruined." And when an actor told him that at the end of Act III Stanislavski, who was rather famous for his crowd scenes, wanted to bring on a woman with a crying baby among the servants who were taking leave of Arkadina, he said: "This is quite unnecessary. It is as if the top of the piano came down with a crash while you were playing a pianissimo passage." In reply to the retort that in real life a forte unexpectedly drowned a pianissimo, he said: "Quite true, but the stage demands a certain amount of convention. You have no fourth wall, for instance. Besides, the stage is art; the stage reflects the quintessence of life. Nothing superfluous should be introduced on the stage."[11]

---

8 Stanislavski, *op. cit.*, pp. 354–5; 358.
9 Magarshack, *op. cit.*, p. 359.
10 *Ibid.*, p. 339.
11 *Ibid.*, p. 332.

Finally, concerning *The Cherry Orchard* Stanislavski wrote: "The Serebriakovs and Gaiev's perished together with that epoch which no one could criticize and condemn like the same Chekhov . . . I know of no greater idealism than that which believes in a better future although it is surrounded by hopeless circumstances."[12] Anyone who is at all familiar with Chekhov's many remarks on his intentions in *The Cherry Orchard* or his absolute insistence that the writer must always be objective and never criticize his character will not be surprised at his opinion of the Moscow Art Theatre's production of the play: "One thing I can say: Stanislavski has ruined my play for me."[13]

Stanislavski failed as both an actor and a director (at least in Chekhov's opinion) because he interpreted each role in terms of the role alone rather than in terms of the play as a whole. If, for instance, the actor takes out of the context of the play, Trofimov's speech at the end of the second act of *The Cherry Orchard* in which the young tutor declaims on working and suffering to build a bright new future for Russia, it is possible to interpret the character as a great idealist. But in context we see that this speech is nothing more than rhetoric and attitudinizing; Trofimov has never worked and never suffered; he only talks. When Trofimov's speech ends with "Here is happiness . . . I can hear its footsteps," Chekhov makes it quite clear that these footsteps are not the brave new world of Russia by undercutting the whole scene ironically. The footsteps turn out to be those of the dull and pious Varya calling the young people with her whining voice.

We find a similar instance in the third act of the same play, when Trofimov tells Lyubov "You mustn't deceive yourself; for once in your life you must face the truth!" To be sure Trofimov has spoken the truth about Madame Ranevsky, but it tells us very little about the Russian equivalent to our perpetual graduate student. After all, it is easy for almost anyone to make that statement about Lyubov (Lopahin has been telling her the same thing from the beginning of the first act); what is important to an understanding of the character of Trofimov is how he reacts when Lyubov rebuffs him: "This is awful! I can't stand it! I'm going. (*Goes off, but at once returns*) All is over between us!" The melodramatic quality of his exit shows him to be a comic butt and

---

[12] Stanislavski, *op. cit.*, p. 348.
[13] Magarshack, *op. cit.*, p. 382.

Chekhov underscores this by having Trofimov run out of the room and fall down the stairs in the midst of a chorus of laughter.

Or, to take a final example. Stanislavski always interpreted Treplev, the young playwright in *The Sea Gull,* as the embodiment of Chekhov and a great dramatic artist. He singles out Treplev's soliloquy on the theatre as Chekhov's statement on the condition of the nineteenth century Russian theatre. Part of that passage reads:

> To my mind the modern theatre is nothing but tradition and conventionality. When the curtain goes up, these great geniuses represent how people eat, drink, love, and move about, and wear their jackets; when from these commonplace sentences and pictures they try to draw a moral—a petty moral, easy of comprehension and convenient for domestic use, I run away. We need new forms of expression. We need new forms, and if we can't have them we had better have nothing.

Now all that Treplev says may be true, but just the fact that he says it does not make him Chekhov and certainly does not make him a great playwright. The proof of this is shown later in the act when Treplev gives us an example of his new form of expression:

> Men, lions, eagles and partridges, horned deer, geese, spiders, silent fish that dwell in the water, starfishes and all living things, all living things, having completed their cycle of sorrow, are extinct . . . I am alone. Once in a hundred years I open my lips to speak and my voice echoes mournfully in the void, and no one hears . . . You, too, pale lights, hear me not . . .

This is pure and unadulterated "Stimmung" variety drivel! Stanislavski defends it with: "Nina Zarechnaya is the cause of the failure of Treplev's talented play. She is not an actress."[14] Eleanora Duse could not have saved that speech. Poor writing is poor writing and Stanislavski was unable to recognize Treplev's play for the symbolic garbage that it is. The likelihood that Chekhov may have wished to show the disparity between what Treplev says about the theatre and what he produces for the theatre never entered Stanislavski's mind.

It is precisely because of Stanislavski's intuitive approach to building a character—an approach which depends upon natural truth rather than artistic rightness—that he misinterpreted Chekhov's plays so badly. His is a system which tends to isolate each character in a vac-

---

[14] Stanislavski, *op. cit.,* p. 355.

uum;[15] and if the actor does this, then the only pertinent data he has to work with are the lines which the character he is portraying speaks. Using this approach, the actor becomes susceptible to the character's rationalizations. And most important for a Chekhov play, with such an approach the actor fails to understand the rhetorical quality of so many of the character's speeches. T. S. Eliot is very sound on this point in his essay on "Rhetoric and Poetic Drama" when he writes:

> Speechmaking in a play can serve useful dramatic ends. Genuine rhetoric is a device of great effect when it occurs in situations where a character in a play *sees himself* in a dramatic light. In plays of realism we often find parts which are never allowed to be consciously dramatic, for fear, perhaps, of their appearing less real. But in actual life, in many of those situations in actual life which we enjoy consciously and keenly, we are at times aware of ourselves in this way, and these moments are of very great usefulness to dramatic verse. They are valuable because they give us a new clue to the character, for we discover the angle from which he views himself.[16]

It is here that Stanislavski and so many interpreters of Chekhov miss the point. Chekhov's characters are continually dramatizing themselves in this way; but it is important for the actor and the director to distinguish between the way the character sees himself and the way the dramatist sees him.

Chekhov was not a cross old man who could never be satisfied; but he was a dramatic artist who was trying to express something very definite in his plays. Because Stanislavski, in the final analysis, failed to distinguish between art and nature, because he was more concerned with creating *natural truthfulness* of character rather than expressing with *artistic rightness* the role of a character who served a specific function in the playwright's formulation of a statement about life in

---

15 Stanislavski's system, if carried to its logical conclusion, would require that each actor have absolutely no knowledge of the other characters, and that in an ideal production each actor would be trained individually and then all would be brought together on the stage for the first time on opening night. The validity of this conclusion is based upon the fact that the moment an actor uses the other roles in the play to assist him in creating his part he is no longer being true to nature but is taking into account formal considerations which are not natural but artistic.

16 T. S. Eliot, "Rhetoric and Poetic Drama," *Selected Essays*, New York, 1932. p. 28.

theatrical terms, it was inevitable that Stanislavski would be a failure as an actor and director of Chekhov's plays.

This failure is inherent in Stanislavski's approach to the written text of the playwright, for he was never able to realize the script's true significance. Ultimately, this stems from Stanislavski's failure to understand that a play is someone's idea about life. For this reason, if actors are to serve a play properly, their chief function is to communicate to an audience the idea of the play. It is the play's structure and meaning —its artistry—and not the individual actor's approach to a role as a human personality which must in the end always determine the actor's success in building a character.

Farce

BY VSEVOLOD MEYERHOLD

"Mystery in the Russian Theatre" is the title given by Benois to one of his "Letters on Art."[1] One might think that in this article he is discussing a production of one of Alexei Remizov's plays written in the style of a medieval mystery play. Or, perhaps, Scriabin has already realized one of his dreams, and Benois is hastening to announce to the public the greatest event on the Russian stage—the appearance of a new theatrical form reviewing the mystic rites of ancient Greek culture.

It seems that neither Remizov nor Scriabin has written a mystery; according to Benois the Moscow Art Theatre has produced a mystery with its performance of *The Brothers Karamazov*. But just what characteristics of the medieval mystery plays could be found in the performance of *The Brothers Karamazov?* Perhaps here the purified ancient Greek mysteries were combined with the visual edification of the medieval mystery play?

In Dostoevsky's novel the traits of purification and edification are present, but they are contained in the ingenious structure of thesis and antithesis: God and the devil. These two inseparable elements of the novel are to be found in Zossima and the Karamazovs, the symbol of divinity and the symbol of the devil.

On the stage, the center of gravity in the development of the plot is shifted to Dimitri. In transforming Dostoevsky's novel into a play, the intricate interrelationships of Zossima, Aliosha, and Ivan have been lost. *The Brothers Karamazov* becomes simply the dramatized plot

---

[1] A. N. Benois, well-known painter, art critic, and art historian, wrote regularly his "Letters on Art" for the newspaper *Rech.* (Trans.)

of the novel, or more accurately—several chapters from the novel. Such a transformation is not only a sacrilege against Dostoevsky, but also against the idea of the authentic mystery play (if the directors wanted to make this production into a mystery play).

If one is to expect a "mystery" from the Russian theatre, who but Remizov or Scriabin would write it? But the question is, has the time arrived? And here is another question: Is the theatre ready for a "mystery"?

Scriabin in his first symphony sang a hymn to art as religion. In his third symphony he revealed the force of the liberated spirit. And in his *Poem of Ecstasy*[2] man is seized with joy at the realization that he has passed the thorny path, and that the hour of creation has arrived. In each of these works Scriabin gathered valuable material which might be used for a majestic ritual called a "mystery," where music, dance, light, and the intoxicating scent of wild flowers combine into a single work.[3] Realizing how miraculously fast Scriabin has passed from his first symphony to his *Prometheus,* one can say with assurance that he is ready to present a "mystery" to the public. But if *Prometheus* has not united the contemporary audience into a single community, will Scriabin want to present a "mystery"? Not without reason does the author of *Prometheus* long for the banks of the Ganges. He has not yet found an audience for a "mystery." He has not yet gathered around himself the initiated and faithful.

I am convinced that until the writers of contemporary mysteries break their ties with the theatre and leave the theatre entirely, the mystery play will only hinder the theatre, and the theatre the mystery.

Andrey Bely is right. Analyzing the contemporary symbolical theatre he comes to the following conclusion: "Let the theatre remain the theatre, and the mystery remain the mystery." He clearly sees the danger in mixing these two opposing types of performance. And recognizing that a rebirth of the real mystery play is impossible in our age of religious inertia, Andrey Bely hopes "that the traditional theatre will be revived on its own modest merits."

The revival of the traditional theatre is hindered by the public itself which has formed an alliance with the so-called dramatists—those playwrights who transform literature for reading into literature for the

---

[2] Scriabin's fourth symphony. (Trans.)

[3] At his death in 1915 Scriabin left such a *Mystery* uncompleted. (Trans.)

theatre. In the public's mind there is already enough confusion about the theatre. And Benois, by calling the performance of *The Brothers Karamazov* a mystery, creates only greater confusion.

Certain lines in Benois' article give the key, if not to what he meant by a mystery, then at least to an understanding of his relationship to the theatre. Benois writes: "And so I repeat that the Moscow Art Theatre, as well as Dimitri, is incapable of lying." And further on: "The Comédie Française has found success, and so may Reinhardt and Meyerhold, in illusion and 'cabotinage'; this is foreign to the Art Theatre."

Benois gives a negative meaning to the word "cabotinage." He thinks the people concerned with reforming the contemporary stage deceive the public by inventing some fiction about a regenerated theatre. Only the Moscow Art Theatre, Benois thinks, "is incapable of lying." He considers "cabotinage" an evil in the theatre. To those "incapable of lying" (the directors of the Art Theatre) illusion and "cabotinage" are foreign.

However, what is the theatre without "cabotinage," and what is this "cabotinage" which Benois hates? Cabotin was a wandering comedian. He was a relative of the mimes, *histriones,* jugglers. Cabotin possessed a miracle-working acting technique. Cabotin was the upholder of the tradition of the authentic acting art. With his assistance the western theatre (the seventeenth-century Spanish and Italian theatre) attained its greatness. Benois is delighted with the renaissance of the mystery play on the Russian stage, but writes scornfully about "cabotinage"; whereas even the mysteries sought the assistance of the "cabotins." The "cabotin" appeared wherever performances were given, and the producers of mystery plays expected him to help with all the difficult tasks of a mystery. From the history of the French theatre we know that an interpreter in a mystery play found it impossible to solve his problems without the aid of a juggler. At the time of Philip le Beau a farce about the improper pranks of Renard, the Fox, suddenly appeared among religious plays. And who could play this farce except the "cabotin"? With the gradual development of processional mystery plays new subjects appeared which demanded more and more technique from the actors. Only the "cabotin" could solve the most complicated problems of a mystery play. So we can see that "cabotinage" was not alien to the mystery plays, and that the "cabotin" played an important role in their development.

As the mystery play gradually included the popular elements of miming it was forced to leave the church; first the pulpit, then the porch and graveyard, and finally it passed into the market place. Wherever the mystery play tried to make an alliance with the theatre, it had to rely on miming elements, and as soon as it became allied to the actor's art, it ceased to be a mystery play.

Probably it is always true that—no "cabotin," no theatre; and vice versa—as soon as the theatre rejects the fundamental laws of theatricality, then it feels capable of existing without "cabotins."

For Benois, evidently, the mysteries can help save the Russian theatre from decline, but "cabotinage" only harms the theatre. I think the reverse is true: the mystery play, which Benois describes, is harmful to the theatre, and "cabotinage" might save it. In order to rescue the Russian stage from becoming a slave to literature it is necessary to return to the stage the cult of "cabotinage."

But how can this be done?

First of all, I think, one must study and revive those former theatres in which the cult of "cabotinage" reigned.

Our playwrights are totally ignorant of the laws of the authentic theatre. Instead of the old vaudeville[4] of the nineteenth-century Russian theatre, we have brilliant dialectics, *pièces à thèse*, realistic plays, and plays of mood.

The novelist is reducing the number of descriptive passages and, for the liveliness of the story, increasing the characters' dialogue, until he finally invites his reader to pass from the library into the auditorium.

---

[4] I am referring to the old vaudeville not because it must be brought back to the theatre at all cost, but because I consider this form to be an example linked not with literary, but with theatrical traditions on the one hand, and with popular taste on the other. One must remember that vaudeville came to us from France, and we know that French vaudeville was created in the following manner (see Fournel, *Spectacles popul et artistes des rues,* pp. 320–21): "An improvisational, popular theatre performed for a long time near the Porte St. Jacques; the people came in crowds to hear the gay songs, and to watch three merry performers. All three had come from Normandie; all three were apprentices in the baker's guild, had come to Paris to try their fortune, and had brought to the capital the bawdy and clever popular Normandie songs and verses which consequently introduced vaudeville to France. Everyone knew and loved them, and their names—Gaultier Garguille, Turlupin, and Gros. Guillaume—will forever be remembered in the history of French humor." So we see that vaudeville arose from popular songs and humor.

Does the novelist need the services of the "cabotin"? Of course not. The readers themselves can come onto the stage, assume parts, and read aloud to the audience the dialogue of their favorite novelist. This is called "a harmoniously performed play." A name is quickly given to the reader-transformed-into-actor, and a new term, "an intelligent actor," is coined. The same dead silence reigns in the auditorium as in the library. The public is dozing. Such immobility and solemnity is appropriate only in a library.

To transform the novelist who is writing for the stage into a playwright, he should be compelled to write a few pantomimes. A good "antidote" to the superfluity of words! But the playwright need not fear that he will have no opportunity to speak. He will be allowed to give words to the actor, but only after the scenario has been written. When will the following law be added to the commandments of the theatre—*words in the theatre are only a design on the canvas of motion?*

Somewhere I read that the "drama in reading is mainly dialogue, controversy, intense dialectic. Drama on stage is mainly action, intense struggle. Here words are only overtones of action, so to speak. They must involuntarily burst from the actor who is caught by the elemental motion of the dramatic conflict."

The organizers of medieval mystery ceremonies recognized perfectly well the magic power of the pantomime. The most touching scenes in the French mystery plays of the late fourteenth and the early fifteenth centuries were always dumb shows. The movements of the actors explained the subject matter of the show much better than profuse discourses in verse or prose.[5] It is instructive to note that as soon as the

---

[5] An episode from another period recalls the meaning and power of pantomime: "According to the words of a Roman writer, in Nero's reign a foreign ruler was attending a pantomime performance in which a famous actor performed the twelve labors of Hercules with such expressiveness and clarity that the foreign ruler understood everything without any explanation. He was so surprised, that he begged Nero to give him this actor as a present. Nero was very much astonished at this request, but then the guest explained that next to his kingdom lived a wild tribe whose language no one could understand. The savages, likewise, could not comprehend what their neighbors wanted from them. With pantomime this remarkable actor could make the savages understand what was wanted from them, and they undoubtedly could grasp his meaning well." *Tantsy, ikh istoriia i razvitie s drevnykh vremen do nashikh dnei* (Dances, their History and Development from Ancient Times to Our Days), St. Petersburg, 1902, p. 15, Po Viuile.

mystery play passed from the dry rhetoric of religious ceremonies to a new form of action filled with emotional elements (first to the miracle play, then to the morality, and finally to the farce)—then immediately pantomime and the juggler appeared on stage.

Pantomime shuts the mouth of the rhetorician whose place is on the rostrum and not in the theatre; and the actor proclaims the self-sufficiency of the acting craft—the expressiveness of gesture and bodily movement. The juggler demands for himself a mask, plenty of rags for a bright costume, plenty of balloons, feathers, and bells, plenty of everything that lends brilliance and noise to the performance.

Although the organizers of religious performances were pious, they nevertheless presented three nude girls as sirens at the festivities for the entry of Louis XI; at the entry of Queen Isabelle of Bavaria, in the midst of a religious setting, the good burghers enacted the great battle of King Richard against Saladin and the Saracens; at the entry of Queen Ann of Bavaria, an actor appeared addressing the crowd with a prologue in verse. Each of these examples shows the important role played by "cabotinage" in the spectacles. Processions, battles, prologues, parades, even mystery plays could not forego these elements of true theatricality.

The beginning of the theatre must be sought in just such periods of highly developed "cabotinage." It would be a mistake to think that the theatre in the Hospital of the Holy Trinity,[6] for example, originated from mystery plays. No. It originated among the street mimes at the festive entries of kings.

At present most stage directors are turning to pantomimes and prefer this kind of theatre to spoken drama. This is not mere chance, nor is it just a matter of taste. Nor are the directors trying to cultivate this genre because a very special charm is hidden in the pantomimes. In reconstructing the theatre of former times, the modern director finds it necessary to begin with pantomimes because in staging these wordless plays the primary force of the theatre is revealed to the actors—the power of masks, gestures, movements, and plot.

Mask, gesture, movement, and the plot are ignored completely by the modern actor. He has lost all connection with the tradition of the

---

[6] Les Confrères de la Passion of The Community of the Holy Trinity, in sixteenth-century Paris, moved indoors and gave performances on a platform stage. (Trans.)

great masters of the acting art. The modern actor has been transformed into an "intelligent reader." "The play will be read in costume and make-up" could be written on our programs. The new actor plays without mask and juggling technique. The mask is replaced by make-up which has to reproduce accurately the features of the face as it is in real life. The modern actor does not need the juggler's technique because he never "acts" but only "lives" on the stage. He does not understand "acting," the theatre's magic work, because an imitator is not capable of improvisation based on technique.

The cult of "cabotinage," which I am sure will come back with the restoration of the traditional theatre, will help the modern actor understand the fundamental laws of theatricality.

The restorers of old scenarios, deriving their knowledge from forgotten theories of scenography, from old theatrical chronicles and iconography, are attempting to make the actor believe in the strength and importance of acting.

Just as the novelist interested in a certain style reconstructs the past from old chronicles which he embellishes with his own fantasy, so the actor from material gathered for him, can re-create the craft of the forgotten comedians.

Enthusiastic over the simplicity, the refined nobility, and the great artistry of the old yet eternally new acting methods practiced by the *histriones, mimi, atellani, scurrae, jaculatores,* and *ministrelli,* the actor of the future can and must (if he wants to remain an actor) coordinate his emotions and his craftsmanship within the traditional framework of the theatre.

Whenever the revival of old styles is mentioned, one always hears how boring it is for the modern playwright to be forced to compete with the old-fashioned Cervantes *intermedia,* Tirso de Molina dramas, or Carlo Gozzi tales. If the modern playwright does not want to follow the traditions of the old theatre, if, for a time, he leaves the theatre which seeks its regeneration from the past, then the modern theatre will be benefited. The actor who is bored with practicing his trade in defunct plays will soon want not only to act, but even to compose for himself. In this way the Theatre of Improvisation finally makes its appearance. If, however, the playwright wants to help the actor, the dramatist's role will be confined to the seemingly simple, but in reality very intricate, role of inventing the scenarios and the prologues which present to the public the outline of what the actor is going to perform. I hope the playwright will not be humiliated by such a role. Did Carlo Gozzi lose anything when, after giving a scenario to the Sacci Company, he permitted the actors to improvise monologues and dialogues?

I am asked: Why is it so necessary for the theatre to have all these prologues, parades and the like? Isn't a single scenario sufficient?

The prologue and the parade that follows, as well as the concluding address to the audience so favored by the Italians and Spaniards of the eighteenth century and the French vaudevillists—all these elements of the traditional theatre compelled the spectator to regard the performance as nothing but play. Whenever the actor had enticed the spectator too deeply into the land of fiction, the actor, as quickly as possible, by some unexpected remark or a long aside, reminded the audience that everything presented was only "a play."

While Remizov and Scriabin are waiting for their place in the new theatres, while their mysteries are awaiting the initiated, the theatre which restores the juggler will wage a desperate fight with realistic and dialectical dramas, with *pièces à thèse,* and plays of mood. The new Theatre of Masks will learn from the Spaniards and Italians of the seventeenth century how to build its repertory on the laws of the farce where amusement comes before instruction, and movement is valued more highly than words. Not without reason was pantomime the favorite dramatic expression of the "Clercs de la Basoche."[7]

Schlegel maintained that in ancient Greece pantomime attained an incredible perfection. And M. K. added that "pantomime could develop and be brought to perfection only by a people who so successfully practiced the plastic arts, and only a country whose many statues imparted grace to all things."[8]

Will not a constant preoccupation with the art of pantomime bring us to these wonders of grace even though we do not have the sky and the sun of ancient Attica?

II

There are two kinds of puppet theatres.

The director of one wants his puppets to resemble the human being

[7] The Clercs de la Basoche, in the middle of the fifteenth century in Paris were a guild of legal scribes famous for their performance of satirical farces. (Trans.)

[8] *Opyt istorii teatra* (An Experiment in the History of the Theatre) Moscow, 1849, p. 126.

in all its features and peculiarities, just as the heathen wants his idol to nod its head, and the toymaker wants his doll to make sounds resembling the human voice. In his desire to reproduce reality, the director continues to perfect his puppets until he realizes that there is a simpler solution to this complex problem, namely, to transform them into a man.

The other director sees that the audience in his theatre is amused not only by the witty plays performed by his puppets, but probably more by the puppets' movements which, however much they try to imitate life, never entirely resemble what the audience sees in life.

When I watch the performance of modern actors, it is always clear to me that I see before my eyes the perfected puppet theatre of the first of these two directors—the one where man has replaced the puppet. Here man equals the puppet in its efforts to imitate life. The human being has been called upon to replace the puppet because in copying reality the human being can be more successful than the puppet.

The other director, who also tried to make his puppet resemble a living person, noticed quickly that when he began to improve his puppet's mechanism, it lost some of its charm. It even seemed to him that the whole nature of the puppet opposed this barbarous alteration. This director realized in time that there are limits to a transformation which, if exceeded, will inevitably lead to the replacement of the puppet by man.

But is it possible to part company with the puppet which has succeeded in creating such an enchanting world in the theatre with expressive gestures governed by a special, bewitching technique and with an angularity of movement that cannot be compared to anything else?

I have described two puppet theatres in order to force the actor into a thoughtful mood: should he replace the puppet and continue in a subservient role which gives no freedom to his own personal creativity, or should he fashion a theatre such as the puppet could defend, refusing to submit to the director's attempts to transform his nature? The puppet did not want to be an exact image of man because the world the puppet reflects is a wonderful imaginary world, and the character it reflects is an imaginary character, and the stage it moves on is like a sounding board along which lie the strings of its skill. The puppet's stage is as it is not because of the puppet's nature, but because of its will, and its will is not to imitate but to create.

When the puppet cries, its hand holds the handkerchief but does not touch its eyes; when the puppet kills, it pierces its opponent so gently that the tip of the sword does not touch his chest; and when the puppet slaps someone, the color does not fade from his cheek; and the puppet lovers embrace with such reserve that the spectator, observing their caresses from a considerable distance, does not ask his neighbor how these embraces end.

But when a human being appears on stage, why does he blindly subject himself to a director who wants to turn him into a puppet of the naturalistic school? The human does not wish to present *his art* on the stage. The contemporary actor refuses to understand that the comedian-mime is supposed to lead the audience into the land of imagination, and on his way entertain with his technical brilliance.

The invented gesture, suitable only in the theatre, the stylized movement, conceivable only in the theatre, the artificiality of stage elocution—all this is being criticized by the public as well as the critics because the idea of "theatricality" has not yet been divorced from the acting of the so-called "actors of mood."

The "actor of inner mood" wants to depend only on his own state of mind. He does not want his will to command his technique. He is proud of bringing to the stage the brilliance of his improvisation, and naïve enough to believe that his improvisation has something in common with the improvisation of the old Italian comedy. He does not know that the *commedia dell'arte* performers cultivated their improvisations only on the basis of a refined technique. He resolutely denies all technique. "Technique hinders the freedom of the creative act"—is how this actor speaks. Only the moment of unconscious creativity based on emotion has any value to him. If there is such a moment, then there is success; without it—no success.

But does an actor's intellect really hinder the display of emotion? It was a living man who acted and danced around the altar of Dionysus; his emotions were aroused; the altar fire raised his feelings to ecstasy. However, the ritual dedicated to the god of wine has pre-established meters and rhythms, and certain prescribed methods of movement and gesture. Here the actor's reasoning did not obstruct his temperament. The dancing Greek, although obliged to observe a whole series of traditional rules, could nevertheless introduce into his dance many innovations.

Not only does the contemporary actor lack all rules of the comedian's art (for art is only that which is governed by laws; according to Voltaire "dancing is an art because it is governed by rules"), but he also has created a frightful chaos in his art. As if this were not enough, he considers it his duty to bring chaos into the other spheres of art. If he wants to enter the field of music, he invents recitation to music. If he reads poetry from the stage, he pays attention only to the subject of the poetry, and arranges the logical stresses without concerning himself in any way with meter and rhythm, caesura and pauses, or musical intonation.

Modern actors, in their attempt at reincarnation, set themselves the problem of destroying their "I" and of producing an illusion of life on the stage. Why, then, are the names of the actors announced on the placards? When the Moscow Art Theatre produced Gorky's *Lower Depths,* instead of an actor a real tramp was brought onto the stage. The tendency toward reincarnation reached a point where the actor was relieved of his function altogether. Why was the name of the actor performing the role of Teterev printed on the posters? Is it possible to call someone an "actor" when he appears on the stage as he is in real life? Why deceive the public?

The public comes to the theatre to see the art of man, but what kind of art is it to walk on the stage as one really is? The public expects fantasy, acting, skill, and instead sees either life or a slavish imitation of it.

Once having discarded the shelter of one's surroundings, does not man's art on the stage consist of skillfully selecting a mask and a decorative costume, and of dazzling the public with the technical brilliance of either a dancer, or an intriguer (as at a masquerade ball), or a simpleton of the old Italian comedy, or a juggler?

The mask's magic power becomes apparent after one reads carefully the forgotten collections of scenarios, those of Flaminio Scala (1613), for example.

Harlequin, a native of Bergamo, the servant of a stingy doctor, is forced by his master's avarice to wear a suit of many-colored patches. Harlequin is the silly fool, the cunning servant who seems always merry. But look what is hidden under his mask—Harlequin, the mighty magician, sorcerer, and wizard; Harlequin, the representative of the infernal powers. The mask is capable of hiding more than just these two opposing figures. These two aspects of Harlequin are two poles between which lie infinite varieties. How is this great diversity shown to the spectator? By the mask.

The actor in control of the art of gesture and movement (here lies his strength!) will wear the mask in such a way that the spectator knows clearly who is before his eyes: the silly fool from Bergamo, or the devil. This chameleon quality, hidden under the comedian's fixed mask, provides the theatre with an enchanting play of light and shade. Is it not the mask which aids the spectator to fly into the land of fantasy? The mask makes the spectator see not only one particular Harlequin, but all the Harlequins in his memory. In Harlequin the spectator sees all the people who in any way resemble this image. But is the mask the only source of the theatre's fascination? No.

It is the actor who, with his art of gesture and movement, compels the spectator to be whisked into a fairyland where the bluebird flies, where the beasts talk, and where the loafing, roguish, or infernal Harlequin is transformed into a simpleton who performs wonderful tricks. Harlequin is an acrobat, sometimes a rope walker. His leaps are exceedingly dextrous. His improvised jokes startle the audience by an exaggerated improbability which even the dramatists did not dream of. The actor is a dancer. He can dance the graceful *monferrina*[9] as well as the coarse English jig. The actor can make you cry and a few seconds later laugh. He carries the fat Doctor on his shoulders and jumps around with him as if there were nothing to it. Now he is soft and flexible, now clumsy and awkward. The actor has at his command a thousand different intonations with which he does not imitate specific characters, but which he uses rather to decorate and supplement. He can speak fast, when playing the role of a rogue, or slowly and in a drawl when imitating the pedant. On the stage he can trace geometric figures with his body, or he can leap happily and recklessly as if flying through air.

The face of the actor is covered by a mask, but by his skill he can use it in such ways, and contort his body in such positions that the dead mask becomes alive.

Since the appearance of Isadora Duncan, and even more since Jacques Dalcroze's eurhythmic theory, the modern actor has gradually begun to understand the meaning of gesture and movement. However, a mask still interests him very little. Whenever the subject of masks

---

[9] *La monfrina, or monferrina*—a popular Italian dance. (Trans.)

204 / *Theatre in the Twentieth Century*

arises the actor asks: is it possible for the mask and cothurn of the ancient theatre to reappear on the contemporary stage? To the modern actor, the mask is something which once was used to overcome poor acoustical conditions, or was used to emphasize a role in an exaggerated but stereotyped way.

We are still waiting for the time when an actor without a mask will arouse the indignation of the public, as was the case in the reign of Louis XIV, when the dancer Hardel was the first who dared appear without a mask. But at present the modern actor will under no circumstances recognize the mask as a symbol of the theatre—and not only the actor.

I have made the experiment of interpreting the figure of Don Juan according to the principles of the Theatre of Masks.[10] But even such an art critic as Benois did not understand the mask of Don Juan's face.

"Molière loves Don Juan. Don Juan is his hero, and as with all heroes, he is even a little Molière's portrait. To substitute for this hero some satyr type is not only a mistake, but something worse."[11]

This is how Benois regards Molière's Don Juan. He would like to see in Don Juan the image of the "Seville seducer" as portrayed by Tirso de Molina, Byron, and Pushkin.

In his wanderings from one poet to the next, Don Juan preserved the basic features of his character, but he reflected, as a mirror, the diverse natures of his authors, the life of the most divergent countries, and the expression of various social ideals.

Benois forgets completely that Molière was attracted to the character of Don Juan not as a goal, but as a means to an end.

Molière wrote *Don Juan* after *Tartuffe* had aroused a storm of indignation among the clergy and nobility. He was accused of a number of base offenses, and the poet's enemies were anxious to find a worthy punishment for him. He could fight this injustice with his only weapon, the theatre. In order to ridicule the bigotry of the clergy and the hypocrisy of the aristocracy which he hated so intensely, he grasped Don Juan as a drowning man clutches a straw. A number of scenes and separate sentences, though inconsistent with the mood of the ac-

---

[10] My revival of Molière's *Don Juan* was first given in the Imperial Alexandrinsky Theatre, November 9, 1910.

[11] In the newspaper *Rech*, No. 318, November 19, 1910.

tion and the characteristics of the protagonist, are introduced by
Molière as a revenge on those who had hampered the success of
Tartuffe. Molière exposes to ridicule and abuse this very "jumping,
dancing and grimacing Lovelace"[12] in order to make him a target for the
poet's bitter attacks against pride and vanity. And at the same time
Molière places in the mouth of this frivolous dandy, whom he had
just ridiculed, a brilliant characterization of the period's prevailing
vices—hypocrisy and bigotry.

One more consideration should not be forgotten. Just at the time
when Molière was greatly distressed by the withdrawal of *Tartuffe* from
the stage, the poet suffered a family tragedy. "His wife, little capable of
appreciating her husband's genius, was unfaithful to him with the
most unworthy rivals, falling in love with *salon* gossipers whose noble
birth was their only distinction. Even before this, Molière had never
missed an opportunity to hurl gibes at the *Marquis ridicules*."[13] Now he
uses the figure Don Juan for new attacks on his rivals.

Molière needed the scene with the peasant girls, not so much for
characterizing Don Juan, as for drowning with the intoxicating wine
of comic scenes the drama of a man deprived of family happiness by
such flippant and egotistical "breakers of women's hearts."

It is only too clear that for Molière Don Juan is a puppet necessary
to the author for settling his accounts with his numerous enemies. To
Molière Don Juan is a wearer of masks. We see him wearing the masks
of licentiousness, contempt for religion, cynicism, and hypocrisy which
were worn by the cavaliers of the Sun King's court. He wore the mask
of the author-accuser; the nightmarish mask which was stifling the
author himself, and the torturing mask which Molière had to wear at
court spectacles or before his deceitful wife. Only at the very end of
the play does the author give to his puppet the mask reflecting the
features of *El Burlador de Sevilla* as he was originally conceived.

The greatest compliment which the director and designer who staged
Molière's *Don Juan* could dream of was paid them by Benois when
he called the performance a "dressed-up farce." The Theatre of Masks is
always a farce, and the idea of the actor's art, based on a worship of
mask, gesture, and movement, is indissolubly linked with the idea of

12 *Ibid.*
13 *Artist*, No. 9, 1890.

the farce. The farce is eternal. If its principles are for a time expelled from the walls of the theatre, we nevertheless know that they are firmly engraved in the lines of the manuscripts left by the theatre's greatest writers.

Translated by Nora Beeson

Psychopathic Characters
on the Stage

BY SIGMUND FREUD

IF THE FUNCTION OF THE drama, as has been assumed since Aristotle, is to excite pity and fear, and thus bring about a "catharsis of the emotions," we may describe this same purpose a little more fully if we say that the question is one of opening up sources of pleasure and enjoyment from within the sphere of life, just as wit and the comic do from within the sphere of the intellect, through the action of which many such sources had been made inaccessible. Certainly the release of the subject's own affects must here be given first place, and the enjoyment resulting therefrom corresponds on the one hand to the relief produced by their free discharge, and on the other, very likely, to the concomitant sexual stimulation which, one may suppose, occurs as a by-product of every emotional excitation and supplies the subject with that feeling of a heightening of his psychic level which he so greatly prizes. The sympathetic witnessing of a dramatic performance fulfills the same function for the adult as does play for the child, whose besetting hope of being able to do what the adult does, it gratifies. The spectator at the play experiences too little; he feels like a "Misero, to whom nothing worth while can happen"; he has long since had to moderate, or better direct elsewhere, his ambition to occupy a central place in the stream of world events; he wants to feel, to act, to mold the world in the light of his desire—in short, to be a hero. And the playwright-actors make all this possible for him by giving him the op-

Reprinted with permission from The Psychoanalytic Quarterly, XI, 1952, *p. 459–464.*

portunity to identify himself with a hero. But they thus spare him something also; for the spectator is well aware that taking over the hero's rôle in his own person would involve such griefs, such sufferings and such frightful terrors as would almost nullify the pleasure therein; and he knows too that he has but a single life to live, and might perhaps perish in a single one of the hero's many battles with the Fates. Hence his enjoyment presupposes an illusion; it presupposes an attenuation of his suffering through the certainty that in the first place it is another than himself who acts and suffers upon the stage, and that in the second place it is only a play, whence no threat to his personal security can ever arise. It is under such circumstances that he may indulge in the luxury of being a hero; he may give way unashamedly to suppressed impulses such as the need for freedom in religious, political, social or sexual respects, and may let himself go in all directions in each and every grand scene of the life enacted upon the stage.

These are prerequisites for enjoyment, however, which are common to several forms of creative art. Epic poetry subserves above all the release of intense but simple feelings—as does, in its sphere, the dance; the epic poem may be said to make possible the enjoyment in particular of the great heroic personality in his triumphs; drama, however, is supposed to delve deeper into emotional possibilities, to manage to transform even the forebodings of doom into something enjoyable, and it therefore depicts the embattled hero rather with a masochistic satisfaction in succumbing. In fact, one might characterize drama by this very relation to suffering and misfortune, whether as in the play mere apprehension is aroused and then allayed, or as in tragedy actual suffering is brought into being. The origin of drama in sacrificial rites (goat and scapegoat) in the cult of the gods cannot be without appositeness to this meaning of drama; it assuages as it were the beginning revolt against the divine order which decreed the suffering. The hero is at first a rebel against God or the divine; and it is from the feeling of misery of the weaker creature pitted against the divine might that pleasure may be said to derive, through masochistic gratification and the direct enjoyment of the personage whose greatness nevertheless the drama emphasizes. This is the Prometheus attitude of man, who in a spirit of petty compliance would be soothed for the time being with a merely momentary gratification.

All varieties of suffering are therefore the theme of drama, which promises to create out of them pleasure for the spectator; whence arises the first condition which this art form must fulfill, that it shall cause the spectator no suffering, and that it must know how to compensate by means of the gratifications which it makes possible for the pity which it arouses—a rule against which modern dramatists have particularly often been offenders. But this suffering is soon restricted to mental anguish only, for nobody wants to witness physical suffering who knows how soon the bodily sensations thus stimulated put an end to all mental enjoyment. He who is ill has but one desire: to get well, to get over his condition; the doctor must come with his medicine; the arresting of the play of fantasy must cease—that arrest which has spoiled us to the extent of letting us extract enjoyment even out of our suffering. When the spectator puts himself in the place of the sufferer from physical illness, he finds nothing within himself of enjoyment or of psychological give and take; and it is on this account that a person physically ill is possible on the stage only as a property, but not as the hero—excepting as some particular psychic aspect of illness is susceptible of psychic elaboration, as for example the abandoning of the sick Philoctetes, or the hopelessness of the sick in the plays of Strindberg.

Mental suffering we recognize, however, chiefly in relation to the circumstances out of which it has developed; hence drama requires an action from which this suffering derives, and begins by introducing to the audience this action. It is only an apparent exception that such plays as *Ajax* and *Philoctetes* present mental suffering as already in existence, for because of the familiarity of the matter to the audience the curtain always rises in the Greek drama in the middle of the play, as it were. Now, it is easy to define the conditions which this action must fulfill. There must be a play of contending forces; the action must contain within itself a striving of the will and some opposition thereto. The first and most grandiose fulfilling of these conditions was exemplified in the struggle against divinity. It has already been said that the essence of this tragedy is revolt, with dramatist and spectator taking sides with the rebel. The less that is then ascribed to the divine, the more accrues to the human element, which, with ever increasing insight, is made responsible for suffering; and so the next struggle, that of the hero against the social community, becomes the social tragedy. Still another fulfilling of these conditions is seen in the struggle between men themselves, that is, the character drama, which contains within itself all the characteristics of the *agon*, and, enacted preferably between outstanding personalities freed from the restrictions of human institutions, must accordingly have more than one hero. Combinations of these two are of course perfectly permissible, in the form of a struggle on the part of the hero against institutions of which strong characters are the embodiment. The pure drama of character is lacking in the sources of enjoyment afforded by the theme of rebellion, which in social plays, such as those of Ibsen, is again as powerfully to the fore as in the historical plays of Greek classical times. If religious, character, and social drama differ from one another chiefly with respect to the arena in which the action takes place from which the suffering has its origin, we may now follow the drama to still another arena, where it becomes the psychological drama. For it is within the soul of the hero himself that there takes place an anguished struggle between various impulses—a struggle which must end, not with the downfall of the hero, but with that of one of the contending impulses, in other words, with a renunciation. Every combination of this situation with that in the earlier type of drama, that is the social and the character drama, is of course possible insofar as social institutions evoke just such an inner conflict, and so on. It is here that the love drama belongs, insofar as the suppressing of love—whether on the score of the mores, the conventions or the conflict, familiar from opera, between "love and duty"—forms the starting point for an almost endless variety of conflictual situations, as infinite in their variety as the erotic daydreams of mankind. The possibilities multiply still further, however, and the psychological drama becomes the psychopathological, when the source of the suffering which we are to share and from which we are to derive pleasure is no longer a conflict between two almost equally conscious motivations, but one between conscious and repressed ones. Here the precondition for enjoyment is that the spectator shall also be neurotic. For it is only to him that the release and, to a certain extent, the conscious recognition of the repressed motivation can afford pleasure, instead of making merely for unacceptance. In the non-neurotic this will meet only with unacceptance, and will induce a readiness to repeat the act of repression, for in his case the latter has been successful. The repressed impulse is kept in complete counterbalance by the original force of repression. In the neurotic, on the other hand, repression is by way of failing; it is unstable, and requires ever renewed effort, an effort which is spared by recognition. It is only in the neurotic that such a struggle exists as can become the subject of drama; but in him

also the dramatist will create not only the pleasure derived from release but resistance as well.

The foremost modern drama of this kind is *Hamlet,* which deals
with the theme of a normal man who, because of the particular nature
of the task enjoined upon him, becomes neurotic—a man in whom an
impulse hitherto successfully repressed seeks to assert itself. *Hamlet* is
distinguished by three characteristics which seem of importance to our
discussion: 1) that the hero is not psychopathic, but becomes so only
in the course of the action we are going to witness; 2) that the repressed desire is one of those that are similarly repressed in all of us, the
repression of which belongs to an early stage of our individual development, while the situation arising in the play shatters precisely this
repression. Because of these two features it is easy for us to recognize
ourselves in the hero. For we are victims of the same conflict as is he;
since "he who doesn't lose his reason under certain provocations has no
reason to lose." 3) But it appears to be one of the prerequisites of this
art form that the struggle of the repressed impulse to become conscious, recognizable though it is, is so little given a definite name that
the process of reaching consciousness goes on in turn within the spectator
while his attention is distracted and he is in the grip of his emotions,
rather than capable of rational judgment. In this way resistance is
definitely reduced, in the manner seen in psychoanalytic treatment,
when the derivatives of the repressed ideas and emotions come to consciousness as a result of a lessening of resistance in a manner denied to
the repressed material itself. And indeed the conflict in *Hamlet* is so
deeply hidden that at first I could only surmise it.

Possibly it is because of the disregarding of these three requisite
conditions that so many other psychopathic characters become as useless for the stage as they are for life itself. For the sick neurotic is to
us a man into whose conflict we can obtain no insight (empathy)
when he presents it to us in the form of the finished product. Conversely, if we are familiar with this conflict, we forget that he is a sick
man, just as when he becomes familiar with it he himself ceases to be
sick. It is thus the task of the dramatist to transport us into the same
illness—a thing best accomplished if we follow him through its development. This will be particularly needful when the repression is
not already existent in ourselves and must therefore be effected *de
novo*—which represents a step beyond *Hamlet* in the utilization of
neurosis upon the stage. Where the full-blown and strange neurosis

confronts us, in real life we call the physician and deem the person in question unsuitable as a stage figure.

In general, it may perhaps be said that the neurotic liability of the public, and the art of the dramatist in making use of resistances and supplying forepleasure, alone determine the limits of the utilization of abnormal characters upon the stage.

Translated by HENRY ALDEN BUNKER

3. The Critic:
Analysis and Appraisal

The Possibilities and Perils
of Modern Tragedy

BY JOHN GASSNER

I

A QUESTION THAT CONTINUES TO agitate literary circles is whether it is possible to write tragedy in modern times and whether indeed it has been possible to produce tragedies at all ever since Ibsen's generation abandoned romanticism. The subject has become a veritable vested interest of academic criticism, but has also involved nonacademic critics and creative writers. It has been impossible to declare a moratorium on the question because it thrusts itself into the foreground of discussions of the worth and pretensions of the modern theatre. Playwrights and critics who deplore the vogue of realism or the absence of poetry on the stage are especially inclined to make the impossibility of writing tragedy for the commercial theatre an article of faith. And it appears to be an absolute conviction on the part of some commentators that modern drama should be excluded from the aristocracy of letters altogether. Since tragedy is the most aristocratic of dramatic genres, it is a fore-gone conclusion of the literary mandarins that a tragic playwright cannot thrive in the theatre of the populace.

It is not the theatre, however, but the modern world that receives criticism's first and most devastating fire. How indeed should the exalted art of tragedy, which has traditionally dealt with the fate of singular individuals, flourish in the age of the common man? How should the grandeur of the tragic hero and the splendor of the tragic

This article is a somewhat revised version of the author's Amos Taylor, Jr. Memorial Lecture given on January 20, 1957 at The John Hopkins University.

vision survive in a world leveled down by democracy and cheapened by mass production and mass consumption, a world in which even emotions and ideas have been converted into commodities gaudily packaged for the buyer? At the same time, the leaders of this mandarin brand of criticism, many of whom have cherished ideals of classic or medieval unity, have been wont to observe that this world characterized by a distressing sameness is paradoxically a divided one. It is said to be incapable of providing the individual with a coherent view of himself and of his place in the universe. The same critics who disdain a world grown irrevocably common are apt to deplore the absence of communion in it. They regret the absence of tradition and belief in our mongrel culture. With no myth or cult to assure the continuity of time-honored values, with no religion to relate the individual unequivocally to the universe, with no fixity of class structure to bind men to their place, we presumably cannot have significant dramatic action: it cannot be significant because it cannot be communally meaningful. The high concern with human fate that has characterized tragic art in past ages must therefore make way for considerations of temporary and local conflict between ant-men who are paradoxically common without being representative.

A commonplace realism, then, takes the place of the ideality to which the art of tragedy aspires by historical example since the time of Aeschylus and by critical prescript since the time of Aristotle. And it is a rare event indeed when the language of the modern stage does not reflect the commonplace view of mankind. The plot may pulsate with exciting events, as in the plays of O'Neill, but the language limps behind the action and limits its tragic resonance. The inarticulateness so often postulated by realism as a result of its idolatry of verisimilitude dooms the characters to a level of consciousness too low to sustain an impressive personality and a significant action. And that inarticulateness is itself mainly a concomitant of the selection of low-grade personalities for dramatic representation as well as of a low view of humanity. Rarely do the modern plays assume or demonstrate that greatness of spirit we discover in an Antigone and Oedipus or a Hamlet, Othello, and Lear. Henry James was surely correct when he declared in one of his prefaces that "the agents in any drama are interesting only in proportion as they feel their respective situations," and feeling communicates itself mainly through language. The prose of modern drama, often commonplace if not indeed barbarically colloquial, is both a symptom of the absence of tragic art and a cause of its absence.

So runs the argument, which is fortified by the critics' dismal view of modern liberalism, which entertains nontragic premises insofar as it puts its trust in rationalism, science, and sociology. When behavior is explained largely by heredity, instinct, and environment, man is deprived of any genuine responsibility for his actions that would make dramatic conflict humanistically relevant and calamity morally significant. There can be no tragic heroes in the bleak commonwealth of conditioned animals. Nor is the individual given materially greater significance when he is treated as a psychological case history. His writhings in the grip of a neurosis or psychosis may gratify our curiosity but not our moral sense. He may be interesting as a specimen of morbidity, but his plight—his error and his suffering—will exalt neither the character nor spectator. A heroic view of man, then, is the last thing that sociology and psychopathology can supply whereas it has been the peculiar triumph of tragic art in the past to affirm the wonder of man. For ages, tragedy has been a high mystery by means of which defeat has been transformed into victory for the human spirit. In this mystery which converts despair over the human condition into reconciliation with fate and leaves us exhilarated rather than dismayed, the protagonist is the sacrifice, and the sacrifice must be worthy of the rite. With respect to both the protagonist or sacrificial victim and the humanity which the rite redeems modern rationalistic inquiry is held to be altogether too disillusioning. But if the modern viewpoint is too depressing, it is also too optimistic for tragedy, for modern liberalism has been inveterately melioristic. Denying that evil and suffering are absolute and unalterable, the liberal viewpoint has proposed to remove or moderate the very conditions that make tragedy possible and its ministrations welcome, if not indeed imperative. The modern viewpoint, then, appears to be both too hard and not hard enough for tragedy.

The critics of liberal modernism cannot, however, be completely represented by the above-given arguments, for they have set up their batteries not only on the literary heights but on the summits of theological disputation. They have wondered, for example, how a modren writer of the liberal persuasion can expect to write tragedy while rejecting the doctrine of original sin, failing to make characters feel accountable to God, or depriving man of an inviolable ethos and of the solace of belief that his suffering has spiritual significance. And some critics have also become amateur anthropologists in emphasizing the ritualistic character of a tragic performance. They seem to believe that because tragedy developed out of religious ritual in Greece, the modern theatre, which is not at all pyramided upon any religious rites, is unable to engender tragic art. The error in this kind of reasoning is the familiar "genetic fallacy," which assumes that a thing must remain what it was at its inception. The proponents of this view are also inconsistent: they certify many Elizabethan and seventeenth-century plays as true tragedies, although neither the Elizabethan nor the neoclassic French theatre had any marked ritualistic basis or character.

The genetic fallacy, however, is not always conspicuously advanced. It is apt to be screened from view by the argument that a community of values (as best expressed in religion and ritual) is essential to the development of tragedy, and this is, on the surface, a reasonable belief. If the tragic experience demonstrates the calamitous results of a character's conduct, that conduct must obviously constitute a violation of a more or less accepted norm. In a community which sanctioned parricide and incest, for example, Oedipus would not be a tragic character. And if a tragically misguided character is to arrive at restorative perceptions or redeeming realizations in the course of his suffering, these must meet with agreement from the public. The emphasis upon the need for a community of values, however, becomes an argument against the possibility of writing tragedy today as soon as the critic implies that the agreement must be strict enough to disallow modern diversity and scepticism, if not strict enough indeed to constitute a religious or quasi-religious sanction. It is doubtful that such "communion" was ever absolute in the individualistic Athenian and Elizabethan periods, and it might be contended that communion is a religious experience that ought not to be confused with social conformity. History indeed supplies many examples of ancient despotisms and modern totalitarian societies that failed to produce tragic art. Conformity, however, does not seem to disturb contemporary neo-ritualists, provided the commonly held values are approvable; and they are apt to be approved if only they are pre-modern and traditional. The neo-conservative position, as laid down in previous decades by Hulme and T. S. Eliot, is indeed the final emplacement from which traditionalists offer resistance to the idea that playwrights whose thought has been contaminated by modern science or sociology can compose tragedy.

The position of the traditionalists on this issue tends to be inflexible. They rarely admit that any modern dramatist has written a true tragedy, and a play dealing "tragically" with a commoner's fate such as *Death of a Salesman* is treated as pretentious vulgarity. A more moderate position grants a few deviations into tragedy by Ibsen, O'Neill, and perhaps a few other writers. But the advanced and more persistent traditionalist view holds that realistic dramaturgy and prose are incompatible with tragedy, as are liberalism, meliorism, sympathy with ordinary persons, skepticism, and modern individualism. According to this view, the would-be tragedian, unless he renounces the ambience of modern thought and popular art, will end up only with melodrama, propaganda, pathology, pathos and sentimentality, or just plain nastiness and bathos. Tragic art, according to this view, has been achieved in the modern age by only two species of writers—the primitive and the ultra-sophisticated: by a Synge and Lorca, on the one hand, or a Cocteau, Yeats, and Eliot, on the other. The primitives have escaped modernity while the ultra-sophisticated have passed beyond it and returned to mystery, legend, ritual, and the racial unconscious.

II

That, in brief, is one side of the argument concerning tragedy in the modern theatre, and it is not difficult to understand why it should be punctuated with so much intellectual artillery. The fire is directed at the modern spirit, which presumably cannot have much worth if it does not produce tragic art—an assumption which would of course invalidate all but the three brief periods of human history which produced Attic, Elizabethan, and neo-classic French tragedy of the latter part of the seventeenth century. But the other side of the argument, though less often maintained, has also been vigorously advanced. Implicit in the theatre's hopes and endeavors for the past three quarters of a century has been the conviction that tragedy could be revitalized by sinking its roots deeper in modern consciousness and by relating it more closely to the immediate life of the times. I do not know of any comprehensive statement that adequately presented this viewpoint until Herbert J. Muller published his vigorous book *The Spirit of Tragedy* late in 1956. Presentations of the modern liberal position have been scattered in a variety of prefaces, letters, diaries, and reviews; and liberal doctrine concerning tragedy has never been particularly impressive, even though such important writers as Hebbel, Zola, Strindberg, Galsworthy, and

Arthur Miller have contributed to it. The real force of the argument must be sought in the works to which the theories were prefatory or supplementary; it resides in whatever realizations of modern tragedy can be found in the plays of Ibsen, Strindberg, Tolstoy, Curel, Hauptmann, O'Neill, Galsworthy, O'Casey, and other playwrights.

A fundamental premise has been the opinion that a great deal of the tragic art of the past, while excellent as far as it went, belongs to the past. The pagan beliefs that served Attic tragedy twenty-five centuries ago are no longer acceptable to modern man. Neither are the beliefs of the Elizabethan period and the age of Louis XIV. There is simply no single true philosophy of tragedy any more than there is a single inviolable tragic form. Tragic art is subject to evolutionary processes, and tragedy created in modern times must be modern. The fact that it will be different from tragedy written three, five, or twenty-five centuries ago does not mean that it will no longer be tragedy; it will merely be different. It will be as different from earlier tragic literature as *Hamlet*, let us say, is different from *Oedipus Rex*, or as *Phaedra* is different from Euripides' *Hippolytus*. Aristotle himself did not presume to legislate on tragedy for all time, but spoke modestly about tragic art as he knew it from the works of a handful of Athenian playwrights. He spoke of tragedy as it had developed up to his time in Greece, rather than of an everlasting and invariable type of drama. In generalizing about tragic method he spoke of optimal approaches rather than of absolutes; in the *Poetics*, he even countenanced a turn of fortune from bad to good as a possible, though not as the most effective, pattern of a tragedy. It was apparent to him that the Greek plays differed in kind and degree of tragic artistry, whatever their external structural similarities. It could be apparent to us, too, if we did not invite the hobgoblin of consistency into literary theory and attributed to Greek tragedy a single form, quality, and effect. The leaders of the modern theatre after 1870 rejected esthetic absolutism. They envisaged not only the possibility of writing tragedy with modern minds, but of extending its range and enlarging its potentialities as a study of man and his world.

The modern view started, sensibly enough, with considerations of character and environment. Tragic art was allowed to focus on all, rather than on only class-privileged representatives of the human race. By 1870, the destiny of nations was no longer being shaped exclusively or even predominantly by a dynasty or an aristocracy. It was virtually granted by then that a character's station in society was secondary in importance to his stature as a human being. Of first importance was his capacity to manifest desires and engage in actions that could reveal human nature and its strivings significantly. Ibsen and his successors did not intend to repeat the error of early writers of "bourgeois tragedy" such as Diderot and Lillo who made common characters commonplace in feeling, will, and destiny. Many writers proceeded to endow them with passion-charged personalities, as Ibsen proved himself capable of doing when he created Hedda Gabler and O'Neill when he created Christine and Lavinia, the modern Clytemnestra and Electra of his *Mourning Becomes Electra*. Moreover, even examples from the past favored latitude. It had been possible for Shakespeare to plumb human destiny with so hesitant and divided a character as Hamlet. It had even proved possible to create tragedy with essentially anti-heroic figures such as Richard II and Euripides' Orestes and Electra. If the modern playwright tended more and more to focus on characters of divided will and thwarted desire, he was under no necessity to renounce all intention of giving them tragic prominence. The generally nonheroic character could be revealed as heroic in some central aspect. Strindberg's mentally tormented Captain in *The Father*, for example, is a clinical case. Yet he could be fully analyzed without lessening the force of his defense of masculinity in an overfeminized society. His personality and experiences were too intensely realized by Strindberg to generate pity without also producing fear; he, the protagonist, fought too strenuously against his wife Laura, his antagonist, and he resisted his fate too forcefully to engender pathos rather than passion. Thus, too, the Willy Loman of *Death of a Salesman* could be tethered to the satchel of a traveling salesman, could be made to swallow the mental garbage of a materialistic society, could be drawn in all his littleness as a business failure, and yet be allowed to draw attention to the soaring part of his personality. His self-regard or ideal of himself wills him to assert his sense of worth against his own littleness and makes him rage like a caged lion in his suburban home—and suburban mind. According to liberal doctrine, indeed, modern dramatists could reveal more, rather than fewer, facets of humanity.

That communication with modern audiences was henceforth to be attained on the maximum levels of understanding available to modern consciousness was indeed the ruling conviction of Ibsen, Strindberg, Shaw, Hauptmann, Curel, and other pioneers of the late nineteenth-century theatre, to which our own is still very largely bound. In their view it was preposterous to compose tragedy according to histrionic notions of heroism, and they consequently broke with romanticism as firmly as romantic writers had broken with neo-classicism. The moderns, moreover, could admire Shakespeare without believing that the Elizabethan world-picture was correct or meaningful for the modern world; and they could find merit in classic tragedy or even employ its retrospective dramatic structure, as Ibsen did in *Ghosts*, without subscribing to Greek notions of Fate. It seemed sounder as well as more honest to attempt to translate ancient concerns into present ones and old concepts into new ones. Aeschylus and Euripides had not hesitated to do so, and there was no particular reason why Ibsen and Strindberg or O'Neill and Arthur Miller, after them, should.

The proponents of modern drama, moreover, could contend that they met the fundamental requirements of tragic art with considerable fidelity. They approached their subject with high seriousness, motivated human conduct, refrained from mere pathos by studying social and psychological causation, avoided melodrama, and made calamity a means for achieving significant revelations concerning the individual and his milieu. For them error, evil, and suffering were never ends in themselves, useless in providing the audience with a *frisson* and the playwright with an income. They knew that perception was a necessary element in the tragic experience and proposed to provide realization not by rote but by critical inquiry and by a realistic testing of the alternatives of action. Sometimes it was the main character who was led from passion to perception or from suffering to understanding; sometimes the final comprehension belonged to a group of secondary characters whose role was not radically different from that of a Greek chorus; sometimes it was the audience that was expected to understand what the characters could not express. The means might differ in respect to the situation and the intelligence of the character, but suffering was not allowed to be devoid of meaning. In one way or another, some means was to be found for compensating calamity with insight. And direct or indirect means were sought for supplying the tragic awareness that the protagonist of a modern play could not articulate because he could not be convincingly given the self-conscious intelligence of a Hamlet or the eloquence of persons in the more formal tragedies of the past.

Articulateness on the part of the characters was indeed very much the concern of the modernists, for, as critics impatient with prose in the theatre tend to forget, verse-drama had become quite decadent in the nineteenth century before it was abandoned. (Nor was it abandoned so absolutely that an Ibsen, Hauptmann, or Maxwell Anderson would not go back to verse.) Pioneers of the modern theatre found it necessary to reject verse and rhetorical prose not merely for the sake of "fourth-wall" verisimilitude, but for the sake of simple artistic integrity. They could not countenance the customary use of eloquence as a screen for hollow content and commonplace feeling and thought. The decision to write prose-drama was the result of clear deliberation on Ibsen's part. The author of *Brand* and *Peer Gynt* laid aside a considerable reputation as a poet and a hard-won success as a playwright when he entered upon the realistic and prose part of his career in his fiftieth year. That his prose in *A Doll's House* and the plays that followed became a very powerful instrument demonstrating the mental and emotional processes of his characters is evident even in translation. The planning of the dialogue, the verbal exchanges between the speakers, the innuendo or double-meaning of many a line, and the stress on key words and phrases do not indicate indifference to the role of language in the drama. The cumulative effect of his and other writers spare dialogue could provide the articulateness that had previously been allocated to the set speeches, harangues, and soliloquies of characters in the pre-realistic drama. Motivations could be found, moreover, for some distinctly infectious speeches when characters addressed an assembly or summarized a passionately held conviction. Ibsen's successors, among whom there were such masters of dialogue as Shaw and O'Casey, continued to prove that prose could be written for the theatre with compelling *brio*. Many a verse-drama of the past three centuries sounds exceedingly flat with its familiar tropes and metronomic regularity by comparison with the verbal explosions of modern realistic and expressionist plays. And to dramatic excitement could be added a variety of effects capable of lending nuance, poetic reverberation, and Chekhovian counterpoint. Peasant dialect, as in the plays of Synge, could be relied upon to yield a new music and a new imagery for the theatre, as could even the colloquialism of the city streets. And symbolism could be imbedded in the soil of realism whenever a playwright was capable of composing a *Rosmersholm* and *The Master Builder*.

Nor does the search for a poetically charged prose exhaust the effort to ensure expressiveness on the modern stage. Developments in physical production and in the art of acting have contributed imaginativeness and power to the stage. We have supplemented the verbal element of the drama with the so-called *poésie de théâtre,* ever since the turn of the century when Gordon Craig called for expressive stage design and Stanislavsky for *inner* realism in acting. The masters of this "poetry of the theatre" could give scenic atmosphere and visual symbolization to a tragic action. "A good scene design should not be a picture but an image," wrote Craig's American disciple Robert Edmond Jones, and it could create "an expectancy, a foreboding, a tension" in the theatre. That acting could add emotional depth and dramatic stature to a playwright's character was evident, of course, whenever a Duse or Nazimova played an Ibsen part.

Finally, we should not overlook the modern playwright's search for new dramatic form, especially in the turbulent expressionist mode which is marked by fantastic invention, explosive dialogue, and expressive distortion of scenes and characters. There have been expressionist attempts to write tragedy as well as realistic ones, ever since the turn of the century. Playwrights who gravitated toward expressionism tended to concern themselves with such contemporary themes as the Oedipus complex, the alienation of the individual in a cheapened world, and the crises of war and revolution. One could maintain indeed that the boundaries of tragic art were extended by the adoption of modern expressionist technique in such plays as *The Spook Sonata, The Hairy Ape,* and *Death of a Salesman,* as well as by naturalistic presentations of character and environment that closed a ring of inevitability around the dramatic action of the individual. If this argument does not at all prove that modern playwrights have written better tragedies than Sophocles and Shakespeare did (and the reverse is obviously the case), it does suggest that modernity may be relieved of the charge that it has extinguished the art of tragedy—which is one more charge added to the general indictment of our civilization or, rather, of the democratic and scientific spirit.

III

To mediate between the conflicting claims of the pro-modern and anti-modern factions is no easy matter. The value we place on specific works is the first and last consideration. There is no difficulty in claiming that the modern age can produce tragedy if we are prepared to qualify a considerable number of modern plays as "tragedies." And, conversely, it is easy enough to maintain that the modern spirit cannot support tragic writing once we disqualify them.

An agile disputant can easily sustain his aristocratic distaste for the world of the common man by invalidating almost any modern play. All he has to do is to insist on absolute standards of high tragedy derived from a few masterpieces of the past and prove that the modern work deviates from them. He can then protest, often with good reason, that the hero of some particular play written since *A Doll's House* lacks the magnitude of mind or spirit that could give him the "tragic stature" needed to dignify humanity even in the character's descent from grace and fall from good fortune. With respect to many a modern stage character from Ibsen's Oswald Alving to O'Neill's "Yank" and Miller's Willy Loman it has been possible for very intelligent critics to say, with Henry James, that "Our curiosity and our sympathy care comparatively little for what happens to the stupid, the coarse, and the blind." The critic may indeed multiply his strictures without ever being entirely wrong. The plays may impress him as depressing rather than exalting, and as topical rather than universal. They may also strike him as too prosaic, too intellectual or too unintellectual, too active or too passive, too optimistic or too pessimistic. Any one of these attributes can be easily identified, torn out of context, and used to invalidate the tragic status of such modern pieces as *Ghosts, Hedda Gabler, The Father, The Power of Darkness, The Lower Depths, The Hairy Ape, Desire Under the Elms, Mourning Becomes Electra, The Iceman Cometh*— and even *Saint Joan*. Advocates of a scrupulously restricted category of tragedy would probably certify only plays produced at some remove from the liberal-scientific spirit or deliberately set against it. They would certify peasant drama set in regions remote from our industrial civilization such as Synge's Aran Islands, off the west coast of Ireland, or Lorca's Spanish countryside. They would also qualify formally structured plays, preferably suggestive of ritual and rooted in theology or in myth: Among these would be Eliot's *Murder in the Cathedral* and *Family Reunion*, some short poetic pieces by Yeats patterned after medieval Japanese drama, and a few anti-realistic French plays such as Giraudoux' *Electra* and Cocteau's *The Infernal Machine*, which one young American enthusiast recently recommended to us as *the* model for modern tragedy. To this, one may add a genre of neo-romantic verse-drama represented by Maxwell Anderson's Elizabethan trilogy, *Elizabeth the Queen, Mary of Scotland, Anne of the Thousand Days*, and his *Winterset*—plays well patterned after a conventional tragic blueprint.

A strenuous exponent of the realistic and more or less liberal persuasion, however, could, in turn, cut a good deal of the ground from under the literary opposition. Turning to specific works, he could show, for instance, that Anderson's achievement in the historical field, and similar achievements in other countries, are tragic only by rote, posture, and imitation. He could maintain, too, that *Winterset*, despite its powerful second act, was only factitiously tragic; that it consists of a forced marriage between poetic rhetoric and gangster melodrama, and that the playwright evades his Sacco and Vanzetti theme with rather transparent borrowings from *Hamlet* and *Romeo and Juliet*. These animadversions would probably win the endorsement of members of the literary élite of our day, since they have even less use than the liberal realists for popular romanticism. But the latter would promptly turn on their allies to remind them that literary formalism, too, has proved vain. On the one hand, we have had the example of so great a poet as Yeats withdrawing from the modern drama in order to compose tragic one-act plays intended for private performance, an admittedly thin harvest for the man who had helped to establish the Abbey Theatre and had discovered Synge and O'Casey for the Irish national stage. On the other hand, we have had the example of Cocteau and other French sophisticates leaning toward contrived tragicality and arriving at cleverness or virtuosity in the theatre much more conclusively than they have arrived at tragedy. And the argument would gravitate toward T. S. Eliot, the high priest of anti-modernism in our time, who abandoned the rigors of high tragedy with *The Cocktail Party* and edged closer to Noel Coward than Sophocles with drawing-room lines and scenes. This after having composed two tragedies with a marked ritualistic and theological basis, *Murder in the Cathedral* and *Family Reunion*, which owed a good deal to Shaw and Coward respectively in virtually all scenes in which the plays came to life as theatre. It will be apparent, then, that the uncertainties of tragic writing in the present world are not altogether on one side. And if the peril of trying to write tragedies under the modern liberal dispensation is an unliterary descent into *banality*, the peril of creating it under any other dispensation is a literary ascent into *futility*.

Which is the greater evil cannot be determined, I suppose, without bias. (My own is, on the whole, democratic, while that of some men of letters for whom I have entertained the greatest admiration is largely aristocratic.) Nevertheless, the two factions are not fated to remain completely apart, and there are areas of agreement available to reasonable exponents of either viewpoint. The "liberals" can agree that variable degrees of inadequacy have attended the efforts of O'Neill, Ibsen, and the sociological playwrights to produce tragic literature, while "conservatives" have been known to concede some measure of tragic power to Ibsen, Strindberg, and O'Casey. It would certainly appear from the divergent enthusiasms of the partisans that, in one way or another, it has been possible to write tragic drama—that is, some clearly definable tragedies and many plays more or less tragic in feeling such as Chekhov's *The Three Sisters.*

Agreement could be reached especially if we first noted that there are degrees of tragic ascent today and that some are more favored than others. And this should not disturb us particularly, for there were, after all, degrees of tragic ascent even in the great ages of tragic literature— as we may observe, for instance, by comparing Sophocles' *Electra* with Euripides' *Electra* or *Macbeth* with *Richard II.* Modern playwrighting is apt to fall into a category of "middle tragedy" or perhaps "low tragedy" instead of "high tragedy," a term suitable for some (and only for some) of the tragic pieces of the Attic, Elizabethan, and French neoclassic periods of the theatre. With agreement on this subject, we could then settle down to the essential business of encouraging and creating the plays, regardless of degree, that may best express the tragic and near-tragic understanding of which we are capable in our time and place.

We may also arrive at the conclusion that there is really no compelling reason for the modern stage to *strain* toward tragedy. There are other ways of responding to the human condition. There is, for one thing, the time-honored way of comedy. Shaw followed it so creditably in his so-called comedies of ideas that his plays have overshadowed the work of many a tragedian of modern, Victorian, or Elizabethan times. The writing of comedies is as serious a business as the writing of tragedies; comedy, too, constitutes a criticism of life, incorporates values, and affords a catharsis. The comic viewpoint is at least as relevant as the tragic to man's life in society and perhaps even more representative of human conduct. Nor does the comic playwright have to spare us glimpses into the abyss of human nature or encounters with what Nietzsche called "the terrible wisdom of Silenus." Comedy is an art of notable variety, and its complexion runs from light to dark and from sweet to bitter.

There is also the way of *drame,* of serious drama without tragic pretensions. Many provocative social and psychological dramas as diversified as *Awake and Sing* and *The Children's Hour*, as well as imaginative works such as *Our Town* and *The Skin of Our Teeth*, have filled a place in our theatre without conveniently fitting into pigeonholes of tragedy. Generally, indeed, our age has found its sensibility and mood most adequately expressed by amalgamations of grave and comic writing. We have been partial to a mixed genre represented at its best, perhaps, by several of Chekhov's masterpieces, although "mixed drama" is not at all exhausted by Chekhov's highly individual style. We can only conclude that if plays such as *The Cherry Orchard, Heartbreak House, Juno and the Paycock, The Glass Menagerie* and *Six Characters in Search of an Author* have not conformed to any blueprints of tragedy (and there was no intention on their authors' part to achieve such conformity), this has been no loss to the theatre of our century. It is the value of the specific work and not the *genre* that really and finally matters to the playgoer, and not to prefer a distinguished nontragic composition to an undistinguished tragic one would be pedantry rather than responsible criticism.

Tragedies of one kind or another have been contributory to the interest and power of the modern theatre. But the creative spirit of an age should be allowed, and indeed expected, to engender its own dramatic forms or to modify existent ones. Overawed, it would seem, by premises and promises of tragic grandeur, playwrights from D'Annunzio to Maxwell Anderson (nor would I acquit O'Neill when he composed *Dynamo* and *Lazarus Laughed* or Miller when he wrote *A View from the Bridge*) have strained too much to produce standardized high tragedy with a contemporary fillip of interest. They would have been well advised to leave some tragic motifs and trappings alone, and they should have refrained from endeavoring to lift some of their characters and situations out of the nontragic categories that would have suited them better. Critics and scholars have been prone to compound confusion for playwrights by harping on categories of drama, glorifying one of these above all others, and paying insufficient heed to the fact that tragedy has been infrequently produced throughout the ages and rarely in pure form. And since everybody has been infected at some time or other with the desire to see the modern drama live beyond its spiritual income, it may yet become necessary to stress the perils rather than the possibilities of tragedy.

The Theatre of
the Absurd

BY MARTIN ESSLIN

THE PLAYS OF SAMUEL BECKETT, Arthur Adamov, and Eugène Ionesco have been performed with astonishing success in France, Germany, Scandinavia, and the English-speaking countries. This reception is all the more puzzling when one considers that the audiences concerned were amused by and applauded these plays fully aware that they could not understand what they meant or what their authors were driving at.

At first sight these plays do, indeed, confront their public with a bewildering experience, a veritable barrage of wildly irrational, often nonsensical goings-on that seem to go counter to all accepted standards of stage convention. In these plays, some of which are labeled "anti-plays," neither the time nor the place of the action are ever clearly stated. (At the beginning of Ionesco's *The Bald Soprano* the clock strikes seventeen.) The characters hardly have any individuality and often even lack a name; moreover, halfway through the action they tend to change their nature completely. Pozzo and Lucky in Beckett's *Waiting for Godot*, for example, appear as master and slave at one moment only to return after a while with their respective positions mysteriously reversed. The laws of probability as well as those of physics are suspended when we meet young ladies with two or even three noses (Ionesco's *Jack or the Submission*), or a corpse that has been hidden in the next room that suddenly begins to grow to monstrous size until a giant foot crashes through the door onto the stage (Ionesco's *Amédée*). As a result, it is often unclear whether the action is meant to represent a dream world of nightmares or real happenings. Within the same scene the action may switch from the nightmarish poetry of high emo-

229

tions to pure knock-about farce or cabaret, and above all, the dialogue tends to get out of hand so that at times the words seem to go counter to the actions of the characters on the stage, to degenerate into lists of words and phrases from a dictionary or traveler's conversation book, or to get bogged down in endless repetitions like a phonograph record stuck in one groove. Only in this kind of demented world can strangers meet and discover, after a long polite conversation and close cross-questioning, that, to their immense surprise, they must be man and wife as they are living on the same street, in the same house, apartment, room, and bed (Ionesco's *The Bald Soprano*). Only here can the whole life of a group of characters revolve around the passionate discussion of the aesthetics and economics of pinball machines (Adamov's *Ping-Pong*). Above all, everything that happens seems to be beyond rational motivation, happening at random or through the demented caprice of an unaccountable idiot fate. Yet, these wildly extravagant tragic farces and farcial tragedies, although they have suffered their share of protests and scandals, do arouse interest and are received with laughter and thoughtful respect. What is the explanation for this curious phenomenon?

The most obvious, but perhaps too facile answer that suggests itself is that these plays are prime examples of "pure theatre." They are living proof that the magic of the stage can persist even outside, and divorced from, any framework of conceptual rationality. They prove that exits and entrances, light and shadow, contrasts in costume, voice, gait and behavior, pratfalls and embraces, all the manifold mechanical interactions of human puppets in groupings that suggest tension, conflict, or the relaxation of tensions, can arouse laughter or gloom and conjure up an atmosphere of poetry even if devoid of logical motivation and unrelated to recognizable human characters, emotions, and objectives.

But this is only a partial explanation. While the element of "pure theatre" and abstract stagecraft is certainly at work in the plays concerned, they also have a much more substantial content and meaning. Not only *do* all these plays make sense, though perhaps not obvious or conventional sense, they also give expression to some of the basic issues and problems of our age, in a uniquely efficient and meaningful manner, so that they meet some of the deepest needs and unexpressed yearnings of their audience.

The three dramatists that have been grouped together here would probably most energetically deny that they form anything like a school or movement. Each of them, in fact, has his own roots and sources, his own very personal approach to both form and subject matter. Yet they also clearly have a good deal in common. This common denominator that characterizes their works might well be described as the element of *the absurd.* "Est absurde ce qui n'a pas de but . . ." ("Absurd is that which has no purpose, or goal, or objective"), the definition given by Ionesco in a note on Kafka,[1] certainly applies to the plays of Beckett and Ionesco as well as those of Arthur Adamov up to his latest play, *Paolo Paoli,* when he returned to a more traditional form of social drama.

Each of these writers, however, has his own special type of absurdity: in Beckett it is melancholic, colored by a feeling of futility born from the disillusionment of old age and chronic hopelessness; Adamov's is more active, aggressive, earthy, and tinged with social and political over-tones; while Ionesco's absurdity has its own fantastic knock-about flavor of tragical clowning. But they all share the same deep sense of human isolation and of the irremediable character of the human condition.

As Arthur Adamov put it in describing how he came to write his first play *La Parodie* (1947):

> I began to discover stage scenes in the most commonplace everyday events. [One day I saw] a blind man begging; two girls went by with-out seeing him, singing: "I closed my eyes; it was marvelous!" This gave me the idea of showing on stage, as crudely and as visibly as possible, the loneliness of man, the absence of communication among human beings.[2]

Looking back at his earliest effort (which he now regards as unsuccess-ful) Adamov defines his basic idea in it, and a number of subsequent plays, as the idea "that the destinies of all human beings are of equal futility, that the refusal to live (of the character called N.) and the joyful acceptance of life (by the employee) both lead, by the same path, to inevitable failure, total destruction."[3] It is the same futility and point-lessness of human effort, the same impossibility of human communica-tion which Ionesco expresses in ever new and ingenious variations. The two old people making conversation with the empty air and living in the

---

[1] Ionesco, "Dans les Armes de la Ville," *Cahiers de la Compagnie Made-leine Renaud-Jean-Louis Barrault,* No. 20 (October, 1957).

[2] Adamov, "Note Préliminaire," *Théâtre II,* Paris, 1955.

[3] *Ibid.*

expectation of an orator who is to pronounce profound truths about life, but turns out to be deaf and dumb (*The Chairs*), are as sardonically cruel a symbol of this fundamentally tragic view of human existence as Jack (*Jack or the Submission*), who stubbornly resists the concerted urgings of his entire family to subscribe to the most sacred principle of his clan—which, when his resistance finally yields to their entreaties, turns out to be the profound truth: "I love potatoes with bacon" ("J'adore les pommes de terre au lard").

The Theatre of the Absurd shows the world as an incomprehensible place. The spectators see the happenings on the stage entirely from the outside, without ever understanding the full meaning of these strange patterns of events, as newly arrived visitors might watch life in a country of which they have not yet mastered the language.[4] The confrontation of the audience with characters and happenings which they are not quite able to comprehend makes it impossible for them to share the aspirations and emotions depicted in the play. Brecht's famous "Verfremdungseffekt" (alienation effect), the inhibition of any identification between spectator and actor, which Brecht could never successfully achieve in his own highly rational theatre, really comes into its own in the Theatre of the Absurd. It is impossible to identify oneself with characters one does not understand or whose motives remain a closed book, and so the distance between the public and the happenings on the stage can be maintained. Emotional identification with the characters is replaced by a puzzled, critical attention. For while the happenings on the stage are absurd, they yet remain recognizable as somehow related to real life with *its* absurdity, so that eventually the spectators are brought face to face with the irrational side of their existence. Thus, the absurd and fantastic goings-on of the Theatre of the Absurd will, in the end, be found to reveal the irrationality of the human condition and the illusion of what we thought was its apparent logical structure.

If the dialogue in these plays consists of meaningless clichés and the mechanical, circular repetition of stereotyped phrases—how many meaningless clichés and stereotyped phrases do we use in our day-to-day

---

[4] It may be significant that the three writers concerned, although they now all live in France and write in French have all come to live there from outside and must have experienced a period of adjustment to the country and its language. Samuel Beckett (b. 1906) came from Ireland; Arthur Adamov (b. 1908) from Russia, and Eugène Ionesco (b. 1912) from Rumania.

conversation? If the characters change their personality halfway through the action, how consistent and truly integrated are the people we meet in our real life? And if people in these plays appear as mere marionettes, helpless puppets without any will of their own, passively at the mercy of blind fate and meaningless circumstance, do we, in fact, in our over-organized world, still possess any genuine initiative or power to decide our own destiny? The spectators of the Theatre of the Absurd are thus confronted with a grotesquely heightened picture of their own world: a world without faith, meaning, and genuine freedom of will. In this sense, the Theatre of the Absurd is the true theatre of our time.

The theatre of most previous epochs reflected an accepted moral order, a world whose aims and objectives were clearly present to the minds of all its public, whether it was the audience of the medieval mystery plays with their solidly accepted faith in the Christian world order or the audience of the drama of Ibsen, Shaw, or Hauptmann with their unquestioned belief in evolution and progress. To such audiences, right and wrong were never in doubt, nor did they question the then accepted goals of human endeavor. Our own time, at least in the Western world, wholly lacks such a generally accepted and completely integrated world picture. The decline of religious faith, the destruction of the belief in automatic social and biological progress, the discovery of vast areas of irrational and unconscious forces within the human psyche, the loss of a sense of control over rational human development in an age of totalitarianism and weapons of mass destruction, have all contributed to the erosion of the basis for a dramatic convention in which the action proceeds within a fixed and self-evident framework of generally accepted values. Faced with the vacuum left by the destruction of a universally accepted and unified set of beliefs, most serious playwrights have felt the need to fit their work into the frame of values and objectives expressed in one of the contemporary ideologies: Marxism, psychoanalysis, aestheticism, or nature worship. But these, in the eyes of a writer like Adamov, are nothing but superficial rationalizations which try to hide the depth of man's predicament, his loneliness and his anxiety. Or, as Ionesco puts it:

> As far as I am concerned, I believe sincerely in the poverty of the poor, I deplore it; it is real; it can become a subject for the theatre; I also believe in the anxieties and serious troubles the rich may suffer from; but it is neither in the misery of the former nor in the melancholia of the latter, that I, for one, find my dramatic subject matter. Theatre is for

me the outward projection onto the stage of an inner world; it is in my dreams, in my anxieties, in my obscure desires, in my internal contradictions that I, for one, reserve for myself the right of finding my dramatic subject matter. As I am not alone in the world, as each of us, in the depth of his being, is at the same time part and parcel of all others, my dreams, my desires, my anxieties, my obsessions do not belong to me alone. They form part of an ancestral heritage, a very ancient storehouse which is a portion of the common property of all mankind. It is this, which, transcending their outward diversity, reunites all human beings and constitutes our profound common patrimony, the universal language. . . .[5]

In other words, the commonly acceptable framework of beliefs and values of former epochs which has now been shattered is to be replaced by the community of dreams and desires of a collective unconscious. And, to quote Ionesco again:

. . . the new dramatist is one . . . who tries to link up with what is most ancient: new language and subject matter in a dramatic structure which aims at being clearer, more stripped of non-essentials and more purely theatrical; the rejection of traditionalism to rediscover tradition; a synthesis of knowledge and invention, of the real and imaginary, of the particular and the universal, or as they say now, of the individual and the collective . . . By expressing my deepest obsessions, I express my deepest humanity. I become one with all others, spontaneously, over and above all the barriers of caste and different psychologies. I express my solitude and become one with all other solitudes. . . .[6]

What is the tradition with which the Theatre of the Absurd—at first sight the most revolutionary and radically new movement—is trying to link itself? It is in fact a very ancient and a very rich tradition, nourished from many and varied sources: the verbal exuberance and extravagant inventions of Rabelais, the age-old clowning of the Roman mimes and the Italian *Commedia dell'Arte*, the knock-about humor of circus clowns like Grock; the wild, archetypal symbolism of English nonsense verse, the baroque horror of Jacobean dramatists like Webster or Tourneur, the harsh, incisive and often brutal tones of the German drama of Grabbe, Büchner, Kleist, and Wedekind with its delirious

---

5 Ionesco, "L'Impromptu de l'Alma," *Théâtre II*, Paris, 1958.

6 Ionesco, "The Avant-Garde Theatre," *World Theatre*, VIII, No. 3 (Autumn, 1959).

language and grotesque inventiveness; and the Nordic paranoia of the dreams and persecution fantasies of Strindberg.

All these streams, however, first came together and crystallized in the more direct ancestors of the present Theatre of the Absurd. Of these, undoubtedly the first and foremost is Alfred Jarry (1873–1907), the creator of *Ubu Roi*, the first play which clearly belongs in the category of the Theatre of the Absurd. *Ubu Roi*, first performed in Paris on December 10, 1896, is a Rabelaisian nonsense drama about the fantastic adventures of a fat, cowardly, and brutal figure, *le père* Ubu, who makes himself King of Poland, fights a series of Falstaffian battles, and is finally routed. As if to challenge all accepted codes of propriety and thus to open a new era of irreverence, the play opens with the defiant expletive, *"Merdre!"* which immediately provoked a scandal. This, of course, was what Jarry had intended. *Ubu*, in its rollicking Rabelaisian parody of a Shakespearean history play, was meant to confront the Parisian bourgeois with a monstrous portrait of his own greed, selfishness, and philistinism: "As the curtain went up I wanted to confront the public with a theatre in which, as in the magic mirror . . . of the fairy tales . . . the vicious man sees his reflection with bulls' horns and the body of a dragon, the projections of his viciousness. . . ."[7] But Ubu is more than a mere monstrous exaggeration of the selfishness and crude sensuality of the French bourgeois. He is at the same time the personification of the grossness of human nature, an enormous belly walking on two legs. That is why Jarry put him on the stage as a monstrous pot-bellied figure in a highly stylized costume and mask—a mythical, archetypal externalization of human instincts of the lowest kind. Thus, Ubu, the false king of Poland, pretended doctor of the pseudoscience of Pataphysics, clearly anticipates one of the main characteristics of the Theatre of the Absurd, its tendency to externalize and project outwards what is happening in the deeper recesses of the mind. Examples of this tendency are: the disembodied voices of "monitors" shouting commands at the hero of Adamov's *La Grande et la Petite Manoeuvre* which concretizes his neurotic compulsions; the mutilated trunks of the parents in Beckett's *Endgame* emerging from ashcans—the ashcans of the main character's subconscious to which he has banished his past and his conscience; or the proliferations of fungi that invade the married

---

[7] Jarry, "Questions de Théâtre," in *Ubu Roi, Ubu Enchaîné,* and other Ubuesque writings. Ed. Rene Massat, Lausanne, 1948.

couple's apartment in Ionesco's *Amédée* and express the rottenness and decay of their relationship. All these psychological factors are not only projected outwards, they are also, as in Jarry's *Ubu Roi*, grotesquely magnified and exaggerated. This scornful rejection of all subtleties is a reaction against the supposed *finesse* of the psychology of the naturalistic theatre in which everything was to be inferred between the lines. The Theatre of the Absurd, from Jarry onwards, stands for explicitness as against implicit psychology, and in this resembles the highly explicit theatre of the Expressionists or the political theatre of Piscator or Brecht.

To be larger and more real than life was also the aim of Guillaume Apollinaire (1880–1918), the great poet who was one of the seminal forces in the rise of Cubism and who had close personal artistic links with Jarry. If Apollinaire labeled his play *Les Mamelles de Tirésias* a "*drame surrealiste*," he did not intend that term, of which he was one of the earliest users, in the sense in which it later became famous. He wanted it to describe a play in which everything was *larger than life*, for he believed in an art which was to be "modern, simple, rapid, with the shortcuts and enlargements that are needed to shock the spectator."[8] In the prologue to *Les Mamelles de Tirésias*, a grotesque pamphlet purportedly advocating an immense rise in the French birthrate, Apollinaire makes the Director of the Company of Actors who perform the play, define his ideas:

> For the theatre should not be an imitation of reality
> It is right that the dramatist should use
> All the illusions at his disposal . . .
> It is right that he should let crowds speak, or inanimate objects
> If he so pleases
> And that he no longer has to reckon
> With time and space
> His universe is the play
> Within which he is God the Creator
> Who disposes at will
> Of sounds gestures movements masses colors
> Not merely in order
> To photograph what is called a slice of life
> But to bring forth life itself and all its truth . . .

Accordingly, in *Les Mamelles de Tirésias* the whole population of Zanzibar, where the scene is laid, is represented by a single actor; and

---

8 Apollinaire, *Les Mamelles de Tirésias*, Preface.

the heroine, Thérèse, changes herself into a man by letting her breasts float upwards like a pair of toy balloons. Although *Les Mamelles de Tirésias* was not a surrealist work in the strictest sense of the term, it clearly foreshadowed the ideas of the movement led by André Breton. Surrealism in that narrower, technical sense found little expression in the theatre. But Antonin Artaud (1896–1948), another major influence in the development of the Theatre of the Absurd, did at one time belong to the Surrealist group, although his main activity in the theatre took place after he had broken with Breton. Artaud was one of the most unhappy men of genius of his age, an artist consumed by the most intense passions; poet, actor, director, designer, immensely fertile and original in his inventions and ideas, yet always living on the borders of sanity and never able to realize his ambitions, plans, and projects.

Artaud, who had been an actor in Charles Dullin's company at the Atelier, began his venture into the realm of experimental theatre in a series of productions characteristically sailing under the label *Théâtre Alfred Jarry* (1927–29). But his theories of a new and revolutionary theatre only crystallized after he had been deeply stirred by a performance of Balinese dancers at the Colonial Exhibition of 1931. He formulated his ideas in a series of impassioned manifestos later collected in the volume *The Theatre and Its Double* (1938), which continues to exercise an important influence on the contemporary French theatre. Artaud named the theatre of his dreams *Théâtre de la Cruauté*, a theatre of cruelty, which, he said, "means a theatre difficult and cruel above all for myself." "Everything that is really active is cruelty. It is around this idea of action carried to the extreme that the theatre must renew itself." Here too the idea of action larger and more real than life is the dominant theme. "Every performance will contain a physical and objective element that will be felt by all. Cries, Wails, Apparitions, Surprises, *Coups de Théâtre* of all kinds, the magical beauty of costumes inspired by the model of certain rituals. . . ." The language of the drama must also undergo a change: "It is not a matter of suppressing articulate speech but of giving to the words something like the importance they have in dreams." In Artaud's new theatre "not only the obverse side of man will appear but also the reverse side of the coin: the reality of imagination and of dreams will here be seen on an equal footing with everyday life."

Artaud's only attempt at putting these theories to the test on the stage took place on May 6, 1935 at the Folies-Wagram. Artaud had made his own adaptation ("after Shelley and Stendhal") of the story of the Cenci, that sombre Renaissance story of incest and patricide. It was in many ways a beautiful and memorable performance, but full of imperfections and a financial disaster which marked the beginning of Artaud's eventual descent into despair, insanity, and abject poverty. Jean-Louis Barrault had some small part in this venture and Roger Blin, the actor and director who later played an important part in bringing Adamov, Beckett, and Ionesco to the stage, appeared in the small role of one of the hired assassins.

Jean-Louis Barrault, one of the most creative figures in the theatre of our time, was in turn, responsible for another venture which played an important part in the development of the Theatre of the Absurd. He staged André Gide's adaptation of Franz Kafka's novel, *The Trial*, in 1947 and played the part of the hero K. himself. Undoubtedly this performance which brought the dreamworld of Kafka to a triumphant unfolding on the stage and demonstrated the effectiveness of this particular brand of fantasy in practical theatrical terms exercised a profound influence on the practitioners of the new movement. For here, too, they saw the externalization of mental processes, the acting out of nightmarish dreams by schematized figures in a world of torment and absurdity.

The dream element in the Theatre of the Absurd can also be traced, in the case of Adamov, to Strindberg, acknowledged by him as his inspiration at the time when he began to think of writing for the theatre. This is the Strindberg of *The Ghost Sonata, The Dream Play* and of *To Damascus*. (Adamov is the author of an excellent brief monograph on Strindberg.)

But if Jarry, Artaud, Kafka, and Strindberg can be regarded as the decisive influences in the development of the Theatre of the Absurd, there is another giant of European literature that must not be omitted from the list—James Joyce, for whom Beckett at one time is supposed to have acted as helper and secretary. Not only is the Nighttown episode of *Ulysses* one of the earliest examples of the Theatre of the Absurd—with its exuberant mingling of the real and the nightmarish, its wild fantasies and externalizations of subconscious yearnings and fears—but Joyce's experimentation with language, his attempt to smash the limitations of conventional vocabulary and syntax has probably exercised an even more powerful impact on all the writers concerned.

It is in its attitude to language that the Theatre of the Absurd is most revolutionary. It deliberately attempts to renew the language of drama and to expose the barrenness of conventional stage dialogue. Ionesco once described how he came to write his first play. (Cf. his "The Tragedy of Language," *Tulane Drama Review,* Spring, 1960.) He had decided to take English lessons and began to study at the Berlitz school. When he read and repeated the sentences in his phrase book, those petrified corpses of once living speech, he was suddenly overcome by their tragic quality. From them he composed his first play, *The Bald Soprano.* The absurdity of its dialogue and its fantastic quality springs directly from its basic ordinariness. It exposes the emptiness of stereotyped language; "what is sometimes labeled the absurd," Ionesco says, "is only the denunciation of the ridiculous nature of a language which is empty of substance, made up of clichés and slogans. . . ."[9] Such a language has atrophied; it has ceased to be the expression of anything alive or vital and has been degraded into a mere conventional token of human intercourse, a mask for genuine meaning and emotion. That is why so often in the Theatre of the Absurd the dialogue becomes divorced from the real happenings in the play and is even put into direct contradiction with the action. The Professor and the Pupil in Ionesco's *The Lesson* "seem" to be going through a repetition of conventional school book phrases, but behind this smoke screen of language the *real* action of the play pursues an entirely different course with the Professor, vampire-like, draining the vitality from the young girl up to the final moment when he plunges his knife into her body. In Beckett's *Waiting for Godot* Lucky's much vaunted philosophical wisdom is revealed to be a flood of completely meaningless gibberish that vaguely resembles the language of philosophical argument. And in Adamov's remarkable play, *Ping-Pong,* a good deal of the dramatic power lies in the contrapuntal contrast between the triviality of the theme—the improvement of pinball machines—and the almost religious fervor with which it is discussed. Here, in order to bring out the full meaning of the play, the actors have to act *against* the dialogue rather than with it, the fervor of the delivery must stand in a dialectical contrast to the pointlessness of the meaning of the lines. In the same way, the author implies that most of the fervent and passionate discussion of real life (of political controversy, to give but one example) also turns around empty and meaningless clichés. Or, as Ionesco says in an essay on Antonin Artaud:

---

[9] Ionesco, "The Avant-Garde Theatre."

As our knowledge becomes increasingly divorced from real life, our culture no longer contains ourselves (or only contains an insignificant part of ourselves) and forms a "social" context in which we are not integrated. The problem thus becomes that of again reconciling our culture with our life by making our culture a living culture once more. But to achieve this end we shall first have to kill the "respect for that which is written" . . . it becomes necessary to break up our language so that it may become possible to put it together again and to re-establish contact with the absolute, or as I should prefer to call it, with multiple reality.[10]

This quest for the multiple reality of the world which is real *because* it exists on many planes simultaneously and is more than a mere uni-directional abstraction is not only in itself a search for a re-established *poetical* reality (poetry in its essence expressing reality in its ambiguity and multidimensional depth); it is also in close accord with important movements of our age in what appear to be entirely different fields: psychology and philosophy. The dissolution, devaluation, and relativiza-tion of language is, after all, also the theme of much of present-day depth psychology, which has shown what in former times was regarded as a rational expression of logically arrived at conclusions to be the mere rationalization of subconscious emotional impulses. Not everything we say means what we intend it to mean. And likewise, in present-day Logical Positivism a large proportion of all statements is regarded as devoid of conceptual meaning and merely emotive. A philosopher like Ludwig Wittgenstein, in his later phases, even tried to break through what he regarded as the opacity, the misleading nature of language and grammar; for if all our thinking is in terms of language, and language obeys what after all are the arbitrary conventions of grammar, we must strive to penetrate to the real content of thought that is masked by grammatical rules and conventions. Here, too, then is a matter of getting behind the surface of linguistic clichés and of finding reality through the break-up of language.

In the Theatre of the Absurd, therefore, the real content of the play lies in the action. Language may be discarded altogether, as in Beckett's *Act Without Words* or in Ionesco's *The New Tenant*, in which the whole sense of the play is contained in the incessant arrival of more and more furniture so that the occupant of the room is, in the end,

---

[10] Ionesco, "Ni un Dieu, ni un Demon," *Cahiers de la Compagnie Made-leine Renaud-Jean-Louis Barrault,* No. 22–23 (May, 1958).

literally drowned in it. Here the movement of objects alone carries the dramatic action, the language has become purely incidental, less important than the contribution of the property department. In this, the Theatre of the Absurd also reveals its anti-literary character, its endeavor to link up with the pre-literary strata of stage history: the circus, the performances of itinerant jugglers and mountebanks, the music hall, fairground barkers, acrobats, and also the robust world of the silent film. Ionesco, in particular, clearly owes a great deal to Chaplin, Buster Keaton, the Keystone Cops, Laurel and Hardy, and the Marx Brothers. And it is surely significant that so much of successful popular entertainment in our age shows affinities with the subject matter and preoccupation of the avant-garde Theatre of the Absurd. A sophisticated, but nevertheless highly popular, film comedian like Jacques Tati uses dialogue merely as a barely comprehensible babble of noises, and also dwells on the loneliness of man in our age, the horror of overmechanization and overorganization gone mad. Danny Kaye excels in streams of gibberish closely akin to Lucky's oration in *Waiting for Godot*. The brilliant and greatly liked team of British radio (and occasionally television) comedians, the Goons, have a sense of the absurd that resembles Kafka's or Ionesco's and a team of grotesque singers like "Les Frères Jacques" seems more closely in line with the Theatre of the Absurd than with the conventional cabaret.

Yet the defiant rejection of language as the main vehicle of the dramatic action, the onslaught on conventional logic and unilinear conceptual thinking in the Theatre of the Absurd is by no means equivalent to a total rejection of all meaning. On the contrary, it constitutes an earnest endeavor to penetrate to deeper layers of meaning and to give a truer, because more complex, picture of reality in avoiding the simplification which results from leaving out all the undertones, overtones, and inherent absurdities and contradictions of any human situation. In the conventional drama every word means what it says, the situations are clearcut, and at the end all conflicts are tidily resolved. But reality, as Ionesco points out in the passage we have quoted, is never like that; it is multiple, complex, many-dimensional and exists on a number of different levels at one and the same time. Language is far too straightforward an instrument to express all this by itself. Reality can only be conveyed by being *acted out* in all its complexity. Hence, it is the theatre, which is multidimensional and more than merely language or literature, which is the only instrument to express the bewildering complexity of the human condition. The human condition being what it is, with man small, helpless, insecure, and unable ever to fathom the world in all its hopelessness, death, and absurdity, the theatre has to confront him with the bitter truth that most human endeavor is irrational and senseless, that communication between human beings is well-nigh impossible, and that the world will forever remain an impenetrable mystery. At the same time, the recognition of all these bitter truths will have a liberating effect: if we realize the basic absurdity of most of our objectives we are freed from being obsessed with them and this release expresses itself in laughter.

Moreover, while the world is being shown as complex, harsh, and absurd and as difficult to interpret as reality itself, the audience is yet spurred on to attempt their own interpretation, to wonder what it is all about. In that sense they are being invited to school their critical faculties, to train themselves in adjusting to reality. As the world is being represented as highly complex and devoid of a clear-cut purpose or design, there will always be an infinite number of possible interpretations. As Apollinaire points out in his Preface to *Les Mamelles de Tirésias:* "None of the symbols in my play is very clear, but one is at liberty to see in it all the symbols one desires and to find in it a thousand senses—as in the Sybilline oracles." Thus, it may be that the pinball machines in Adamov's *Ping-Pong* and the ideology which is developed around them stand for the futility of political or religious ideologies that are pursued with equal fervor and equal futility in the final result. Others have interpreted the play as a parable on the greed and sordidness of the profit motive. Others again may give it quite different meanings. The mysterious transformation of human beings into rhinos in Ionesco's latest play, *Rhinoceros,* was felt by the audience of its world premiere at Duesseldorf (November 6, 1959) to depict the transformation of human beings into Nazis. It is known that Ionesco himself intended the play to express his feelings at the time when more and more of his friends in Rumania joined the Fascist Iron Guard and, in effect, left the ranks of thin-skinned humans to turn themselves into moral pachyderms. But to spectators less intimately aware of the moral climate of such a situation than the German audience, other interpretations might impose themselves: if the hero, Bérenger, is at the end left alone as the only human being in his native town, now entirely inhabited by rhinos, they might regard this as a poetic symbol of the gradual isolation of man growing old and imprisoned in the strait jacket of his own habits and memories. Does Godot, so fervently and vainly awaited by Vladimir and Estragon, stand for God? Or does he merely represent the ever elusive tomorrow, man's hope that one day something will happen that will render his existence meaningful? The force and poetic power of the play lie precisely in the impossibility of ever reaching a conclusive answer to this question.

Here we touch the essential point of difference between the conventional theatre and the Theatre of the Absurd. The former, based as it is on a known framework of accepted values and a rational view of life, always starts out by indicating a fixed objective towards which the action will be moving or by posing a definite problem to which it will supply an answer. Will Hamlet revenge the murder of his father? Will Iago succeed in destroying Othello? Will Nora leave her husband? In the conventional theatre the action always proceeds toward a definable end. The spectators do not know whether that end will be reached and how it will be reached. Hence, they are in suspense, eager to find out *what* will happen. In the Theatre of the Absurd, on the other hand, the action does not proceed in the manner of a logical syllogism. It does not go from A to B but travels from an unknown premise X toward an unknowable conclusion Y. The spectators, not knowing what their author is driving at, cannot be in suspense as to how or whether an expected objective is going to be reached. They are not, therefore, so much in suspense as to *what* is going to happen *next* (although the most unexpected and unpredictable things do happen) as they are in suspense about what the next event to take place will add to their understanding of *what is happening*. The action supplies an increasing number of contradictory and bewildering clues on a number of different levels, but the final question is never wholly answered. Thus, instead of being in suspense as to what will happen next, the spectators are, in the Theatre of the Absurd, put into suspense as to *what* the play *may mean*. This suspense continues even after the curtain has come down. Here again the Theatre of the Absurd fulfills Brecht's postulate of a critical, detached audience, who will have to sharpen their wits on the play and be stimulated by it to think for themselves, far more effectively than Brecht's own theatre. Not only are the members of the audience unable to identify with the characters, they are compelled to puzzle out the meaning of what they have seen. Each of them will probably find his own, personal meaning, which will differ from the solution found by most others. But he will have been forced to make a mental effort and to evaluate an experience he has undergone. In this sense, the Theatre of the Absurd is the most demanding, the most intellectual theatre. It may be riotously funny, wildly exaggerated and oversimplified, vulgar and garish, but it will always confront the spectator with a genuine intellectual problem, a philosophical paradox, which he will have to try to solve even if he knows that it is most probably insoluble.

In this respect, the Theatre of the Absurd links up with an older tradition which has almost completely disappeared from Western culture: the tradition of allegory and the symbolical representation of abstract concepts personified by characters whose costumes and accoutrements subtly suggested whether they represented Time, Chastity, Winter, Fortune, the World, etc. This is the tradition which stretches from the Italian *Trionfo* of the Renaissance to the English Masque, the elaborate allegorical constructions of the Spanish *Auto sacramental* down to Goethe's allegorical processions and masques written for the court of Weimar at the turn of the eighteenth century. Although the living riddles the characters represented in these entertainments were by no means difficult to solve, as everyone knew that a character with a scythe and an hourglass represented Time, and although the characters soon revealed their identity and explained their attributes, there was an element of intellectual challenge which stimulated the audience in the moments between the appearance of the riddle and its solution and which provided them with the pleasure of having solved a puzzle. And what is more, in the elaborate allegorical dramas like Calderón's *El Gran Teatro del Mundo* the subtle interplay of allegorical characters itself presented the audience with a great deal to think out for themselves. They had, as it were, to translate the abstractly presented action into terms of their everyday experience; they could ponder on the deeper meaning of such facts as death having taken the characters representing Riches or Poverty in a Dance of Death equally quickly and equally harshly, or that Mammon had deserted his master Everyman in the hour of death. The dramatic riddles of our time present no such clear-cut solutions. All they can show is that while the solutions have evaporated the riddle of our existence remains—complex, unfathomable, and paradoxical.

To Hell with Society

BY HENRY ADLER

BOTH IN THE UNITED STATES and in the United Kingdom, the keen discussion about the degree to which the theatre should be socially committed has been confused by the vague, ambiguous, and tendentious use of focal words like "society," "politics," "realism," "humanity." In England the bid by one group to impose politics on the theatre in a narrow and a party sense under the guise of solicitude for social principles has been made evident on at least two occasions. The first was the shouting in the theatre when *The Tenth Chance*, an immature first play by a young writer named Stuart Holroyd, was tried out at the Royal Court for a single Sunday night performance. The play dealt with the reactions to persecution in a totalitarian state of three imprisoned men: a rationalist, a religious mystic, and a moronic tough. It shows the tough, lacking in mental resources, breaking first and the mystic, buoyed up by faith in some extra-personal force, outlasting the rationalist who relies unsuccessfully on his vulnerable brain. What Holroyd was getting at was similar to Shaw's aim in *Saint Joan* and other plays. But the performance of Holroyd's play embodying these familiar principles was assailed by shouts of protest from Christopher Logue, a Brechtianesque poet, who was apparently outraged by this aspersion on the staying powers of Socialist rationalists and by Mrs. Kenneth Tynan who, although an *afficionada* of bullfighting, declared herself repelled by the play's "sadism," (the application of ketchup to the face to simulate blood in the style made familiar by such plays as *Oedipus Rex* and *King Lear*). Mr. Tynan himself, who was present as dramatic critic for the *London Observer*, denied taking part in this demonstration and, as evidence that the hostility of his subsequent notice of the play had not been motivated by political opposition to its thesis, cited

245

testimony that he had made program notes faulting the play early in its performance.

Now, in principle, Mr. Tynan was perfectly in his rights as a critic to say that he personally found the play "offensive" because the mystic (in his mistaken reading) "found God through torture." (In fact, the play showed the mystic holding out, not through torture, but in spite of torture.) But Mr. Tynan's critical reactions in this case were valid because they were honestly personal, and not concealed by any doctrinaire smoke screen—although he would have to revise them if he were to value any play by, say, Eliot, Claudel, Montherlant. In fact, however, doctrinaire preconceptions do blur his judgment in the case of Holroyd, and Eliot, and, as we shall see, Strindberg. They are also inconsistent with his pronouncements on other occasions. (For example, he recommends Brecht's didactic plays but rejects Eliot's *The Elder Statesman* for its didacticism.) But in the ensuing correspondence on *The Tenth Chance*, he went further. He refuted the possible accusation that he had rejected the play because of Holroyd's declaration on another occasion that he favored government by an elite, which (wrongly again) Mr. Tynan believes to be tantamount to Fascism. Mr. Tynan went on to clarify his views by saying that, although he deplored Shaw's views on dictatorship, he venerated the author of *Heartbreak House*. The implication is that, confronted by a play that in his opinion advocated dictatorship, Mr. Tynan would have condemned it for its political views irrespective of its dramatic qualities.

What a play says in political terms must be separated from the success or failure of the playwright's expression of them in a coherent, unified drama. And indeed, the value of political or any other kind of opinion will be remorselessly exposed in the character, the plot, the inner life, the credibility and appeal of the work of art. Mr. Tynan makes almost the same point when he says that he deplores Ezra Pound's racial views but enjoys his poetry. I believe Arthur Miller has said as much. This raises an interesting point. It implies that Pound speaks truer through his poetry than through his politics, that one can sift true from false more accurately if one listens to what he says through his art rather than through his polemics. Another writer might speak more cogently through his politics than through his plays. But both are to be judged within their own framework, the politics as politics, the play as a play. This is what Ionesco means by the truth of a play to its nature. And from this aspect, we shall be free from those idiotic discussions about Shakespeare's anti-Semitism in portraying Shylock. To condemn a play because of its human values seems to be justifiable. That is, one may protest at the way Shylock is treated by the characters in the play but not that Shylock is represented at the outset as a miser. One must accept the dramatic hypothesis in order to study what conclusions arise from it (and, as critics, watching that the apparent conclusions do arise from it in terms of human truth and dramatic logic). Mr. Tynan was not justified in complaining about Holroyd's play that the agnostic succumbed to religion, for that was Holroyd's thesis, although Mr. Tynan was justified in expressing his opinion that plays do tend to be cliché-ridden by presenting agnostics as inevitably succumbing to religion in the last act and within his rights to criticize the plausibility of the conversion. But even Mr. Tynan's opposition to clichés seems to be influenced by his social-political affinities, for his opposition to such clichés as reforming agnostics and drug-addicted Negroes seems to impel him to imply that all agnostics are rationalists honestly finding the truth, and that all Negroes are perfect gentlemen like Sidney Poitier. The result is that he favors plays which "are in the business of healing," of curing "pain, fear, and sadness," plays which are humanitarian and which are linked with politics to the degree that democracy is "good" and dictatorship is "bad," and he works from a confused glossary of words like "rational" and "human."

Apart from the vagueness and confusion of these terms, they vitiate his whole approach to the drama. It may be right to reject a play because its effect in the playing seems repulsive or false to his experience of life. But that is not the same thing as saying that it is repulsive or false because it conflicts with his preconceived political codification of life. One wants a personal response and not a conditioned reflex which causes a snarl at words like "dictatorship" and saliva at the mention of "rationalism," even before the curtain goes up. More, I would say that one should suspend disbelief in the theatre to a greater extent than in political argument precisely because the theatre is the place where we go to see other views, hear other opinions.

In explaining why he rejects Strindberg's *The Dream Play*, Mr. Tynan writes: "If a man tells me something which I believe to be an untruth, am I forbidden to do more than congratulate him on the brilliance of his lying?" Does Mr. Tynan really go around calling people liars when their opinions differ from his own? All art is, in a sense, lies. According to a photograph, Van Gogh is a liar. According to the history of Hamlet, Shakespeare is a liar. But more relevant than this is the question of how far we should tolerate a view of life which we find antagonistic. For example, Shaw the Socialist declared himself repelled not by the snob values of *The Importance of Being Earnest* but by its lack of humanity, the mechanical humor. "Unless comedy touches me as well as amuses me, it leaves me with a sense of having wasted my evening." But he could see value in Henry James' *Guy Domville*, which was execrated by every other critic, in spite of its social views which were antipathetic to Shaw's own. On the other hand, Shaw indicated what the Socialist-committed writer would have done to ruin his own play, *Widowers Houses:*

> . . . cut out the passages which convict the audience of being just as responsible for the slums as the landlord is; make the hero a ranting Socialist instead of a perfectly commonplace young gentleman; make the heroine an angel instead of her father's daughter only a generation removed from the washtub; and you have the successful melodrama of tomorrow.

In short, consistent with Shaw's general views that the conscience and conduct of man develop irrespective of doctrine, which made him as a Socialist so inconvenient a colleague to Socialist doctrinaires, he wanted a free theatre unbedeviled by political preconceptions.

In contradiction to those who want to make the theatre a close reflection of what is vaguely termed "life" and to those who misread Shaw's personal didacticism to mean a doctrinaire didacticism, I believe that the justification of the theatre is precisely that it is at one stage removed from life, so that I may listen to Shaw's didacticism, Eliot's didacticism, Brecht's didacticism, review issues in debate, view the world from new or strange or unpleasant aspects, have character—whether Jew or Gentile, Fascist or Communist—revealed to me as sympathetic or unpleasant against my antagonistic or sentimental expectations, recognize the evil in good, the good in evil, see compressed and unified in the microcosm of a play the pattern and interconnection which are lost in the life outside the theatre where argument is too angry and hasty and too closely connected with immediate action to permit consideration, where the human values are buried beneath policies, and the pattern and meaning are lost in the tangle of events and the delayed consequences of time. As against the open and shut case for political action advocated by Brecht (a policy which he aban-

doned), I want a play to be the "playing out" of the thoughts and
emotions and experiences of life, for the same reasons as the Greeks
invented this vicarious experience.

Tynan has done a tremendous deal to raise the standard and increase the human relevance of the theatre. If I oppose his conception of
social relevance, it is partly because it is crippled by defective terminology. As we shall see, in this vague and ambiguous glossary, apart
from the confusion of social relations with politics, which are the
administration of social relations, there is the false equation of "social"
with "sociological," of men with Man, of humanity with humanitarianism, of reason with the rational, of rationalism with rationalization, of
reality with naturalism. All this confusion emerged in the now famous
Tynan-Ionesco debate which was published in the *London Observer* in
the weeks beginning June 22, 1958. And it also became clearer that
Mr. Tynan's social commitment took the specific form of a pinkish
Welfare State socialism in contradistinction with which all opinion
was liable to derogation as anti-democratic or Fascist. First, Mr. Tynan
accused M. Ionesco of being divorced from "reality." What Mr. Tynan
meant was "objective reality" or the facts of life. He explained:

> The broad definition of a realistic play is that its characters and events
> have traceable roots in life. Gorki and Chekhov, Arthur Miller and
> Tennessee Williams, Brecht and O'Casey, Osborne and Sartre have all
> written such plays. They express one man's view of the world in terms
> of people we can all recognize.

He immediately backpedals by admitting that Brecht employed stylized
production techniques but goes on to accuse Ionesco of being "ready
to declare that words were meaningless and that all communication between human beings was impossible" and to pour scorn on the critics
who had praised the plays of Ionesco and Beckett as "authentic images
of a disintegrated society."

But was it not Chekhov who first wrote plays of inarticulacy, of
pauses in which lives came together or parted because people had no
words or because there were no words, and was not that inarticulacy
the result and expression of a disintegrated society? Chekhov as much
as Ionesco recognized that reality lay behind the sociological approach.
And when Ionesco pointed out in his reply that "a work of art has
nothing to do with doctrine. I have already written elsewhere that any
work of art which was ideological and nothing else would be pointless,

tautological, inferior to the doctrine it claimed to demonstrate," he was corroborated by Arthur Miller, one of Mr. Tynan's selected realists, who says in the Introduction to his *Collected Plays*: "I do not believe that any work of art can help but be diminished by its adherence at any cost to a political program, including its author's, and not for any other reason than that there is no political program—any more than there is a theory of tragedy—which can encompass the complexities of real life." Miller goes on to say much more to the same effect and concludes: "It is merely that a writer of any worth creates out of his total perception, the vaster part of which is subjective and not within his intellectual control." Ionesco echoes this by saying: "An ideological play can be no more than the vulgarization of an ideology. In my view, a work of art has its own unique system, its own means of directly apprehending the real." And he goes on to accuse Mr. Tynan of affirming (in an interview in *Encounter*) only one plane of reality, what is called the social plane which "to me," says Ionesco, "seems the most external, in other words, the most superficial . . . But that is not all: One must also, apparently, be a militant believer in what is known as progress." And Ionesco says:

> This would considerably restrict the planes of reality . . . I believe that what separates us all from one another is simply society itself, or, if you like, politics . . . the true society, the authentic human community, is extra-social—a wider, deeper society, that which is revealed by our common anxieties, our desires, our secret nostalgias. . . . No society has been able to abolish human sadness, no political system can deliver us from the pain of living, from our fear of death, our thirst for the absolute; it is the human condition which directs the social condition and not vice versa. . . . If anything needs demystifying it is our ideologies. . . . It is these ideologies which must be continually re-examined in the light of our anxieties and our dreams, and their congealed language must be relentlessly split apart in order to find the living sap beneath . . . I could take almost any work of art, any play, and guarantee to give it in turn a Marxist, a Christian, a Buddhist, an Existentialist, a psychoanalytical interpretation. . . . For me this proves . . . that every work of art outside ideology is not reducible to ideology. . . . The absence of ideology in a work does not mean an absence of ideas; on the contrary, it fertilizes them. In other words, it was not Sophocles who was inspired by Freud but, obviously, the other way round. A work of art is the source and the raw material of ideologies to come. . . . He [the critic] must look at it, listen to it and simply say whether it is true to its own nature . . .

Whether or not it is what you would like it to be—to consider this is already to pass judgment, a judgment that is external, pointless and false. A work of art is the expression of an incommunicable reality that one tries to communicate—and which sometimes can be communicated. That is its paradox and its truth.

In his reply, Mr. Tynan narrowed his social commitment by equating it with political commitment. "Even buying a package of cigarettes has social and political repercussions." He ought to remember that one may not be able to reach back from a repercussion to the original sound of the human voice. Human relations involve more than their schematization. However, one sees that he means the whole complex of human relationships and that he recognizes that redemption by faith cannot be separated from redemption by works. He goes on to assert that art is not, as Ionesco has it, the source of ideology, but that art is parasitic on life, that art and ideology spring from the same source. To quote Tynan's words:

> To say that Freud was inspired by Sophocles is the direst nonsense. Freud merely found in Sophocles confirmation of a theory he had formed on the basis of empirical evidence.

Mr. Tynan goes on to say of M. Ionesco:

> His aim is to blind us to the fact that we are all in some sense critics who bring to the theatre not only those "nostalgias and anxieties" by which, as he rightly says, world history has largely been governed, but also a whole series of new ideas, moral, social, psychological, political— through which we hope some day to free ourselves from the rusty hegemony of *Angst*.

Mr. Tynan parodies the proposition that the audience is merely to say whether or not a play is true to its nature: "'Clear evidence of cancer here, sir.' 'Very well, leave it alone: it's being true to its nature.'" "A play," says Mr. Tynan, "is a statement . . . addressed in the first person singular to the first person plural," and he goes on to claim the right of dissent when, for example, *The Dream Play* presents a version or a view of life which he finds unacceptable. He denies that one must accept an alien view of life in a play merely because the artist's vision is vivid.

If a man tells me something which I believe to be an untruth, am I forbidden to do more than congratulate him on the brilliance of his lying? . . . I shall be looking . . . for evidence of the artist who concerns himself, from time to time, with healing. M. Ionesco correctly says that no ideology has yet abolished fear, pain or sadness. Nor has any work of art. But both are in the business of trying. What other business is there?

This subjective-objective demarcation has been absurdly exaggerated in this debate, as, I think, Mr. Tynan realizes. If he has overstated his case it is because he fears that Ionesco may let in a crowd of lesser disciples, of whom there is already some sign. Ionesco and Beckett and N. F. Simpson diagnose and dissect man's loneliness, his metaphysical inanity, his inability to convey all he feels, his personal life rendered so absurd by an absurd society that words between two people in the same room are not communications of personal reality but become sound waves sent out across the desert to break the silence and conceal the void. But the minor followers are tending to make easy fun of uneducated inarticulate people and their surrealist effects result from superficial verbal humor. Had I to choose between one school of playwrights and another, I would follow Mr. Tynan.

But we have to recognize that in reacting against subjectivism, Mr. Tynan makes a false distinction between realism and nonrealism. Arthur Miller himself disclaims narrow realism as much as Brecht does and in Miller's introduction to his *Collected Plays,* he describes how he will use expressionism or any other means to telescope time, to break down the barriers against empathy so as to enable us to penetrate to the raw suffering soul of Loman. Tennessee Williams says much the same thing in his preface to *The Rose Tattoo.* Not only Brecht but also O'Casey is expressionistic and Osborne is indebted to Brecht both in *The Entertainer* and *The World of Paul Slickey.* The most literal of the realists mentioned by Mr. Tynan are Gorky, the old time social realist, and the ponderous Sartre. The reason why, externally realistic though they often are, the other writers cease to be naturalistic is that, like Ionesco, they are aware that at the core of reality is subjective man. Indeed, in words that might be Ionesco's, Mr. Miller writes: "Ibsen was, after all as much a mystic as a realist. Which is simply to say that while there are mysteries in life which no amount of analyzing will reduce to reason, it is perfectly realistic to admit and even to proclaim that hiatus as a truth." It is. But in fact, Mr. Miller does not express it in his plays, and that is their deficiency. And Mr. Tynan rejects Strindberg's *The Dream Play* as "nihilistic" precisely because it implies that rationalism is limited; it is this rationalism which cripples his critcism.

The conception of subjective man has changed. The tragedy of Oedipus could be played out in a spiritual vacuum. Consequently, the character could be made big enough to encompass the highest common denominator of mankind, embrace all human destiny, and speak with all the eloquence of Sophocles. In Shakespeare, the Aristotelian belief that the universe was God-centered and that the divine order was expressed in the king-centered state enabled his protagonists to speak as mouthpieces of the race. But the development of the machine, of the town, of democracy, the new power of the heretofore dumb and respectful masses has caused the parallel and independent channels of high tragedy and low comedy to fuse and merge. As Miller points out, the ordinary man cannot be presented as fully eloquent and conscious of his relation to universal issues as Oedipus. Modern industrialism has atomized the population into a multitude of uniform human particles so that the large-scale universal representative hero has been replaced by the tiny, individual hero who does not embody mankind but is only a facet reflecting some aspects of it. Objectively, externally, materially, one human being becomes like another.

This new economic and scientific materialism split the intellectuals, not necessarily because one group was socially conscious and committed while the other was in the Ivory Tower. Eliot's writings in the thirties, like his play *The Rock,* were socially aware, although he envisaged a different social cure from the Socialists. Indeed, his description of the dead city men marching across London Bridge into the purgatory of the economic wasteland as "disassociated in sensibility" was paralleled by Marx's "alienation," the disassociation from, the helpless looking-on at, the total social process, which Brecht was to employ theatrically. Nevertheless, the effect of "the wasteland" on some writers was to induce retreat into solipsism, subjectivism, the private world where in Eliot's words, "the dialect of the tribe" might be purified and the time "redeemed." The desiccation and objectification of reality, the apparent meaninglessness of the individual man, the unreality of the agglomeration of facts, the insignificance of time in the succession of repetitive days, have caused the relativity of Einstein to be reflected philosophically in the relativity of individuality in Eliot, Pirandello, Beckett, and Ionesco.

The Marxists, on the other hand, staked all on the remaking of objective reality, the switch-over from a bad to a good economic society and in their vocabulary, rationalism was truth, progress was utilitarian, and art sociological. In came the era of the hero as victim, dominated by the world. The question is: How far has the social world, which starts as a symbol of, an approximation to, a means toward, human fulfillment become an end in itself, a blank wall, a millstone rather than a milestone? Ibsen in *Hedda Gabler* and *Rosmersholm* created tragedy in a bourgeois setting. Mr. Miller tries for tragedy and he fails in his attempt because his work includes just those qualities which, he seems to think, make him Ibsen's superior: his rationalism and his democratic social consciousness. The clear-cut social exposition, the precise Freudian analysis make the situation so clearly judgeable in terms of right and wrong, so diagnoseable in terms of disease and cure that no further dramatic meaning is left. The plays are noble failures but they reveal the limitations of Mr. Miller's approach. In *A View From the Bridge,* Miller shows Ed Carbone fighting irrationally, amorally, in his pagan vitality, his passionate asocial refusal to settle for half in the devitalized democratic way, but Miller ultimately reveals that he believes that the fundamental relationship between man and men, or man and Man, is the sociological mechanism that will manipulate us if we do not manipulate it. His Introduction to the *Collected Plays* is an admirable statement and could not be improved on. In the plays, however, we become aware that the sociological approximation of the world of men seems to Miller to be not merely a schematization, but the whole possible realm of human relations. Society has become sociological, and he believes that the development of society with all its teeming packed populations, with its alienation of man from the product of his work, is not something inherently evil but something that must be adjusted functionally so that men, if not fulfilled, will be able to settle for half.

No more than Loman could Oedipus, or Hamlet, or Rebecca West, walk away from fate. But if Loman does not walk away, it is because he is a barnacle clamped to the hull of society. He is a suffering barnacle and he tears my heart. Miller is a humanitarian and insists that "attention" must finally be paid to this man. So it must. But he tries to make the theatre do it. He revises the theory of tragedy to take in the passive, the inarticulate. And it is true that the passive must be helped, the inarticulate given voice. But not merely that. The theatre should show the ends of man, the purpose to which life should be devoted and not merely be the mouthpiece of the feeblest and weakest. Because Miller narrows down the scope of the drama to the limitation of the pathetic victim of society—and of society viewed particularly as a socio-economic nexus—his plays become a tearing of heart strings, a call for sympathetic attention, so that we turn from them heart and nerves torn, depressed, and not instructed, stimulated, exhilarated by the purpose of life as we do from even the most catastrophic tragedy of Ibsen. It must be ruthlessly said that the purpose of drama is not sympathy for the weakest and most hapless man. It is not humanitarian. All this inversion and narrowness of drama springs from the rationalist, sociological fallacy with its back to front logic which argues that, since all drama is human, everything human is dramatic and therefore art should focus upon the feeblest man if he occurs in sufficient numbers.

The effect on the drama is the apotheosis of ordinariness, the worship of the weakest, the victim as hero and the sentimentalization of the underprivileged, the folk-art dramas of the tenements and police courts with the junkie or hoodlum as hero. From falsity of one kind, the pendulum swings to falsity of another.

Of course, human values are important. Of course, the individual deserves attention. And it is precisely for this reason that the drama must emancipate itself from the narrow rationalism which would confine it within the utilitarian values, from the sentimentalization of the ordinary man simply because he is ordinary and met with in large numbers, and the narrowly political standards of dramatic criticism which would confine the drama within doctrinaire limits. It is a question of scope and of dimension. With his intense humanitarian feeling for men, Miller is overwhelmed by the worlds of inarticulate suffering and experience in drab-suited people whom no one recognizes as having dramatic meaning and who stoically accept the man-made miseries of our society as the inevitable conditions of life. Each of them is a window upon the world, each of them is a personification of life and no one, not even he himself, recognizes the fact. They accept as the will of God a world in which they work from nine to six, day passing day and time lacking significance until they die in a bed-sitting room consoled by the firm's testimonial to their lifetime's punctuality. But even when there is rebellion in the sociological play, it becomes, since it is solely against the economic conditions, a feeble shaking of the bars implying that, once the bars are removed, we shall be out in that kind of technicolored garden suburb depicted in the dream sequence in *West Side Story,* where everyone will walk around dreamily hand in hand and no one will quarrel anymore.

Mr. Miller thinks every man's death is tragic. In a very human sense it is. But although everything tragic on the dramatic scale is human, not everything tragic on the human scale is dramatic, in the sense of being significant. And I do not think Loman's ignorant and narrow love is in any wide sense, and from any aspect other than his own, significant. I repeat that he is pitiable and one weeps for his real love, his private suffering. But are we to respect intensity of emotion, anguish of suffering, however narrow, however misdirected, however passive? Othello and Lear are fools, possibly madmen. But Shakespeare does not vindicate them as individuals. Rather he uses their individualities as springboards for leaps of passion and philosophy over the whole range of human experience. We admire the range of the leap; we do not admire or like Lear or Othello as persons. But we are asked, in terms of almost moral hectoring, to pay "attention" to Willy Loman who achieves none of the general meaning of human experience, contributes nothing to enrich human experience but slumps abjectly upon our pity with attention being demanded by Mr. Miller with his Jewish humanitarian sympathy for passive suffering. Mr. Philip Toynbee, contributing to the Ionesco-Tynan correspondence, did no good to his own argument by attempting to refute Ionesco by saying: "To write that what separates all of us from one another is simply 'society itself' is like writing that the human race is horribly hampered in its freedom of movement by the atmosphere which lies so heavy on our planet." Shades of Brecht! If there was one thing which that most social of playwrights emphasized it was that society could be changed. In fact, he would have pointed out that changing the atmosphere of the planet is already a possibility (even discounting the effect of H-bomb explosions) and may become economically feasible and socially useful. Of course, it is true that what Ionesco was getting at was the mechanization of society which is destroying any real individuality and community. It does not follow that the adjustment of society from bad economics to good social economics will produce better men. Even H. G. Wells, who originally took this line, learned better.

The drama has to be positive and we have to ask whether the righteous indignation behind the cries for human and social justice is enough or whether we have to think in more detail about the purpose and direction of human development. Now that the Soviet Union is losing all the Christian mystique of Communism, and Mr. Khrushchev is aiming at the Utopia of American supermarkets, Russia is becoming as materialistic as any capitalism and the hate-love relationship between the USSR and the USA will spur both countries happily onward to the great goal of technological efficiency and economic abundance that will certainly abolish poverty and disease and, in Mr. Tynan's sense, "pain, fear and sadness." But the repression of human qualities and of man's creative development is as severe in the democratic welfare state as it is in the communist state or the fascist state. The crippling human effects resulting from the conscription of the population into technological production and from the narrow rationalism of utilitarian social improvement will not take the form of poverty or unemployment, except in occasional cycles. Quite the contrary. The present upsurge of world prosperity seems likely to produce a world of good wages, automation, clean model factories and a vast army of well-off workers who will alternate between doing their smooth, repetitive, endless, purposeless jobs like docile automata, disturbed only by a vague boredom and sadness, and exploding with a superficially rationalized violence against bosses, Negroes, Jews, or women, or any other ostensible culprit against whom the pent-up rage caused by the frustrations of death-in-life can explode. The trouble with the sociological play is that it is so buried inside social evils, so centered on the most pathetic of people, that it raises the belief that the weak, lowly, and vicious will be magically transformed when economic and social conditions produce better wages and living conditions, that human progress is all that can be reached by the improvement of production, distribution, and exchange.

In the new world of social democracy there will be discussions about progress, within bounds, of course, and within the social ideology. In none of these social plays is there any hint, let alone discussion, of the personal nature of man, his conscience, his relation to the universe. The values are suburban, and there is no distinction between the values which he should impose upon the world as distinct from the values which will be imposed on him as a solid member of the paternal state. When Brecht preached the beneficence of science (as in *Galileo*), he proclaimed the pious hope that man would control and direct his power, and art and science would, as Mr. Tynan desiderates, join hands. Brecht wrote: "The great buildings of the City of New York are not of themselves enough to swell mankind's sense of triumph . . . It is my belief that he (man) will not let himself be adapted by machines but will himself adapt machines." Let us hope so. But how is it to be done? In our society "science" is no longer interpreted as knowledge in the widest sense. No longer do we believe in the knowledge, the very real "science" of the inner life of man, of the poet and the mystic. Science has to be regarded as what is factual and functional and can be rationalized. And it is rationalized in terms of whatever Big Brother or Big Business paternalism interprets as good for the masses.

In the attempt to cure the economic injustices of society, Mr. Tynan tries to enjoin us to fight back with the same weapons. We get the paradox that it is the sociological values themselves, which are ostensibly designed to aid individuality in the person of a Willy Loman, which destroy individuality in the name of social conformity, reducing, for example, architecture to the production of massive egg boxes (so many cubic feet per human unit). Marxism is the philosophy of the unilinear, of the function and the fact forming the human being. But so is capitalism.

The sociological ideal of both Marxism and capitalism seems at present to be the supply of material benefits, the TV and the refrigerator, the leisure in which from President downwards every man in the population can fulfill himself by searching for a million lost golf balls, or race in the car down the endless arterial road to limbo, or conquer space to find the moon is made of ashes, proving once again the truth of Nietzsche's perception that science always comes up against its own reflection. It is this narrow sociological approach to life, the veneration of the limited rationalistic keyhole view of life as the whole means of human apprehension, the confusion of scientific objectivity with the whole truth, which accounts not only for the limitation of human values but for the limitation of the theatre, the identification of naturalism with realism, of psychology with character, the photographic superficiality and the clinical narrowness of the Method. In an age when all mystery can be probed by the intellect, every problem solved by the appropriate action, every evil potentially curable by skill and knowledge, is not Mr. Tynan right to believe that we can cure pain, fear, and suffering? And should not this be the purpose of art? And if this were so, would not tragedy be a morbid luxury?

Into Nietzsche's Dionysian-Apollonian antithesis in *The Birth of Tragedy*, we can read Marx for Socrates, Brecht for the author of epic, and Mr. Miller for the practitioner of the "inartistic naturalism" of Euripides into which epic declined. Brecht's heart-head dualism is an expression of the romantic-classical dualism. It is true that for the most part Brecht implied that all would be well when there was economic millenium, as at the end of *The Caucasian Chalk Circle* when a good world would grant "the valley to the waterers that it bring forth fruit." But when I talked to him about the play, he said that Grusha represented love. Now love is not a Marxist concept. That Brecht could hold this belief in love is a sign that he was animated by a belief that there was more to the resurrection of society than a technological, an economic, or even an intellectual change. He told me that he saw no end to the dialectical development of man with his world, the vistas which would unfold as love and skill were set against unjust economics and the harsh aloofness of nature. Like Eliot, Brecht sought to integrate intellect and emotion. Since he believed that pleasure at its best was meaningful, the heart-head, man-society, dualism manifested itself (as Nietzsche had said the Socratic approach must manifest itself) in epic: the drama which watches, surveys, studies with detachment the tenuous progress of man across the world, the slow cumulation of consequence of the relationship of heart and head in dealings with other men. It was Brecht's painful repression of his vulnerable humanitarianism, because he saw that mere emotion got you nowhere, that produced his dramatic expression of Marxist "alienation"—the detachment of the artist from his creation, the spectator from the action—and made him, he claimed, a classical writer, controlling his emotion, demonstrating his intention. He ceased to be obsessed with the personal pain and "heroism" of his characters and so alienated himself from what Nietzsche would have called the "inartistic naturalism" of Mr. Miller and the psychological playwrights familiar on Broadway. As I see it, the objection to naturalism is not merely its photographic superficiality but the fact that this superficiality is symptomatic of the sociological approach which makes a hero of the man who suffers, and considers the aim of society to be simply to give him what he wants, and the aim of the drama to proclaim that this is the purpose of society. Indeed, Miller argues that this is the stuff of tragic drama and that we ought to "pay attention." While there is a similarity between Mother Courage trudging with her cart and Willy Loman trudging with his bags, *Death of a Salesman* falls between the stools of epic detachment and naturalistic empathy so that our cool study of Willy is confused by the hectoring of our moral sympathies. That Brecht refused to make this bid for emotion is a sign that he was an artist, that he saw further than Miller.

But although Brecht's canvas is wider than the naturalistic Utopians, while he relegates his characters to the role of personal exemplars of the social process, he still equates the social approximation of the world with the whole human potential for experience of the world, the economic schematization of life with life itself. From this point of view, all human problems become simple material problems. One is led to believe that if Mother Courage had been more sensible, or if society had been better, she would not have become poor but become rich, and healthy, and happy. These are desirable ends but they are not the ultimate ends of human existence. That is the essential flaw in the social drama as practiced in terms of conformity to political doctrine as Mr. Tynan desires. They are schematic, unilinear, and reduce human values to the standards of social or economic efficiency. Shaw and Ibsen so far transcend Brecht because they are aware of the essential problems of human nature, of human development, of the inner conflicts of man's mind and feelings and their outward expression not only in his relations with his fellow men but with his sense of life on this planet in the universe. That meant that they did not merely see the world as something to be understood by astronomical calculation or grasped by technological expansion, but something to be evaluated in terms of the dialectical relationship between man and not merely society, but the human meaning perceived in the world of which society was but an approximation. As Shaw wrote: "[Nietzsche] is easy to a witty man who has once well learnt Schopenhauer's lesson, that the intellect by itself is a dead piece of brain machinery, and our ethical and moral systems merely the pierced cards you stick into it to make it play a certain tune." And as he wrote to the Nun of Stanbrook: "I exhausted rationalism when I got to the end of my second novel at the age of twenty-four and should have come to a dead stop if I had not proceeded on purely mystical assumptions."

What are these mystical assumptions which Miller and the sociological dramatists reject to their cost, and which make Ibsen and Shaw relevant today when the humanitarian plays are forgotten? These assumptions are first of all inspired by the pride, dignity, hardship, and joy of man's lonely task to develop life on this planet. In this sense, the purpose of these playwrights was not to drug the average man against pain, fear, and suffering but instead to embrace pain, fear, and suffering so as better to know the cold bare reality rather than to burrow in to the self-indulgent pleasures which the average man tells himself he is "entitled" to in a snug, smug introverted society directed to the lowest needs of the greatest number.

But the tragedy in the best plays of Ibsen is not, as Mr. Tynan seems naïvely to imply, a matter of unnecessary gloom as tragedy is interpreted in the vulgar sense. Ibsen's tragedy is, as the greatest tragedy always is, exhilarating. And the reason is because of Ibsen's working from the prime factor of the human individuality which must be fulfilled by becoming ever more aware of reality and cutting away all the jungle of words, sentiments, and doctrines to achieve that aristocracy of spirit (not, of course, of rank), which is so unpopular in times when there is obeisance before the average and the popular. From this point of view, Ibsen would have considered Tynan's charge of Fascism as irrelevant nonsense. Both man and Man, individual and society, were to be appraised not by indulgent humanitarianism, nor by an inverted sociology of the lowest need of the greatest number, nor by the treason of intellectuals kowtowing before the hydra-headed monster, but by the degree to which their interrelationship progressed toward fulfilling the best aspirations of life. And to do that one must work from within, and observe the shifting dialectic of human relationships toward a situation. As Rosmer said: "People don't lend themselves to ennobling from without. . . ." True democracy is the machinery by which the truth of human relationships is expressed. Because Ibsen recognized the imponderable, elastic, subtle, and (before Freud) subconsciously tangled motives of men, his dialectic is progressive and not the mechanical either-or of Brecht's dramatization of economic issues. Ibsen anticipated the latest developments of science in perceiving that in the social world, as much as in the atomic world, personal relationships, like atomic relationships, cannot be represented as objectively as in a photograph or as precisely factual as the relationships of mechanical gears but that they change, as we witness them, because we witness them.

Over and above recommending or suggesting any obvious social therapy which would "adjust" his characters in the superficial way Mr. Tynan favors, Ibsen reveals the deep sources of human motivation, the vital force of the good intentions that pave the road to hell so that although we may condemn the hellbent as socially undesirable, we may understand and even admire the mistaken nobility and the misdirected vitality which drive the most powerful spirits there, when the vast majority stay safely at home. As in all great tragedy, evil is energy out of place and that energy is in origin as innocent, as neutral, as justified in its own terms of fulfilling itself as it is in a volcano, a tiger, or (in Mr. Tynan's example) a cancer. It is only when we are at a sufficient distance in time or space that we can appreciate the beauty of the glowing fire, the swift leap, or the self-willed vitality of the proliferating cells. We can combat them just as we combat criminals even while understanding and possibly sympathizing with what makes them act as they do.

Therefore, coupled with the will to avert the danger to man, is an almost aesthetic attitude of understanding, admiration, wonder which is my reason for making a plea for detached observation in the audience, politically disinterested testimony in the author, for a wider view of the phenomena of life than can be compressed in any passionate or narrow doctrine. The play that is evil, or perverted, or mad, or misguided, is better than the politician possessing these traits precisely because the play is in the theatre and not in the market place where the passions are strong, action is immediate, and emotions overcome judgment. The justification for a play, as against the Brechtian exhortation to action (usually on tendentiously presented issues) is precisely that it is at one stage removed from life. And it is worth noting that Brecht himself, while he started off arguing for his didactic *lehrstück,* said in later years ("Kleines Organon"), and quite conscious that he was contradicting his earlier pronouncements, that a play should entertain rather than instruct. He went further: "Pleasure becomes its [the theatre's] noblest function. . . . Even when people speak of higher and lower degrees of pleasure, art stares impassively back at them; for it wishes to fly high and low so long as it can give us pleasure." But for Brecht, as Ionesco, pleasure does not mean merely thoughtless laughter. In both writers there is a union of thought with emotion. If Brecht mocks as he analyzes, Ionesco analyzes as he mocks and there is disturbance behind the laughter. Just as Brecht urges us to:

> Observe the conduct of these people closely
> Find it estranging even if not very strange [and]
> We particularly ask you
> When a thing continually occurs—
> Not on that account to find it natural . . .

so Ionesco would persuade us to contemplate, speeded up, reduced to absurdity, carried logically to its natural illogicality, the falsity in the quasi-reality, to look askance at the death-in-life, of the Willy Loman average man's social world with the blinds pulled down against the disturbing universe.

That is why I want to be able to see any play, even when the social content is not explicit, and which may well seem to be flippant, pernicious, pornographic, or in some way evil. We can indeed consider evil in the theatre in the same detached and interested way that a surgeon will study and find interest, benefit, beauty, in a cancer being true to its nature even while he will try to eradicate it from a man. Just as pure science is separated from applied science, so art is separated from politics and for the same reason. We have to understand from a position of neutrality and also to act according to immediate demands of emergency. We have to understand why men do murder and also to prevent, restrain, and punish the murderer. Political emergency demands hasty, shortsighted, inadequate action. I refuse to side with such narrow loyalties even though I may coöperate when (as in war) action is necessary. My loyalty is to man against his enemies in nature, in men, in himself. But although I would seek to eradicate the cancer, exterminate the rat, or kill a tiger which came too near, I cannot see any reason for hating forms of life because they are irreconcilable with our own. Similarly, although I might side with political action in one form or another (and illogically lose my temper with adversaries), I refuse to adopt political loyalty as the sign of a crusade against tribal enemies. And in the theatre, at least, one can adopt the detached clinical study toward issues which the doctor adopts in his laboratory. Even though, like him, we may take action in the operating theatre it is, or should be, enlightened action derived from the sympathetic understanding of the inner nature of the disease.

Like Mr. Tynan, I believe that Ionesco is limited, although I think his work has value. I too want to see more human relevance in his work even though it need not be overtly or explicitly sociological. But we have to be careful in rejecting work which does not seem to be humanly relevant or sociologically valuable, or we shall find ourselves in the camp of Clement Scott inveighing against the work of Ibsen as an "open sore unbandaged," and on the way to calling Ionesco's work a "cancer" and Strindberg's *The Dream Play* a "lie." I recognized that Mr. Tynan is after a closer communion between thought and feeling, direct statement and sensibility, a closer relationship with the recognizable world rather than a retreat into a personal expression which too often has no personality and is not worth expressing. But if, as M. Ionesco says, "a work of art is the expression of an incommunicable reality that one tries to communicate—and which sometimes can be communicated," it is to that extent a social act. It is valuable that we should know that our fellow man is as lonely as each of us, as full of inexpressible feelings, of subtle irrational inner experiences which he fears or is unable to express because they seem ridiculous in a utilitarian society, or because words are too functional, or because he has no words except the jargon that facilitates action and obscures feeling. This is what Ionesco and Beckett show in those scenes of people imprisoned in silence, of man doomed to solitude in the desert of a small room peering across the table at his family. I cannot accept that the subjective worlds of Strindberg or Ionesco or Beckett are lies because they are not congruous with the social world. After all, their comments being the honest voicing of individual feelings, must (since society consists of individuals) be socially relevant. If they are not, so much the worse for society. And the failure of the individual irrational personal voice to be heard in an increasingly functional and technical society explains the inhumanity, the death-in-life we can witness on all sides in a world where prosperity is linked with depression, suicide, and people who pursue their daily lives as a kind of penance, without meaning. I do indeed want to see a closer subjective-objective relationship between the individual and his world through society. And therefore we have ever to ask ourselves: If the individual is to be committed to society, what then is society to be committed to?

It is because I agree so much with Shaw's and Tynan's efforts to give a backbone of intellect to our wishy-washy theatre of sensibility that I want to raise Mr. Tynan's sights, extend his limits, in his view of society. He would want to make motivation of character, and character itself explicable in social terms. I agree with Strindberg who, anticipating Freud, wrote fifty years ago that evil is the other face of good, and that there is no photographic or moralistic black and white in art, no simplification of motives but only the discretion of the artist who may offer us the strange irrational beauty of the cancer as Dostoevsky offered the lovable aspects of evil, seeing the evil relevant to good, the ugly to the beautiful. I simply cannot follow Mr. Tynan in his dismissal of Strindberg's *The Dream Play*. If ever there was a socially critical play, this is one. But Mr. Tynan is inhibited at the start by his narrow preconception of society and his view that every statement in a play should be explicit and social in this sense. He presumably calls the play "nihilistic" because Strindberg makes the Daughter of Indra come to earth, like the gods in *The Good Woman of Setzuan*, and say, apparently with Strindberg's approval, that "human beings are piti-able." But she says this because, like Fulke Greville writing of the wearisome condition of humanity "created sick and commanded to be sound," she loves and admires them in their struggle: "To be mortal is not easy." Strindberg is animated by no flabby defeatism about the human condition. Child of Brahma and Maya, of heaven and earth, man is seen as both mortal and immortal, physical and yet transcending his limitations by the power of the poet.

Just as Ibsen in *Emperor and Galilean* rejects both the philosophy of empire and the philosophy of spirituality and aims toward the Third Empire, the state of tension and creative conflict in which man's will shall be linked with God's, material strength and spiritual purpose guiding each other, so Strindberg expresses the inadequacy of material life in such terms as:

> ... this mingling of the divine element with the earthly was the Fall from heaven. This world, its life and its inhabitants are therefore only a mirage, a reflection, a dream image. . . . But, in order to be freed from the earthly element, the descendants of Brahma sought renunciation and suffering. And so you have suffering as the deliverer. But this yearning for suffering comes into conflict with the longing for joy, for love. Now you understand what love is; supreme joy in the greatest suffering, the sweetest is the most bitter. Do you understand now what woman is? Woman, through whom sin and death entered into life.
> ... And the outcome?
> ... Conflict between the pain of joy and the joy of pain, between the anguish of the penitent and the pleasure of the sensual. . . . The conflict of opposites generates power, as fire and water create the force of steam.

And when the Poet asks: "But peace? Rest?" she gives no answer. There is no answer. The eternal conflict of man with the world, of the conflicting elements in his nature must go on, and there is no verbal formula or biotic that will settle the conflict, or quiet the ache. It is as usual Mr. Tynan's superficial misreading of the text of the play which makes him see in Strindberg another Claudel, vaporing about other worlds to be reached only by hysteria and self-laceration, and a contempt for the human condition. I dislike Claudel, but I dislike equally Mr. Tynan's assumption about the panacea of welfare sociology.

Mr. Tynan apparently believes that a purely sociological commitment will achieve a formula for living, and "pain, fear, and suffering" will be irrelevant to well adjusted citizens in a prosperous state. There will be no individual hankering in conflict with a world full of good mixers, none of the irrational desires or emotions to feel, to give, to understand, and to suffer reality which drove Socrates, Jesus, Beethoven, and all those squares. Well adjusted, rationalized, obedient to the norm imposed by the technical manager of the Establishment, whether of Right or Left, we should have no strange personal promptings but perform our tasks like puppets conditioned by sociological reflexes to a life that is a phantasmagoria which it would be unsocial to question. Viewed from such an aspect, the officer in *The Dream Play* who waits in every generation for the girl who, like Godot, never turns up, must seem completely ridiculous.

Like Brecht, Strindberg claimed the right of the artist to trace his own pattern in the carpet, and the pattern was no mere arabesque. And like Brecht describing the fall of Icarus in Breughel's painting, where the peasant bends over his earth unaware that even the fall of that man was a great triumph of human endeavor, so Strindberg celebrates the pain and the pleasure of human striving. The relationship of earth to heaven, of man to the gods, is for him not one of earthbound mortality divorced from divinity but aspiring to it. The play is Strindberg's most penetrating analysis of nineteenth-century society. But Mr. Tynan is troubled. Strindberg does not see social reform as the cure-all of human unhappiness and evil. The officer always staring at the mandala of the clover-leaf pattern is seeking some pattern in life, is always wondering what lies beyond the door. But for Mr. Tynan the remedy is social and within society. Apparently, the pain, fear, and suffering which Mr. Tynan says is our business to cure can be removed by social means— pain by biotics, fear by analysis, and suffering not by Ionesco but by UNESCO. On the other hand, Strindberg points out that it is the growing castle (skyscraper?) which absorbs all the energies of man and he implies that the kingdom of heaven on earth will come, the chrysanthemum will blossom in the stone, only when there is a change of heart, and men relinquish, as the people in his play relinquish, their egos which cause them, in Schopenhauer's analogy, to be so many branches strangling the main stem and therefore themselves. When Strindberg speaks of "the joy in pain and the pain of joy," he is not merely anticipating the pleasure-pain principle, the sado-masochistic duality, but the ever-present duality in man to be himself and yet to be more than himself. The Daughter says that what she has most suffered from on earth is the dimmed vision, the dulled hearing, the "luminous thought bound down in a labyrinth of fat. You have seen a brain. What twisting channels, what creeping ways." And she tells the Poet that his language can never express the thoughts of the gods. But he is, in Mr. Tynan's words, in the business of trying. And that is the emancipated purpose of society over and above what Willy Loman may want.

The eternal conflict between the desire to be fulfilled as an individual and the feeling of the inadequacy of individual fulfillment, of wanting to be more than oneself and finding it impossible to be more until you are first fully yourself, the aspiration of earth for heaven, and the recognition that there could be no such heavenly aspiration if there were no earth to aspire is behind Strindberg's social view in *The Dream Play*. Strindberg's philosophy is therefore not nihilistic but creative in the wider social sense of the transformation scenes in a Sean O'Casey view of the new Jerusalem, when the chrysanthemum flowers and the dead stones of a civilization are fertile, because man sees a relation of earth to heaven, because life has, not comfort, but meaning and direction outside the individual ego.

If then Mr. Tynan asks what other business is there than the view of society, I would answer none if society is viewed in this wider sense, plenty if his view of society is as narrow and doctrinaire and pink as it seems to be. Like Blake, Strindberg saw the purpose as the intensification and flowering of the life of the individual man, the development of the senses and the awareness of living and the overcoming of the merely cerebral and rational. It is this pain-pleasure principle which makes tragedy not, as Mr. Tynan believes, a delight in pain or *angst* for its own sake, but exhilarating and a sign of human creativity. It was not *angst* which made the Greeks take to tragedy. In fact, in *The Birth of Tragedy* Nietzsche asks this very question: Why was it that the Greeks, the least morbid, the most confident, vital, and happy of people should have been drawn to tragedy? Nietzsche's answer was that it was precisely their ebullient feeling that they could live forever, embrace all existences, encompass the universe, which made them almost will the friction of adversity as a drunken Irishman will take on the whole bar, drove them to impale the bursting breast upon the thorn, spurred them to the limits of their vitality until they were faced by those limits and what was beyond them. Tragedy, says Nietzsche, originated in this explosive force of life, the desire to wrestle with what might lie just beyond their strength or will or courage or human capacity. But as I have mentioned, Nietzsche pointed out that this Dionysian emotional urge of tragedy was, and inevitably would be, replaced by the Apollonian influence of the Socratic epic, the controlled intellectual scrutiny of life which we know as controlled by science and by Marx and, in the theatre, by Brecht. In a world where we are inclined to believe that everything can be understood if it is dissected, and the stars explained, once we can tread on them, is tragedy relevant or an emotional luxury signifying nothing? At this moment, in London, a modern tragedy, *Rosmersholm,* is drawing packed houses. What is the attraction or relevance of this bourgeois drama set more than fifty years ago? I am not for keeping Fate as a hooded figure. But just as philosophy ceases and science begins when speculation is confirmed by fact, only for philosophy to move on to the fresh mystery revealed by the new knowledge, so whatever is explained in the mysteries of human relationships thereby presents the fresh mystery revealed by our new viewpoint. The loom of Fate assumes new meaning when we see *Rosmersholm* because the complex of relationships in that play cannot be fixed or appraised in the superficial Freudian sense. The tightening of a stitch here loosens a stitch there in that intricate web of interweaving relationships. Each character constantly changes in his own eyes and changes in a different way in ours so that new aspects of a personality continually appear, to be newly appraised by him, by the other characters, by us, to enter new relationships based on the new valuations, which thereby are again changed and revalued. Like Strindberg, like Sophocles, like every great artist, Ibsen divined the ramifications of the subconscious before Freud as Freud himself admitted. Before denying categorically that Sophocles anticipated and guided Freud (as Ionesco and Mr. Harold Clurman have affirmed), Mr. Tynan should have read Volume 5, page 261 of Freud's *Collected Works,* in which he describes *Oedipus Rex* as "a legend whose profound and universal power to move can only be understood if the hypothesis I have put forward with regard to the psychology of children has an equally universal meaning." That is, Sophocles in writing that play gave a description of a situation which was subsequently confirmed by Freud and, moreover, in supplying that early case history, Sophocles invested it with poetry, with dignity, with full meaning and showed the beauty and purpose of the creative tension that might otherwise have been analyzed as a functional disturbance or a pathological perversion. That is the purpose of the artist as against the scientist who can, in the name of scientific detachment and neutrality, only watch from outside, and the sociologist who can only consider whether such relationships are socially useful. It is the case history of Sophocles which shows the real significance of the relationship to Freud clinically studying those fixated children. But Freud goes on:

> If *Oedipus Rex* moves a contemporary audience no less than it did a contemporary Greek one, the explanation can only be that its effect does not lie in the contrast between destiny and human will, but is to be looked for in the particular nature of the material in which that contrast is exemplified. There must be something which makes a voice within us ready to recognize the compelling force of destiny in *Oedipus* while we can dismiss as merely arbitrary such dispositions as are laid down in Grillparzer's *Die Ahnfrau* or direct modern tragedies of destiny. And a factor of this kind is in fact involved in the story of King Oedipus. His destiny moves us because it might have been ours,—because the oracle laid the same curse upon our birth as upon him. It is the fate of all of us, perhaps, to direct our first sexual impulse toward our mother and our first murderous wish toward our father. . . . While the poet, as he unravels the past, brings to light the guilt of Oedipus, he is at the same time compelling us to recognize our own inner minds in which those same strange impulses, though suppressed, are still to be found. . . . Like Oedipus, we live in ignorance of those wishes repugnant to morality, which have been forced upon us by Nature, and after this revelation we may all of us well seek to close our eyes to the scenes of our childhood. . . .
>
> (Vol. 4, p. 262)

> But just as all neurotic symptoms and, for that matter, dreams, are capable of being "over-interpreted," and indeed need to be, if they are to be fully understood, so all genuinely creative writings are the product of more than a single motive, and more than a single impulse in the poet's mind . . . and are open to more than one interpretation. In what I have written, I have only attempted to interpret the deepest level of impulse in the mind of the creative writer.
>
> (Vol. 5, pp. 265–66)

Freud says, as Ionesco says, that Sophocles in writing a play that was "true to its nature," whose meaning was irrational and inexplicable on the surface, nevertheless was conveying through his drama (Fergusson's analogy) a meaning that could be rationalized by the clinical scientist, and that this meaning was only one of many possible meanings implicit in the artist's complex and total response to experience which may afterwards be extricated and clinically analyzed by the psychiatrist, the Marxist, or whomever. Several meanings on several levels capable of several interpretations are possible in all creative art and in citing Grillparzer, Freud gives example of the sterility of the dramatists who write in terms of rationalized case book illustrations of his findings.

I have no wish to discount any such noble attempt as Miller's *A View From the Bridge,* in which an attempt is made to show the drama of psychological impasse and to show the grandeur of a situation in a slum tenement, that might be dignified into tragedy if it were sufficiently distanced in time and place. But the situation is all too clear: Ed Carbone's doomed love is a fixation to be cured, the personal tragedy is the result of social evil resulting from the suppression of immigration. It would be pointless to see the play again, although Miller is sympathetic to the strong asocial, amoral emotions of Ed who will not settle for half. The fixation of Oedipus is, however, but a symptom for something much deeper and more complex. If Sophocles had read his Freud, he might have rationalized it all down to the pathological disturbance of a mother-loving mixed-up kid possibly to be carved out of his brain by lobectomy or blasted out of consciousness by electric shock, with the result that what Sophocles saw as a creative tension might be destroyed in the interest of social conformity. But Sophocles as a poet irrationally, intuitively, without analysis, sensed the poetry and dignity of meaning behind that strange mix-up.

In a similar way, Strindberg and Ibsen anticipated Freud in their interpretations of the human complex and gave a meaning that was not only prior to, but different from, and better (because fuller, richer, with more levels of human significance) than the one-string Freudian fiddle could encompass. (I am not underrating Freud himself who as shown above, and in his comments on *Rosmersholm* reveals his artistic perception. I am only commenting on the limitations of psychoanalytical investigation, which he has himself admitted as quoted above.) When Mr. Tynan demands that every play be a statement, I agree. But what is a statement? A poem is a statement. So is a Beethoven quartet. The poetic statement is the full statement. Rationalism is a codification and the sociological approach as defined by Mr. Tynan is blinkered. Not only does the imaginative ability of the artist anticipate and fully state what is narrowly stated by the scientist, but it is a statement from within and not external and it is a living statement about the relationships with like experiences in other men and with the objective world.

Therefore, we must risk listening to eccentrics and madmen and even charlatans and we must use our judgment as to whether we are getting truth or falsity, Sophocles or Grillparzer, Bosch or bosh.

On the other hand, any statement about man must be relevant to the subjective man in his variable relationship with the objective world. One does not discount the quantitative rationalist approach when one points out that to count is not the same as to evaluate. Ibsen did make a statement but it was not a factual, fixed, once and for all, rational or sociological or liberal statement. I imagine that Brecht's rejection of Ibsen was partly motivated by Brecht's Brandian and Marxist "either-or" view of the objective world where the truth is simply the sum of the facts as against Ibsen's relativism. And I imagine that, if *Rosmersholm* had been the work of a new writer, Mr. Tynan would censure it by asking: Why should rationalism be sneered at? Why ridicule the free-thinking emancipated woman? What is all this morbid, nihilistic, socially unhealthy talk of joint suicide in the mill-race? And why rake up all that stuff about having a love affair with her father?

Yet I would rather have Mr. Tynan's excesses in the cause of a drama with content than the flabby theatre of sensibility and even, let me make myself clear, than the very limited field of subjectivity opened up by Ionesco. We do indeed want art to be in a wide sense a statement about the condition and predicament of man. But the dead end of rationalism is its very clarity. The remedy for the pathological victim in any of the American psychiatric dramas is: Get a doctor. The remedy for sociological suffering is: Change the society. But human nature is complex and it is in the light of human nature that sociology is evaluated. No society is bigger than the individual man and no society can be justified, however wealthy and efficient it is, if a man wakes up in the small hours and wonders in despair why he is living. In the biggest society, each of us is alone. The purpose of all human thought and feeling is to develop the relationship between man through society to the reality of his situation in the universe. In one sense, the universe is as big as the cosmos. In another sense, it is as small as the skull. But it is in that skull, in that flashing electrically charged life, that man comprehends multitudes and himself.

It is not the social play that I am attacking but the sociological approach which would limit and sap the vitality of the drama and the freedom of the playwright as observer and witness. Mr. Tynan writes of the need for abolishing from the drama "pain, fear, and sadness" as though he interpreted tragic drama as being pointlessly wretched. Let us by all means cure the pain of disease, the neurotic fear, the sadness which is only depression. But despite the sociological ostriches, the average-man goodtimers, who cannot bear very much reality, there is the pain, the fear, and the sadness which is the fulfillment of the adult who wants the full awareness of the beauty and sadness of life, its value and its fragility, its vitality and mortality, its greatness and the smallness, its dignity and absurdity, its scope and finiteness. In tragedy the defeat is vindicated by the endeavor which signifies one more gesture and one more advance of mind or body, of intellect or emotion, to the credit of the race though the individual fails. And above any narrow comfort for the average man, there is the greater prize achieved by man imposing meaning on the void.

In the quest for meaning rather than comfort, in the survey of society outside the sentimental doctrinaire limits, Strindberg, Ibsen, and Shaw are social in the ultimate sense of dealing with the relations of man with the world outside in nature and the world inside in his mind for which society is only the provisional intermediary. And in discussing whether, and to what degree, man should be committed to society, we have to discuss what society is to be committed to. If we have the merely Marxist and Brechtian line, we shall have men, in the words of Don Juan in *Man and Superman*, "not social, only gregarious." But the free artists like Strindberg, Ibsen, and Shaw see the shifting dialectical relationship of man and society in the light of the increasing knowledge of the world in nature and the world in man's mind, interdependent, inseparable, and, perhaps, identical. To hell, then, with society that man may be fully social.

Lorca and the Poetry
of Death

BY PEDRO SALINAS

THE READER NO SOONER BEGINS to pry into the poetic world fashioned by Lorca in his lyric poetry, ballads and plays, than he feels himself being immersed in a strange atmosphere. It is an apparently normal setting of popular scenes and people, all perfectly recognizable. But the air is, so to speak, inhabited by forebodings and threats. Metaphors cut across it like birds of ill omen. So, for example, summer "sows rumours of tiger and flame." Day breaks in a most peculiar manner like a shadowy fish: "Great stars of white frost—come with the fish of shadow —that opens the road of dawn." The wind is an enormous man pursuing the maiden "with red-hot sword." These metaphors do not have a decorative function; they are an extension of meaning. They herald what is unusual and mysterious in this world. They proclaim that something is being prepared; they proclaim an imminence of fatality. For the poetic kingdom of Lorca, so brilliantly illuminated and at the same time so enigmatic, is under the rule of a unique, unchallenged power: Death.

Death lurks behind the most normal of actions, and in places where it is least expected. In one poem Lorca says, referring to a tavern: "Death comes in and goes out—and death goes out and comes in." The poet repeats the same simple idea, merely inverting the word-order, as if to point out the fatality of this act, the inevitability of Death's continually coming in and going out—over and over again—not in the concrete place of the tavern, but in the life of man and the work of the poet. The destination of nearly all the characters that Lorca creates, whether in his ballads or in his dramas, is death. Lorca creates them

273

to set them on a road whose only possible end is in dying. In a poem of his youth entitled "Another Dream" he wrote: "How many children has death?—They are all in my breast." Yes, that is where they are, and, as his work grows, those children of death gradually swarm from his breast, transformed into poetic offspring.

In the famous "Sleepwalkers Ballad" two lovers, a horseman and the gypsy girl of the green flesh and green hat who awaits him, look forward with desire to a lover's meeting; she is in her house. But the strange creature and her lover will never meet. For when he finally reaches the house, his breast has been torn open by a wound that will kill him: and the gypsy girl, killed by too much waiting, floats upon the water, borne up by the reflection of the moon. They have not come together in love, but they have in death.

The same end that befalls individuals also lies in waiting for large groups of human beings, for cities. Lorca invents in his magnificent "Ballad of the Civil Guard" a wonderful gypsy city. It is the city of joy, with cinnamon turrets, with lamps and flags bedecking the flat roofs. The poet calls it the festive city. But neither shall it escape the common destiny. The Civil Guards arrive, symbolizing the forces of destruction; they stab women and children, they knock down the cinnamon turrets, and, when dawn breaks, everything is razed to the ground. In this way a city invented by the poet in his imagination comes to an end. But when, years later, Lorca came to New York, in this city, real as it is, in this ceaseless bustle, in this accumulation of different peoples and activities, the poet senses too the terrible destiny of death. The great city bears death within itself. Beneath the quantities, beneath the quantitative weakness, there is blood: "Under the multiplication—there is a drop of duck's blood." And this city of steel and cement, solid as it is, will be destroyed by grief, will die, just like that other one with its cinnamon turrets.

After his phase as a lyric poet Lorca focusses his attention on the theatre. In his dramatic works we shall find the same themes of death, repeated time and again. If he chooses an historical character for his first important drama it can be no other than Mariana Pineda, the figure of a girl who, for embroidering the Republican flag, dies on the gallows.

His three rural tragedies, *Blood Wedding*, *Yerma*, *The House of Bernarda Alba*, tie up and twist the strands of a few people's passions so tightly that only the "tiny knife, the tiny golden knife," sometimes real, sometimes symbolical, can probe the center of the tangle, the center of the conflict. Whom is the bride in *Blood Wedding* destined for? For the bridegroom or for Leonardo, the other man who attracts her with irresistible fascination? The Bride decides in favor of the latter, elopes with him. But who is she, to make the decision? It is Death, disguised as an old beggarwoman, who must decide everything. She brings the two men face to face, makes them fight and die; it is death that carries off all sweethearts. Mortal too is the *dénouement* of *Yerma*. Yerma kills, not only her husband, but in him all her potential children, since she will never belong to any other man.

In *The House of Bernarda Alba* the problem of *Blood Wedding* crops up again. Pepe el Romano, typifying man, the male secretly coveted in the tormented souls of those women, will not give his love to any of the sisters: neither to the one chosen to be his legal spouse, nor to the one who offers to be his mistress in a rapture of passion, and who, seeking to quench her thirst for life in the embrace of a man, falls into the arms of one who is concealed behind him, death.

A poet's work is not a philosophic system; it is not a philosophy, consciously worked out, and conveyed as such in a discursive form. But in the work of no great poet can one fail to find a conception of man and life, just as in paper one finds a watermark, almost invisible, denoting its distinction, individualizing it. All great poets have, one way or another, tried to decipher some secret of the world. Poetry is always a reply to the eternal interrogation addressed to man by the things that surround him. "Here I am," the world, with apparent simplicity, says to the poet. But underneath its simple affirmation of being, the question pulses. "What am I for you?" That is why a poet, up to the moment when *he* is asking the questions, really is replying to what life, in a hushed voice, confidentially asks him about—questions that he alone understands. He is a witness who, in the trial to which the world is eternally brought, gives evidence in its defense or in its prosecution.

The vision of life and man that gleams and shines forth in Lorca's work is founded on death. Lorca understands, feels life through death. This idea may seem paradoxical, but only superficially and at first sight. For in reality the religious and moral tradition of the centuries has offered man as his best guide in life meditation on death. Death is the mentor of life, its teacher. But the nineteenth century has prepared that attitude of thought usually called the cult of life, which entails the regarding of death as a kind of adversary and opponent of life.

Mechanization and vitalism lead to "an estimation of death as some-thing that should be essentially *repressed.*" Existence is exalted as the mere duration of human life, and man is urged to fill it with his satisfaction, enjoyments, and acquisitions, without thinking of the dimension of mortality. Ever since Pasteur, man's existence has been defended by ever-improving means. People surround themselves with comfort and precautions, merely in defence of their material being. The formula "Safety First" has become almost sacred. A kind of conspira-torial silence has been created around the mortal destiny of man. Cemeteries look for new euphemisms and circumlocutions so that they may be called by some other name, for example, Memorial Parks. But, despite all this, one detail of utmost importance proves that men are keeping the vision of death in the bottom of their hearts. However much they pride themselves on keeping it out of mind, on pigeon-holing it in oblivion, the institution of life insurance is spreading throughout the world.

If the value of death was disparaged in the twentieth century, there is no denying that the latest trends of contemporary thought—art, philosophy, poetry, painting—offer evidence of its revaluation. The Pontiff of existentialism, Martin Heidegger, has coined his definitive expression on man's life: "existence for death." Death is an inseparable element of existence. Another German philosopher of our time, Georg Simmel, speaks of "life's needing death inside" and he says that life would not have, without it, either its specific meaning or its specific form. Applying the idea to Shakespeare's characters, he sees their deaths, not as fatal accidents, but as what he calls life's coming-of-age: "The coming-of-age of their destiny, insofar as their destiny expresses their lives, is in itself the coming-of-age of their deaths."

A great modern poet, well known in America, Rainer Maria Rilke, is the best possible example of this tendency converted into poetic experience. His is the distinction between small death and great death; personal death, that proper to an individual, and the death of others, impersonalized and common to all. Hence his famous prayer: "O Lord, grant to each man his own death—a death that proceeds from his life. . . . The great death that each one has inside him—is the fruit around which all revolves." Death is not a misfortune that assails us from without; it is the companion of our life; with it, it develops inside us and grows as we grow. To deny death would be to deny an indis-pensable condition of our life, one which slowly models it, setting it on the path to its final fulfillment. I would suggest that the English word *achievement* denotes perfectly this dual meaning of death: to achieve is to finish, to put an end to something, as dying puts an end to material life; but to *achieve* in English is likewise to fulfill, to complete, to realize.

It should not be thought that I am comparing Rilke with Lorca. They are extremely different poets. What I am pointing out is the coincidence of both seeking in death the center of gravity of their conception of the world and life. But the poet from Prague expresses his obsession with mortality in meditative accents, tinted with hues of melancholy tenderness; Lorca, in violently dramatic shouts and cries, in metaphors flashing with dazzling colors. As an example, one might take the different way they have of rendering objectively an identical thought: the death that lives within us, that we bear inside us. Rilke speaks of a girl's death, and says: "Your death was already old—when your life began." And Lorca, pretending that he has been asked: "What do you feel in your mouth—red and thirsty?" answers "The taste of bones—of my great skull." In the German poet, a concept, expressed by the logical contraposition of the youth of life and the old age of death inside a human being; in the Spaniard, metaphors charged with impressive sensuality, in dramatic contrast, a red mouth and the bones of a skull.

For me the difference between the two poets is to be found in the different origin of each one's obsession with the thought of death. In one case, Rilke is slowly evolving in his poetic conscience, through inner experiences that he analyzes, contemplates, and explores, a sort of *Thanatodicea*, or doctrine of death; he can be seen locked up in his solitude like an alchemist in his cave, distilling feelings, refining visions, in his search for the meaning of death. But Lorca, who expresses the same feeling for death with an undoubted originality and personal accent, has not had to search for it through processes of intellectual speculation along the innermost galleries of the soul. He discovers it all around him, in the native air that gives him breath, in the singing of the servants in his house, in books written in his tongue, in the churches of his city; he finds it in all of his individual personality that has to do with people, with the inheritance of the past. Lorca was born in a country that for centuries has been living out a special kind of culture that I call the "culture of death."

Recognition of the importance of death in the life of Spaniards is a commonplace in many books on travel and the psychology of peoples. We have selected by way of illustration an English writer, Havelock Ellis, who speaks of "the deliberate insistence on the thought of death so congenial to the ethical temper of this people." No superficial or extreme interpretation should be given to this thought of death: it should by no means be regarded as a *Thanatophilia*, or cult of death. Nor should it be construed as indifference to life, or as a denial of life; just the reverse, as Rilke says, since in giving us an awareness of death, it sharpens, intensifies our awareness of life.

What I understand by the "culture of death" is a conception of man and his earthly existence, in which the awareness of death functions with a positive sign; it is a stimulus, and not a hindrance, to living and acting, and it makes possible an understanding of the full and total meaning of life. Within this conception a human being may affirm himself, not only in the acts of life, but in the very act of death. An existence in which the idea of death is hidden or suppressed is like the representation of action on a movie screen, flat, inapprehensible, and lacking in something essential; it is lacking in the dimension of depth, in the dimension that gives life its tone of intensity and drama. Man can only understand himself, can only be entire, by integrating death into his life; and every attempt to expel death, to take no account of it, in order to live, is a falsification, a fraud perpetrated by man on himself.

Few indeed are the great Spanish writers in whom this fraternal relation of life and death is not confirmed. I select as a very typical example, Quevedo. Quevedo did not reject any of the temptations presented to him by this life. On the contrary, his vital experiences reach out to all phases of existence: he advises great lords in palaces, he enjoys the favour of the king, he is a politician and a powerful minister, he pulls strings of intrigue in Italy, he knows at close quarters the common people, the riff-raff, the underdog; he is an accomplished humanist, and writes both Latin and the slang (or *germanía*) of the underworld with equal ease. Prone to fall in love, a great dueller, a practising eroticist, a translator both of Anacreon, the poet of sensuality, and of Seneca, the stoic philosopher; no one can fail to see in Quevedo a burning love of life. Now this man is to be seen ever accompanied by the thought of death. "You begin at one and the same time to be born and to die," he writes on one occasion; and on another "You were born to die, and you spend your life dying." The hours are spades, he will write in another sonnet, that "dig up my monument out of my life." That is to say, it is out of the very earth of life that the monument, the memorial stone, of death is fashioned.

The Spanish public who attended the performances of morality plays saw in them, before their eyes, the figure of Death, represented in brilliant allegorical costume, going, coming, speaking (amidst the other powers of the world). About the same time a character is created —Don Juan, who has come to be universally famous as the hero of life and love. But really, in the intention of his creator and dramatist Tirso de Molina, he is the hero of death. Every year, on the First of November, the drama of the romantic poet Zorrilla, *Don Juan Tenorio,* is put on in most of the theatres of Spain. What the public witnesses year after year, entranced by it as if it were something new, is a drama that first presents man as a hero of untrammeled life, of feats of love piling up on top of one another; but later, in the final apotheosis, it witnesses, in a spectacular, musical, macabre staging, the death of the seducer. A death that leads to his salvation, despite his many sins. The public admires the hero, and enjoys the play, in the scene of his death as well as in those of his life. They feel that Don Juan knows how to die.

This conception is just as discernible in the arts: architecture, sculpture, painting. The most Spanish of architectural monuments, the monastery of the Escorial, includes a royal residence and the royal mausoleum for the Kings of Spain. It has been called "the Palace of Death." In that monastery is a picture by El Greco, which more, perhaps, than any other work of art exemplifies the "culture of death." It is his *Saint Maurice.* According to the legend, Maurice, the leader of the Theban legion, opposed the Emperor's orders to be converted to paganism; and with all his comrades he suffered decapitation for the sake of his religious belief. The theme is portrayed in a surprising way: the actual scene of the sacrifice, of the decapitation, is relegated to the background of the picture, and is painted in modest proportions. The focus of attention in the foreground is given to four knights in armour, who are talking, or rather listening, to Maurice, who, by the expression on his face and by his attitude, is seen to be persuading them to let themselves be killed, is urging them to die. None of the faces reveals any anxiety or fear; gravely, seriously, these people are making a decision, of their own free will and pleasure, to die. Saint Maurice is so firm, so upright in figure and bearing, simply because he is affirming himself in death, with all the fullness of his being. He represents to perfection that dying of one's own death, the great death, as Rilke says.

Velázquez does not paint many religious pictures; but the best of them has as its subject Christ in his death agony, Christ crucified. The portrayal of a dying man? No; as Christian doctrine tells us, the portrayal of eternal life, which is fulfilled in a willingness to die. This death is life's triumph.

We could not speak of a "culture of death" as proper to the Spanish people, if we did not find it not only in the creations of learned art, but also rooted in the most expressive declarations of the popular spirit. It can be seen quite clearly in the popular songs, those transmitted by oral tradition. But I propose to observe it in the fiestas. In the spring two fiestas are celebrated in Seville: Holy Week and the Fair. The first is a religious festival of extraordinary pomp and beauty. The images of the saints that are kept in the churches go forth into the city in processions, carried on litters, and at a slow pace they pass through the streets, where they are admired by a large crowd. And one of those images, one of those splendid seventeenth century wood carvings, is of Christ on the cross. It is impressive to see, over the heads of the people, the naked body of the dying Christ, proceeding step by step, in the night. Anyone who might regard this spectacle as indelicate morbidity, as pleasure taken in the funeral symbol of a dying body, would be wrong. No; as far as the people are concerned, in the death of that God-man, everlasting life is actually being achieved.

When the religious festivals of Holy Week end, the Fair starts in Seville. Its most talked-about attraction is the bullfights. Is fighting bulls a game? Many deny it these qualities—and with some reason. But undoubtedly in it is something of a representation and a mystery. And what it at once conceals and represents is in my view the popular reaction to this "culture of death." To all who attend a bullfight the ring looks like a pageant of magnificent joy and brilliance. Everything rises up to a joyous vitality; to a pulsation of unrestrained happiness. The passes of the toreadors, with their gracefulness, have a suggestion of the dance in them. But soon a hint of mystery begins to appear; blood, the twofold sign of life and death. And the spectators feel, whether they are aware of it or not, that when the bullfighter moves close up to the animal, when the two of them, alone, are engaged in a phase of the fight, another, a third invisible presence is compelling them to look at that game with tremendous emotional tension: it is the presence of death. The bullfighter achieves himself, reaches the full meaning of his existence, so different from that of other men, precisely by revealing to all eyes—even though they may not see it physically—the presence and the Danger of Death. In his performance the people feel the twofold existence of man, the constant possibility for him of living and of dying, concentrated dramatically into a single instant. Only a people having in the depths of its spirit that "culture of death," can find a meaning in such a strange fiesta.

Perhaps that is why Lorca attained one of the peaks of his poetry in the "Lament for the Death of a Bullfighter." The most modern art of surrealist imagery and the most ancient popular tradition of the "culture of death" converge in the poem. So the poet sees the bullfighter, going out of life, as if walking up the stands of the ring "with all his death upon his shoulders."

It is the bullfighter, man, who carries death, just the opposite of the old macabre conception in which Death carries off, kidnaps, man; an example of *personal death,* of *great* death, as Rilke said. A symbol of that conception of living in which the human being advances through time, always the bearer of his death.

Lorca is a modern poet: his sensibility responds to all the tensions of contemporary ways of life; his language illuminates the paths of poetry with a new brilliance. But to me, and this is the point I have tried to emphasize, he cannot be understood in his entirety unless we see him set in that tradition of the "culture of death" that he inherited from great artists of his native land, and that he has passed on to us, made richer with the proud gift of his poetic work.

The Making of a
Dramatist (Shaw: 1892-1903)

BY ERIC BENTLEY

IT WAS CLEAR FROM THE start that Bernard Shaw was a man of ideas. Later it turned out that he was a fabulous entertainer. But few have granted that the two Shaws were one. The old tendency was to allow that he was a publicist, a critic, an essayist, even a philosopher but to add: "not of course a dramatist." The later tendency was to concede that he was a great showman but to discount his thoughtful side. As Egon Friedell said, you could suck the theatrical sugar from the pill of propaganda, and put the pill itself back on the plate.

Neither in the old days, then, nor in the later ones was Shaw considered a dramatist, for even the later generations have only thought him a master of the theatrical occasion, a man with a theatrical line of talk and a theatrical bag of tricks, a highly histrionic jokester—a comedian, certainly, but hardly a writer of serious comedy. The fact is that the shock of that long career in the theatre has still not been absorbed. Shaw has not yet been seen in perspective.

In these circumstances it is interesting to go back and look at what happened in the eighteen nineties. In 1891 Bernard Shaw had still not written a play, though he was 35 years old. A dozen years later, though he could describe himself as "an unperformed playwright in London," he had written *Widowers' Houses* (1892), *The Philanderer* (1893), *Mrs. Warren's Profession* (1893-4), *Arms and the Man* (1894), *Candida* (1894-5), *The Man of Destiny* (1895), *You Never Can Tell* (1895-6), *The Devil's Disciple* (1896-7), *Caesar and Cleopatra* (1898), *Captain Brassbound's Conversion* (1899), *The Admirable Bashville* (1901), and *Man and Superman* (1901-3).

Let us take for granted that these plays are full of ideas and jokes and ask if they do not also meet the demands of dramatic criticism as such. The drama, everyone agrees, presents character in action. Human actions become "an action" in the drama when they are arranged effectively—when, that is, they are given what we can recognize as a proper and praiseworthy structure. Of character dramatic critics have required many different things. One of them is emotional substance.

Let us ask, then, how Shaw, when he set about playwriting, tackled the problem of structure; and let us ask if he gave his characters' existence the requisite emotional substance.

How did Shaw put a play together? To think of questions about Shaw is to think also of the answers he invariably provided to them. In this case, he said: "I avoid plots like the plague . . . My procedure is to imagine characters and let them rip. . . ." The quotation is from his *Table Talk* but (again: as usual) he said the same thing on many other occasions. One always has to ask not what he means (which may be clear) but what he is getting at. All Shaw's critical prose is polemical, as he freely admitted, and his writing on the theatre is devoted to the destruction of some kinds of drama and their replacement by some others (or one other). Here the enemy is the kind of play which had been dominant throughout the latter half of the nineteenth century— "the well-made play" as perfected by Eugène Scribe. In this dramaturgy the Aristotelian doctrine of the primacy of plot had been driven to an improper extreme. The plot was now, not *primus inter pares*, but all that mattered. It lost its originally organic relation to character and theme. So it became anathema to the apostles of the New Drama at the century's close. As late as 1946, when Allardyce Nicoll declared that Shaw was himself influenced by the well-made play, the old playwright went into print to deny it.

If the well-made play is defined as having no serious content, if it is defined by the relation (or lack of relation) of its plot to character and theme, then obviously Shaw did not write well-made plays. Yet Professor Nicoll had a point, and a strong one, which was that, for all the disclaimers, Shaw's plays did have plots and, furthermore, that these plots tended to be old acquaintances for those who knew their well-made play. Actually, the playwright had no need to be scandalized, for no dramatist had been more influenced by the well-made play than his own idol of those days, Henrik Ibsen. The Norwegian had begun his theatrical career by directing a large number of these plays; he made an exact imitation of them in his own *Lady Inger of Ostraat;* and he continued to the end to use many of their characteristic devices. Hence it would have been quite possible for a writer in 1890 to denounce Scribe and Sardou and simultaneously to steal their bag of tricks—from Ibsen. It is doubtful, though, if Bernard Shaw needed to deceive himself in this way. It seems more likely that he took the main situation in *Arms and the Man* from one of Scribe's most successful plays, *Bataille de Dames.*

A situation is not, of course, a plot, and the plot of *Arms and the Man* is not simply lifted from Scribe, even though parts of it may have been. Plagiarism is not the point. The point is that even when Shaw's story diverges from Scribe it remains Scribean. The play *Arms and the Man* is hung, as it were, on the cunningly told tale of the lost coat with the photograph in its pocket. The reader need only go through the text and mark the hints, incidents, accidents, and contretemps of this tale and he will be finding the layout, the plan—yes, the plot—of this play. Or at any rate the plot of what could have been a first draft of the play. Shaw, one gathers, did not write such first drafts but, supposing he had, what would be the difference between the first draft and the final one? In the answer to this question lies the secret of Shavian dramaturgy.

A corollary of the view that "plot is all" is this proposition: the cause of any incident is another incident. It is known that Scribe used to chart out a configuration of incidents and then write his play. This is to go far beyond Aristotle. It is to set no store at all by human initiative and assign to events themselves a kind of fatality: they are a network in which mankind is caught. Granted that the conception might in certain hands have its awesomeness, in Scribe's hands it had only triviality, because he manipulated the events till the issue was a pleasant one. It is curious how often that manipulation had to be arbitrary and drastic. Do events, when given their head, rush downward to disaster? To guarantee a happy ending, the well-making playwrights often needed their emergency weapon: sheer accident. Hence the Shavian complaint that well-made plays were badly made after all.

Hence also Bernard Shaw's first drama, which is an adaptation of an adaptation of a well-made play. The subject is one that Scribe and the younger Dumas brought to the nineteenth-century theatre: marrying, or refusing to marry, money. The immediate source is an unfinished play of William Archer's, *Rhinegold*. Archer's source is *La Ceinture dorée*

by Emile Augier. When a young man discovers that his young lady's inherited money was acquired by her father in an immoral way, what does
he do? William Archer's answer was: he pitches it into the Rhine. One
presumes that Archer's action would have been set on a convenient
balcony beside that river. Augier's hero is not so privileged. To preserve his honor, he would simply have to forego the pleasure of marrying the lady, if the author did not provide him and the play with an
opportune accident (or money *ex machina*). The whole French economy has to meet with a crisis (war breaks out) so that our heroine's
father may be reduced to poverty: it is now honorable for our hero to
propose to our heroine. In the well-made play one incident leads to
another with a logic that is inescapable—except when the author decides
to escape it. Perhaps Shaw's objection was less to the inescapability
than to the egregious, last-minute escapes.

His first play, *Widower's Houses,* may not be great art but it is a
great reversal of custom. Shaw's key decision was to refuse to accept
Augier's ending, to refuse to have accident (masquerading as fate or
otherwise) intervene. Such a refusal leads a man—leads a born playwright at least—back and back into the earlier stages of a story and he
ends up writing an utterly different play—an utterly different *kind* of
play.

Not one but two conceptions of Augier's were being rejected: not
just the solution-by-sheer-accident (which condemns a play to meaninglessness) but also the autonomy-of-incidents—something, by the way,
which was no part of Augier's conscious philosophy but was imposed
on him by the Scribean design. Dramatists are committed to the doctrine of free will. They can say they don't believe in it: but they have
to write their plays as if they did. (In this they resemble human beings
in general, for your most ardent determinist acts on the assumption
that determinism is false.) People in plays have got to be able to make
decisions, and these decisions have got to be both real and influential:
they have to affect events. I see no reason to object to Aristotle's declaration that plot is the soul of the drama, but Aristotle would have ob-
jected to Scribe's attempt to cut the soul off from the body—that is,
from character.

What *does* a young man do when he finds that his bride's dowry
comes from a tainted source? There are two ways for a writer to arrive
at an answer. He can say: "I can think of several answers—on the basis
of several different possibilities of 'theatre.' Answer A will give you Big

Scene X; answer B will give you Ending Y; and so on." Or he can say: "I cannot give you any answer at all until the terms of the proposition are defined, including the term 'tainted.' Above all I need to know who these people are—what bride? what young man?" The first way to arrive at an answer would commonly be thought the playwright's way: the reasoning is "craftsmanlike" and "of the theatre" and would earn a man commendation on Broadway today. The second way is only the human way. That makes it the way of the real dramatist and so of Bernard Shaw.

It could be said that we have this perfectly functioning machine of the well-made play and that a Bernard Shaw is throwing a monkey-wrench into it—the monkey-wrench of character. That is how it must seem from the Scribean viewpoint. From the viewpoint of dramatic art, however, one would say that this particular engine had been revolving all too fast and uselessly: only when a Shaw slips in the clutch can the gear engage and the vehicle prove itself a vehicle by moving.

"My procedure is to imagine characters and let them rip. . . ." The pertinence of this remark may by now be clearer: if the young man has been "imagined," the dramatist can find the decision he would make as to the young lady's money. But at this point we realize that Shaw's words leave out of account the fact that the situation confronting the young man had been established in advance of the imagining of his character. It had been established by Augier and Archer and by Shaw's own decision to use their work. Hence, Shaw's own interpretation is both helpful and misleading—or, perhaps, is helpful only if those who are helped do a lot of work on their own.

Shaw put *Widowers' Houses* together—how? He took from certain predecessors not only a situation but a story, and not only a story but that clever, orderly, and theatrical arrangement of a story which we call a plot. Then he changed the plot—or, as he would have said, let the characters change it for him. Now had he retained Augier's characters they could only have caused him to break off the action one scene earlier than Augier did: instead of the happy ending created by a national emergency, we would get the unhappy ending which the emergency reversed.

Characters in a well-made play are "conventional"—that is, they behave, not according to laws of psychology, but according to the expectations of an audience in a theatre. A type of drama in which the plot is given a free hand cannot afford any less passive or more obtrusive

Arms and the Man with an eye to technique would be to conclude that what we have here is Scribe most subtly interwoven with Shaw. Yet this formulation is inadequate, for who did the interweaving? There was a Scribe in Shaw, and there was a counter-Scribe in Shaw: what makes his works dramatic is the interaction of the two.

The passion and preoccupation of Scribe was the idea of climax: to the Big Scene at the end—or, rather, a little before the end—all his arts are dedicated. In Bernard Shaw there was almost as great a predilection for anti-climax. It is the Shavian "effect" par excellence; no other playwright has come near finding so many possibilities in it. The bit I have quoted from Bluntschli and Raina is an apt example. *Arms and the Man* contains a corresponding scene between Sergius and Louka. Where, in a well-made play, Bluntschli and Louka would have to soar to the heights of Raina and Sergius, in the Shaw play Raina and Sergius drop with a bump to the level of Bluntschli and Louka. Such is resolution by anti-climax. It is dramaturgically effective, and it enforces the author's theme. But this is not all of Shaw: it is only the counter-Scribe. The dual anti-climaxes do not round off *Arms and the Man*. What does? Not the disenchantment of Raina and Sergius but the discovery that Bluntschli the realist is actually an enchanted soul whom nothing will disenchant. He has destroyed their romanticism but is himself "incurably romantic." This is another point that is made in "mere words"—"mere words stuck on at the end," if you wish—and yet stuck on very well, for they are firmly attached to that little tale of the coat and the photograph which gives the work its continuity and shape:

> BLUNTSCHLI.—yes: that's the coat I mean. . . . Do you suppose I am the sort of fellow a young girl falls in love with? Why, look at our ages! I'm thirty four: I don't suppose the young lady is much over seventeen . . . All that adventure which was life or death to me was only a schoolgirl's game to her . . . Would a woman who took the affair seriously have sent me this and written on it: Raina, to her Chocolate Cream Soldier, a Souvenir?
>
> PETKOFF. That's what I was looking for. How the deuce did it get there?
> BLUNTSCHLI. I have put everything right, I hope, gracious young lady.
> RAINA. I quite agree with your account of yourself. You are a romantic idiot. Next time I hope you will know the difference between a schoolgirl of seventeen and a woman of twenty three.

In this scene, plot and theme reach completion together, and the play of thesis and antithesis ends in synthesis.

The supreme triumph of Shaw's dramaturgical dialectics is to be found in *Man and Superman*, and, for all the blarney in the preface about the medieval *Everyman* and the eighteenth-century *Don Giovanni*, the method is the conversion of old materials into nineteenth-century terms, both thematic and technical. Shaw's claim to be returning to a pristine Don Juan is valid to the extent that the theme had originally been less of psychological than of philosophical, indeed theological, interest. It is also true that Don Juan had run away from his women. However, he had run away from them only after possessing them. In Shaw's play, he runs away to prevent *them* from possessing *him*. It is a comic parody of the old motif, embodying Shaw's standard new motif: the courting of the man by the woman. And where the old dramatists and librettists had used the old, "open" type of plot (or non-plot), Shaw substitutes an utterly Scribean "closed" structure.

This very "modern" and "twentieth-century" play is made up of narrative materials familiar to every Victorian theatre-goer. We have a hero who spends the entire evening hotly pursued by his foes; a clandestine marriage celebrated in defiance of a hostile father; a lovelorn hero who sacrifices himself so that the girl will go to his rival; a villain whose function is to constitute for a while the barrier to denouement and happy ending. The sub-plot about the Malone family rests upon two separate uses of the secret skillfully withheld, then skillfully released. Traditional farcical coincidence binds together Straker and Mendoza . . . The play bears every sign of careful workmanship—all of it School of Scribe.

But, as with *Arms and the Man*, as soon as we examine particulars, we find, interwoven with the Scribean elements, those typically Shavian verbal exchanges which constitute further action. Violet's marriage could have been made a secret of in any Scribe play, and Scribe could have been relied on to choose an effective moment for the release of the secret. In Shaw, what creates both the fun and the point of the news release is not the organization of the incidents but their relation to theme:

> TANNER. I know, and the whole world really knows, though it dare not say so, that you were right to follow your instinct; that vitality and bravery are the greatest qualities a woman can have, and motherhood her solemn initiation into womanhood; and that the fact of your not being legally married matters not one scrap either to your own worth or to our real regard for you.

VIOLET (*flushing with indignation*). Oh! You think me a wicked woman
  like the rest . . . I won't bear such a horrible insult as to be compli-
  mented by Jack on being one of the wretches of whom he approves.
  I have kept my marriage a secret for my husband's sake.

An incident which Tanner wishes to use to illustrate his "modern"
philosophy thus comes to illustrate a contrasting thesis: that Violet lives
by a non-modern philosophy.

Simple? Yes, but closely linked to a point that is unsimple enough to
have generally been missed: Tanner is a windbag. Indeed, the mere
fact of the woman courting the man would probably not yield comedy
at all, were it not for a further and more dynamic reversal: the woman,
who makes no great claims for herself, has all the shrewdness, the real
Lebensweisheit, while the man who knows everything and can discourse
like Bernard Shaw is—a fool. Tanner is, in fact, like Molière's Alceste,
the traditional fool of comedy in highly sophisticated intellectual disguise. Ann Whitefield, into whose trap Tanner falls, is the knave—in
skirts.

While Don Juan Tenorio is Superman—or is on the road to him—
John Tanner, M.I.R.C., is merely Man, and as such belongs to The
World As It Is. Of dramaturgical interest is that the kind of plot Shaw
evidently considers capable of giving an image of The World As It Is
should be the kind that is generally considered (by himself, for instance)
artificial, unreal, arbitrary, inane. Shaw the critic championed the new
Naturalism, and among French dramatists especially favored Brieux,
who produced dully literal theatrical documentaries. Yet when Shaw
wrote an essay entitled "A Dramatic Realist to his Critics," the example
of "realism" he gave from his own work was *Arms and the Man*—on
the grounds that the characters respond naturally even if the situations
aren't natural. We are entitled, then, to insist on his choice of "unnatural" situations. He must intuitively have understood something
which, as a critic, he failed to grasp: that plot does not merely reproduce external reality. The violence and intrigue in Shakespeare,
which Shaw the critic declared extraneous, provides the objective correlative of Shakespeare's feelings about life, and "idiocies" of the plot
of *Man and Superman* provide an objective correlative for Shaw's sense
of modern life. The very fact that Shaw despised Scribe helps to explain
the particular use he made of him.

The Don Juan episode in Act Three is neither a well-made play, nor
a portion of a well-made play. It stands apart as something appropri-

ately more austere and august. It is not a traditional work of any kind, not even a Platonic dialogue, the relation between Socrates and his interlocutors being quite different. Nor is it a debate, for two of the speakers, the Commander and Ann, hardly present arguments at all: they simply represent a point of view. Do even the Devil and Don Juan *discuss* anything? A devil is scarcely a being one can convert to a Cause, and if the Don is busy convincing anyone it is himself. Certainly it is the philosophy of Bernard Shaw that he is given to speak, but is persuasion exercised—even on the audience? Rather, the contributions of the four presences come together as a vision of life—and an intimation of super-life.

Man—and superman. The comedy of John Tanner—and the vision of Don Juan Tenorio. Shaw—and counter-Shaw. Thesis and antithesis are, to be sure, of separate interest, and yet, as usual, the great Shavian achievement is to have related one to the other. Tanner seems a wise man and proves a fool. Don Juan passes for a philanderer but proves an explorer and a missionary of the truth. In our trivial, tawdry, clever, Scribean world, intellect is futile and ever at the mercy of instinct. Take away the episode in hell, and Shaw has written an anti-intellectual comedy. The episode assigns to intellect the highest role. No longer, therefore, is Ann the center and source of things—only a possible mother for superman. Here Don Juan dominates. Here (or rather in heaven) intellect is at home, and the Don is cured of that occupational disease of Shavian heroes—homelessness. He "comes to a good end"—only it is not an end, it is an episode, and from these celestial-infernal heights we must descend to earth with the shock of Shavian anti-climax, to earth and to Tanner, from Superman back to Man. One section of the play gets an electric charge from the other.

Of Shaw's "playmaking" one must conclude that he knew how to put together a Scribean plot; that he knew how to subordinate such a plot to his own purposes; and that, in *Man and Superman*, he knew how to take the resultant Shavian comedy and combine it dynamically with a disquisition on (and by) Don Juan.

Emotional Substance

If Shaw's plays are, or begin by being, a parody of the more conventional drama of his time, that parody is by no means confined to the form. We have already seen that the themes, too, tend to get turned around: these compositions not only do the opposite, as it were, but say the opposite.

What of the emotions? Whatever the ultimate purpose of drama, its immediate impact is a strongly emotional one, and one cannot conceive of a story having an emotional effect upon an audience unless it is an emotional story and has a certain emotional structure. I may be forgiven for stating so rudimentary a principle because the Shavian drama presents us with a paradox: it has flooded a thousand theatres with emotion and yet has often been held to be emotionless.

Of course, this common opinion is absurd, bolstered though it can be with remarks of Shaw's own about being a mere "work machine" and the like. What we confront here is originality. Shaw may not have been an original thinker: he tried, rather, to make a synthesis of what certain others had thought. But he was an original person. What fitted him so well for the role of the enemy of convention was that his natural responses were not those of other people but all his own. His emotional constitution was a peculiar one, and that peculiarity is reflected in his plays.

Sex is, without doubt, the crucial issue. Comedy remains fertility worship, however sublimated, and it is fair enough to ask what Bernard Shaw made of the old sexual rigmarole—courtship and the barriers thereto. It is even fair to use any facts about Shaw himself that are a matter of public record.

On the other hand, one is not honor-bound to side with "modern" opinion against "Victorian" as to what is good and bad. The very "modern" Dr. Kinsey implied that human vitality could be measured in statistics on orgasms. Our subject Bernard Shaw will not pass into any Kinseyite paradise. Though he lived to be ninety-four he seems to have experienced sexual intercourse only between the ages of twenty-nine and forty-three. "I lived a continent virgin . . . until I was twenty-nine . . . During the fourteen years before my marriage at forty-three there was always some lady in the case . . . As man and wife we found a new relation in which sex had no part. It ended the old gallantries, flirtations, and philanderings for both of us." This quotation is from a letter to Frank Harris, who, as a Kinseyite before Kinsey, wrote:

> Compare his [Shaw's] private life with Shakespeare's. While Mary Fitton was banished from London Shakespeare could write nothing but

tragedies. That went on for five years. When the Queen died and Shakespeare's Dark Lady returned, he wrote *Antony and Cleopatra*, his greatest love story. As nothing like that happened in Shaw's life we can only get a text-booky, sexless type of play.

A remarkable blend of ignorance, invention, and arbitrary assumption! For actually Shaw concealed from Harris most of his private life; nothing whatever is known about Shakespeare's feelings for any woman; and no critic or psychologist of repute has ever argued that a man's writing has to be "text-booky" and "sexless" unless he is carrying on an adulterous romance; a more familiar argument would be that precisely the abstinent man's imagination might well be crammed with sex. But there is no settling the question a priori.

William Archer declared that Shaw's plays reeked with sex. It is a more suggestive declaration than Harris's. It reminds us that Shaw was able to recreate the sexual charm of both men and women to a degree unequalled by any English dramatist except Shakespeare. To be sure, he doesn't need bedroom scenes to do this. Morell only has to talk and we understand "Prossy's complaint." Undershaft only has to talk and we understand why he is a problem to his daughter. To say nothing of the long line of sirens from Candida to Orinthia! Few of the "sexy" ladies of Restoration comedy, by contrast, have any sex appeal at all. One thing Archer is sure to have had in mind is that the women in Shaw pursue a sexual purpose in a way absolutely unknown to Victorian literature. Of all the reversals in Shavian drama this is inevitably the most famous: the reversal in the roles of the sexes. Shaw once committed himself to the view that all superior women are masculine and all superior men are feminine. In his comedies, most often, the woman is active, the man passive. Perhaps by 1960 the theme has been restated *ad nauseam;* to Archer it was startling. As was Shaw's determination to rub the sore places of the sexual morality of his time. *Mrs. Warren's Profession* was for many years too "raw" a play for production in London, and it created a memorable scandal when it was produced in New Haven and New York in 1905. Like most of the major modern dramatists and novelists, Shaw mentioned the unmentionable. He even claimed to have "put the physical act of sexual intercourse on the stage" (in *Overruled*). Archer may well have felt Shaw could not give the subject of sex a rest: he may not always have been at the center of it but he was forever touching the fringes of it.

Here Frank Harris would have interjected: "He was always *avoiding* the center of it." And the interjection is called for. The impression that a man is unemotional in general and sexless in particular does not come from nowhere. Nor are the kinds of sex I have been noting what the average spectator is looking for if he demands a "sexy" show. *Overruled* does not really "put the physical act of sexual intercourse on the stage," and, even if it did, it would do so comically—depriving the act of precisely that element which people miss in Shaw, which is not sex in general but the torridity of sexual romance. At that, if this element were simply absent, Shaw might very well have got away with the omission. But it is explicitly rejected. It is not that a Shavian couple *cannot* end up in bed but, rather, that they are likely to contemplate the idea— and turn it down. If the characteristic act of the French drama of the period was the plunge into bed, that of the Shavian drama is the precipitate retreat from the bedroom door.

Harris would be right in reminding us that such was Bernard Shaw's emotional constitution. What other writer has ever created all the normal expectations in a scene between a king and his mistress (*The Apple Cart*) only to reveal that their relationship is purely platonic? *Captain Brassbound's Conversion* shows the Shavian pattern to perfection. Is there sexual feeling in the play? There is. The process by which Brassbound and Lady Cicely are brought closer and closer is positively titillating. After which, what happens? They are parted. The play has a superb final curtain. "How marvellous!" says Lady Cicely, "how marvellous!" Then with one of those quick changes of tone that marks the Shavian dialogue: "And what an escape!" Is this unemotional? No. But the emotion is not erotic—rather, it is relief at a release from the erotic. Such is the emotional content of this particular Shavian anticlimax.

As far as conscious intention goes, all Shaw's plays might bear the title he gave to three of them—plays for puritans—for that intention is to show romance transcended by a higher-than-erotic purpose. It is a classic intention—an application, really, of the traditional conflict of love and honor, with honor winning hands down, as it did in Corneille and even in one masterpiece of Racine's—*Bérénice*. We are concerned here, not with philosophic intention, but psychological substance. Where the philosopher insists that Shaw does not cross the threshold of the bedroom, the psychologist asks: why does he hover at the bedroom door?

We know from the correspondence with Mrs. Pat Campbell that

Shaw liked to play with fire. Even the correspondence with Ellen Terry entailed a playfulness not quite devoid of "danger." The boy Shaw had been witness to an odd household arrangement whereby his mother's music teacher contrived to be (it would seem) almost but not quite her lover. A slightly older Shaw has recently been portrayed as the intruder into a friend's marriage like his own Eugene Marchbanks: this is speculation. Let us look at the play *Candida*, which is a fact.

It has a notable Big Scene at the end, which is characterized by an equally notable improbability. A comfortable, sensible, parson's wife doesn't let herself get jockeyed into "choosing" between her husband and an almost total stranger. People—such people at least—don't do such things. A respectable woman's choice was made before the bans were read.

Perhaps Candida is not really respectable? That is the line of interpretation taken by Beatrice Webb who declared her a prostitute. Will the play, taken as a play, bear this interpretation out? A dramatist's license to have the truth turn out different from the impression given to the audience is very limited, for it is to a large extent by giving impressions that he creates characters. Shaw has given the impression that Candida is *not* a prostitute.

Against this it can be urged that Shaw himself took Beatrice Webb's side and attacked Candida—in remarks he made about her in letters to James Huneker, Richard Burton, and others. True, but was that legitimate? He himself admitted that he had no more right to say what his plays meant than any other critic. One might add that he may have had less, for, when an author intervenes to correct our impressions of his work, he is often intervening to change or misinterpret that work.

Outside the play, Shaw is against Candida. Inside it, he is both for and against her, but he is for her effectually, and against her ineffectually, because the direct impression is favorable, while it is only by throwing logic back into the story when it is over that you can reach an unfavorable judgment. This means, I should think, that, though Shaw's intellect is against Candida, his emotions are for her.

What is it that this play has always projected in the theatre, and can always be counted on to project again? The charm of Candida. This is a reality so immediate and all-pervasive that it is hard for any other element in the play to make headway against it. Leading actresses know this and, hearing their director speak of Candida's essential badness, can afford to smile a Candida-smile, strong in the knowledge that there is nothing a director can do about this badness, once that smile has been displayed on stage as well as off.

I would say that it is a confused play but that the confusion goes unnoticed because of Candida's charm and may even be the cause of a degree of emotional tension unusual in Shaw's work. Candida is made out of a Shavian ambivalence: he would like to reject this kind of woman, but actually he dotes on her. One quickly senses that he "is" Marchbanks. One also finds he protests (too much) that he is *not* Marchbanks. "I had in mind De Quincey's account of his adolescence in his Confessions," he wrote, "I certainly never thought of myself as a model." From the empty pretense of being De Quincey, no doubt, comes the prodigious unreality of many of the lines. As a character, Marchbanks must be reckoned a failure. Shaw was hiding. What better image to hide behind than that of the kind of writer he himself was not—a romantic poet? Especially if De Quincey would do the job for him?

It didn't work, of course, except as pure histrionics. (Marchbanks, though a poorly drawn character, is always an effective stage role, and still seems to correspond to the actors' idea of a poet.) But if no one in the play can reject Candida, there is a noteworthy niche in it for the man whom she will reject. This niche Marchbanks can fill nobly, and has his dramatic moment as he marches into it: his final exit is a magnificent piece of action. Possibly everything before that (in this role) is just an improvisation. Shaw could not make us believe in the poet's poetry, but he does make us believe in his pain and his nobility, for at these points he could identify himself with Eugene completely without having to "think of himself as a model."

Dramatists usually speak of their characters individually, and that could be regarded as strange, because the drama, all through the centuries, has done much less with separate persons than with relationships. The traditional characters are, if you will, simplified to the point of crudity. What is not crude, as treated by the old dramatists, is the interaction of these characters: the dynamics of human relations are fully rendered. If what you do not get is the detailed psychological biography, what you do get is the essence of such relations as parent and child, boy and girl, man and wife.

Now modern playwrights, happily, have not departed from the classic patterns as much as they are supposed to have, and what rings true, emotionally, in *Candida* corresponds to Shaw's ability to find and

298 / *Theatre in the Twentieth Century*

re-create some of these elemental relationships. An inner obstacle, one would judge, hampered him when he tried to "do" the Marchbanks-Candida relationship, but the Morell-Candida relation is both clear and challenging. It is, as Shaw himself said, the relationship of Nora and Torvald Helmer turned around: in Shaw's play the man is the doll. But where Ibsen tells the story of a doll who finally comes to life Shaw tells the story of a seemingly-living person who turns out to have been a doll all along. (In other words, the relation of Shaw to Ibsen, instead of being direct as it might seem, is an inverse one, exactly like the relation of Shaw to other nineteenth-century drama.) Into Morell Shaw can put that part of himself (a child) which finds Candida irresistible, just as into Candida he can put that part of Woman which he finds irresistible—the Mother in her. One would have to be as naive a psychologist as Frank Harris to consider the mother and child relation less emotional than that of lovers.

Or less dramatic. Relationships become dramatic not in the degree of their eroticism but to the extent that they contain conflict. Pure love would not be a dramatic subject at all. Love becomes dramatic when it is impure—when the loving element is submerged in a struggle for power. The axis about which *Candida* revolves is that of strength and weakness, not love and hate. And if one knows Shaw's views on the topic of the "weaker sex" in general the conclusion of *Candida* follows naturally: instead of the little woman reaching up toward the arms of the strong man, we have the strong woman reaching down to pick up her child. It is remarkable how far Shaw's thought is from the standard "advanced thinking" of his generation with its prattle of equality and comradeship. He is closer to Nietzsche.

Of the ending of *A Doll's House* it has been said: perhaps Nora has walked out in a mere tantrum and will be back in the morning. How much more savage is the ending of *Candida*! Only Strindberg could have written a sequel to it. The cruelty of the heroine—merely implicit in the present play—would have to come to the surface in any continuation of the story. Candida has chosen to let her husband discover his shame: she, as well as he, will have to take the consequences. Let the stage manager hold razors and strait jackets in readiness!

One reason why Shaw got so little credit for his treatment of the emotions is that the emotions he treats are not the ones people expect. The very fact that his favorite device is anti-climax should tell us that what he most insistently feels is "let-down." It may be retorted that, on the contrary, Bernard Shaw was the most buoyant and vivacious of men. That is also true. The axis "strength-weakness" is not more important to Shaw's content than the axis "elation-depression" is to his form. The dialogue ripples gaily along; then comes the sudden let-down. The circus has familiarized us with the pattern: it is the light of heart who take the prat-fall. Even as the fool pops up in Shavian comedy in the highly intellectualized shape of a Jack Tanner, so the prat-fall is transmuted into an anti-climax that has a positively climactic force. It has been customary to take these anti-climaxes as expressions of an idea—the idea of disenchantment. It is *the* idea of modern literature, and it is inseparable from an emotion far commoner and far more influential than romantic excitement. There seems to be no name for this emotion—and that too is significant. Let us call it desolation.

You cannot be disenchanted without having been enchanted. One is sometimes tempted to believe that our human desolation might have been avoided if only we had not started out so undesolate. It is not the fact that we don't *have* things that worries us but that we have lost them —or rather, been deprived of them. Desolation is the feeling of having been driven from paradise.

A friend of Bernard Shaw's said that when he saw *The Wild Duck* the bottom dropped out of the universe. One difference between Ibsen and Shaw is that the former produced this effect on the audience, whereas the latter produced it on the characters in a play. Just as a character in a melodrama loses a fortune, so a character in a Shaw play loses a universe. The experience may be given a playful treatment, as with Raina and Sergius. In the case of Morell, the treatment is only partly playful. It gets more serious as the play *Candida* proceeds. Morell finally loses his image of his wife and of himself. The curtain has to be rung down to save us from the Strindberg play that would have to follow.

What of *Mrs. Warren's Profession?* The starting point was a treatment by Maupassant of the theme of a girl finding out that her mother is a courtesan. In an early version of the tale Maupassant had the girl kill herself. In the later and better-known text (*Yvette*), he saves her life to engineer for himself an ironic-poignant ending: she becomes a kept woman like her mother before her. Curtain! That is the kind of inversion of a suicidal ending which Shaw did *not* go in for. Or not any more. If Shaw had shown a "surrender to the system" (in comical fashion) in the ending to *Widowers' Houses*, he was now intent on showing a rejection of the system. In the first instance, Vivie Warren's revolt represents Shaw's rational rejection of capitalism, but the play culminates in a scene that has no necessary connection with economics —a scene of family crisis, a scene in which a daughter rejects her mother. Which after all is archetypal Shaw: instead of the emotions of lover and mistress, he renders the emotions of parents and children, and particularly the emotion of the child rejecting the parent. *Major Barbara* is perhaps the grandest example of this archetype. The great last act of *Pygmalion* is the same thing in disguise, for Henry Higgins is the progenitor of the new Eliza, and that is why she must break free of him. Shaw's Joan has a father too—in heaven—and she comes at times almost to the point of breaking with Him. That she does not quite do so is the upshot of a play which, while it shows Joan's isolation from men, ends with a stretching of arms toward the heavenly father . . . Vivie Warren is already a Saint Joan in that the experience Shaw gives her is that of being desolated. It is the experience he felt most deeply —presumably because it was the experience he had most deeply experienced. In any event, the two long scenes between Vivie and Mrs. Warren are passionate playwriting such as England had not seen for a couple of centuries.

The background, however, is blurred. A Scribean climax is arranged to provide élan for the announcement that Vivie's romance is incestuous:

> CROFTS. Allow me, Mister Frank, to introduce you to your half-sister, the eldest daughter of the Reverend Samuel Gardner. Miss Vivie: your half-brother. Good morning.
>
> FRANK (. . . *raising the rifle*). You'll testify before the coroner that it's an accident.
>
> (*He takes aim at the retreating figure of Crofts. Vivie seizes the muzzle and pulls it round against her breast.*)
>
> VIVIE. Fire now. You may.

Direct climax (as against anti-climax) was not really in Shaw's line, and in failing to parody Scribe here, Shaw has himself tumbled into the ridiculous. Perhaps the following act was bound to be an anti-climax in a way not intended—a mere disappointment. Yet it is hard to believe that the particular disappointments it brings are simply the result of a technical miscalculation. Rather, they involve hesitations about the subject. After so strongly creating the impression of incest, Shaw shuffles the notion off in the next act in a surprisingly ambiguous way. It would be easy enough, from a technical viewpoint, to make clear that no incest had been committed. Why did Shaw leave the situation doubt-ful? So that Vivie could dismiss the issue as irrelevant? In that case, what is relevant? Why is she giving Frank up? One can think of possible reasons, but what reason is one *supposed* to think of?

Unclarity in the work of so careful a craftsman, a writer, moreover, who has more than once been accused of excessive clarity, surely bears witness to inner uncertainty and conflict. To think of *Mrs. Warren's Profession* in this personal way is to realize what powerful aggressions it embodies. Shaw combined the themes of prostitution and incest in order to make quite a rational point: our mad society draws back in horror from incest, which is certainly not a pressing menace and per-haps not even a bad thing, while it encourages prostitution, which is a virulent social pestilence. But both themes have a resonance far beyond the bounds of intellect. It is as if they proved to be more than Shaw had bargained for. The incest theme is sounded—all too boldly. Then the young dramatist has no idea what to do with it. He takes it back. Only it is too late. So he half takes it back. After all, what is troubling Vivie does go beyond the rationally established causes . . . Deep water! And Shaw flounders in it. Which has some interest for the student of the emotions. Even where Shaw's plays are faulty, they are not un-emotional. On the contrary, it is because of a certain emotional involve-ment in the material, not because of incapacity for such involvement, that Shaw was not able to resolve certain problems and truly finish certain plays. *Candida* and *Mrs. Warren's Profession* could be cited in evidence. There is material in both which was not successfully "worked through."

Is there similar material in Shaw's collected plays which *was* worked through? To my mind, a good answer would be: yes, *Pygmalion*. This play might well have proved just as ambiguous as the others, for it might have seemed that Eliza must love Higgins, and therefore that her leaving him is but an over-rational afterthought of the author's, like his afterthoughts on Candida. Some people, including the author of *My Fair Lady*, think that is just what the Shavian ending is. I, on the other hand, feel—and it is feeling that is in question—that Eliza's rebellion grows organically out of what preceded. She is Higgins' crea-tion: she cannot *be* at all unless she becomes independent of her creator. If he has "sex appeal," that makes the break more difficult but not less necessary. A girl's father quite normally has sex appeal for her. That is not to justify incest. Here Shaw does cope with incest, and in the best way—by avoiding it.

The ending of *Pygmalion* is the classic Shavian situation: someone is clamorously refusing to enter the bedroom. The friends of Frank Harris are thereby disgusted. That is their right. But there is a point to be made about Shaw's rendering of emotion. Refusal is emotional. There is more turbulence in conflict between Eliza and Higgins as conceived by Shaw than in romance between them as in *My Fair Lady*.

Man and Superman, on the other hand, might seem to be without emotional substance. The attempt made at a straightforward emotional climax is certainly rather unsuccessful:

> TANNER. I love you. The Life Force enchants me: I have the whole world in my arms when I clasp you. But I am fighting for my freedom, for my honor, for my self, one and undivisible.
> ANN. Your happiness will be worth them all.
> TANNER. You would sell freedom and honor and self for happiness?
> ANN. It would not be happiness for me. Perhaps death.
> TANNER. Oh, that clutch holds and hurts. What have you grasped in me? Is there a father's heart as well as a mother's?

If there is capital here, it is the kind that yields no dramatic return, and indeed a criticism of this false climax would lead us to complain of the introduction of the "Life Force" in the first place. There seems no such organic relation between Tanner and Ann as there is between Vivie and her mother, Eliza and Higgins, Candida and Morell. The pair are sometimes compared to Benedick and Beatrice. The comparison is not apt. Shakespeare shows the erotically "dangerous" element in the hostility of his couple. But Tanner and Ann draw no sparks from each other. A cynic might say: here there can be no love since there is no hate. There is really no relationship at all except that she insists on having him and he cannot evade her successfully because the author won't let him. In this case, we have either to conclude that Frank Harris's kind of criticism applies—or that this is "drama of ideas" and we must not ask it to be otherwise.

Emotional substance? The farce of Tanner and Ann, taken in isolation, has very little, but oddly enough the episode in hell has a good deal, and this spreads itself over the work as a whole. Even here, though, there is a discrepancy between intention and achievement. The final effect of the Don Juan scene is not that we find the positive message inspiring. We find it at best important, at worst gallant—a brave effort to make sense of things that cannot be made sense of. It is all rather like a speech made in wartime saying that our side is bound to win because we are right. Perhaps. Perhaps. But the words that burn with irrefutability are all words expressing, not aspiration toward a better future, but recognition of a bad present. Don Juan himself is at his best when denouncing people. The speech that steals the show ("And is man any the less destroying himself . . .") is made by the Devil. Which is because it is not only a very reasonable speech but a very emotional one, a speech that springs from that very desolation which Shaw's best people experience.

This note of personal poignancy is seldom, or never, heard after *Saint Joan* (1923). So much the worse for the later plays. They have considerable merit, yet they often lack urgency even when the author makes Urgent Statements in them. And it is interesting that they lack not only dynamic and turbulent personal relationships but also close structure. There had been a connection between the emotional and the dramaturgic construction of the earlier plays; and when one went, so did the other.

I am not proposing a complete theory of the Shavian drama. Certainly, it should not be implied that this drama is dominated by the emotional conflicts of its author, much less that it ought to be. For that matter, I have had to remark that unresolved conflict sometimes resulted in unresolved art. What I am affirming is, first, that some Shaw plays communicate personal feeling of great intensity and, second, that even some Shaw plays which are less overtly emotional do embody profound feelings, though not of the kind that is usually expected.

Public and Private
Problems in Modern
Drama

BY RONALD PEACOCK

IT HAS BECOME COMMON TO view drama in the post-Ibsen period as falling into two broad categories. On the one hand there was a strong and persistent tradition of the *A Doll's House* type of play, called for convenience "social problem plays," and on the other a number of diverse styles of drama that represent counter-realism; plays in verse, expressionism, formalistic styles as in Yeats' plays, revivals of myths, fantastic drama, surrealism, plays of Freudian psychology, Cocteau-ish *poésie de théâtre,* and so on, all of which, however different from each other, have in common that they turn away both from social problems and from the dramatic style associated with them. They do not necessarily, however, renounce realism for "romance," or for something "poetic" in the escapist sense. Neither are the themes they treat always without relevance to the social situation. The point is that the social situation changed radically in the decade of World War I, making social problem drama of the older kind and its particular mold of realism out of date. But the antiquated forms had no monopoly on all realism or all social problems. The new forms, superficially judged to be anti-realistic, often represent in fact an artistic adjustment to a new soical situation. In Georg Kaiser, in Cocteau, in Giraudoux, in Eliot, there can be no question of evasion of reality, or of the contemporary

Reprinted with permission from the *Bulletin of the John Rylands Library,* Vol. 36, No. 1, September, 1953.

world, or of society. Their works depict these things and express their feelings about them. They were strange at first only because the realities shown had not yet been perceived by others. The world of *A Doll's House* and plays like it was real to Ibsen; it was the world he experienced. But it was no longer real in 1918 to Kaiser, for whom the middle-class home, with a certain set of private beliefs and social attitudes, had been pushed out of the center of the picture to give place to the new reality of highly technical and industrial social organization. In order to show this he devised his expressionistic form which presents not private lives and homes but the skeletal structure of a whole society which in that contemporary situation was more real than the surfaces of bourgeois life. In a similar way Eliot's plays contain a view and a criticism of a given society. They are determined by a religious interpretation, which means that the judgment is one of several possible ones. But the interpretation is neither fanciful nor wilful; it does refer to a social reality. The argument applies also to the work of Giraudoux which to a superficial glance seems to seek refuge in "myths" in order to say something "universal" about life, transcending the localized contemporary situation, but it is in fact profoundly rooted in that situation.

There are some plays that deal, in the strictest sense, with "social problems." Examples are better found in Shaw, perhaps, than anywhere else. *Widowers' Houses* is one. It deals with a problem arising directly from the economic organization of society. Many more plays, while not exactly formulating a social problem, treat a social theme in the sense that a comment on society is implicit in their picture. *The Cherry Orchard* comes under this head. The plays of Ibsen that most influenced the social problem type may themselves in fact be grouped more comfortably under this general head than as examples of purely *social* problems. It is more accurate to say of them that they focus moral problems having social implications. For the crux of the matter nearly always is not so much a specific "social problem" as the situation of the individual in relation to the society he lives in. Ibsen attacks beliefs and the people—persons, human beings—who hold them. If institutions or social customs crack under his criticism it is because the antecedent beliefs on which they rest show up as hollow. This subtlety of moral relationships between individual beliefs and social practices is the very fibre of Ibsen's drama.

It is this relationship between an individual's world and a social world that I want to analyze in connection with a few plays of this century. To isolate a body of plays as social problem drama is not enough in view of the omnipresence of the social theme in various forms. For the larger perspective shows a continuous process of social change and a continuing preoccupation with it in the drama. In that process the emphasis is sometimes on the person and sometimes on society, but always both are involved. The plays I shall use to illustrate the argument are Ibsen's *A Doll's House*, Kaiser's *Gas*, Giraudoux' *La Guerre de Troie n'aura pas lieu*, and Eliot's *The Family Reunion*.

A Doll's House and plays close to it, like *Ghosts, Pillars of Society, The Wild Duck*, and others, present a cumulative picture of society and it is one illumined by angry lights. Ibsen's imagination is always haunted by a great ideal of what man might be if he could realize his humanity to perfection. This ideal, dominated to a large extent by the romantic spirit inherited from the late eighteenth century, implied a number of qualities such as freedom, integrity, joyous creativeness, natural innocence and dignity, the sense of right, that are in fact rarely or never found together but have nevertheless great power and suggestiveness as a composite ideal. Ibsen knew too much about human nature to make the mistake of trying to portray his ideal directly in idealized characters; but he most certainly and ruthlessly measured people against his nostalgic moral aspiration and only late in his life and work did he soften his judgments and begin to inculcate a doctrine of charity. His feelings about the ideal are focused in characters who, although portrayed convincingly as real people, that is, human beings both frail and strong, reflect his own aspiration and undergo an illumination; such are Nora and Mrs. Alving. His feelings of moral despair, on the other hand, are reflected in his picture of a corrupt society; and indeed in these plays the insistence on corruption is so emphatic that one feels Ibsen wanted to give physical reality to the moral stench and assail his audience—the society he attacked—with it. In *A Doll's House* Dr. Rank, embittered by his disease, fulminates against the rottenness lying just beneath the surface in nearly every family, while physical horror is exploited to the utmost in *Ghosts*.

Ibsen's dramatic pattern combines incisive moral analysis with an expressive unburdening of the feelings. To achieve the former he uses his principal character as a pivot. Nora Helmer has been, before the beginnings of her crisis, part of the milieu which arouses Ibsen's indignation; she then emerges from it through a subtle development of her selfhood and awareness of herself in relation to others, particularly her husband; until finally Ibsen has focused in her protestations his own analysis of what society calls "marriage" and "love."

The particulars of Nora's situation may have lost most of their power to move us, since the relations between men and women both in and outside marriage have changed so much. To appreciate the sheer dramatic effect of her decision to leave home, which rested on the horror of the audience at the mere thought of such a step, we have to recall the social ostracism incurred by a woman who took it in an age when the professions were not open to women. This effect has been lost. On the other hand we can still hear, and possibly with keener ears, the lapidary note in the great discussion scene with which the play reaches its climax and in which Nora discloses herself as the type of the protestant rebel.

> NORA. . . . I can no longer content myself with what most people say, or with what is found in books. I must think things over for myself and get to understand them.
>
> HELMER. Can you not understand your place in your own home? Have you not a reliable guide in such matters as that?—have you no religion?
>
> NORA. I am afraid, Torvald, I do not exactly know what religion is.
>
> HELMER. What are you saying?
>
> NORA. I know nothing but what the clergyman said, when I went to be confirmed. He told us that religion was this and that, and the other. When I am away from all this, and am alone, I will look into that matter too. I will see if what the clergyman said is true, or at all events if it is true for me.

When Helmer accuses her further of having no moral sense she answers in the same vein of simple honesty, admitting ignorance but expressing willingness to work the problem out for herself. She admits Helmer's charge that she doesn't understand the conditions of the world in which she lives:

> NORA. No, I don't. But now I am going to try. I am going to see if I can make out who is right, the world or I.

Helmer's answer to this: "You are ill, Nora; you are delirious; I almost think you are out of your mind," is the comment of those who live in darkness.

The history of prophets and poets can show more exalted examples of spiritual birth or rebirth. Yet however modest the person and circumstances of Ibsen's obscure middle-class young wife, she assumes heroic stature in this scene. Step by step, with simplicity and logic, she strips every pretense from her life, her marriage, and her love. But this she does in the spirit of affirmation, not of destruction; and so a great dramatic and moral exhilaration radiates from her discovery of her self and her responsibility. To her age she appeared as the representative of all womanhood about to engage in a struggle for emancipation. But Ibsen has put himself into her actions and words. Through the local particulars of dress and period in his play we see that Nora's case is that of man altogether, liberating himself from falsehood in order to start afresh and work out his salvation with gods and men.

It is fatally easy to assimilate Ibsen to the sociological thought of the later nineteenth century. Since his plays do contain a criticism of "society" they seem to fall pat into a broad picture of social change. But Ibsen as far as beliefs are concerned is situated before the age of "economic and social" man. Society to Ibsen is not a sociological conception but a moral one. It is the herd with its system of subterfuges for protecting its weaknesses and selfishness. His rebels are made to hold out against this herd and judge it. There is in his picture certainly a sense of social pressures, including economic ones. Nora's crisis is precipitated partly by her economic dependence which led her to dishonest ways of procuring money. But Ibsen's world is innocent of the play of "social," i.e. extra-individual, forces as that idea has since his time been understood. His people are not the products of such forces. They are weak, cowardly, selfish, gregarious, but they are individuals with a potential will of their own. Ibsen's indignation is not aroused by the faulty organization of society—for that we have to look to Shaw —but by men defacing their own nature with those grimaces of beasts that Rubek, in *When We Dead Awaken*, portrayed in his sculpture. Man is here still conceived in the traditional image of a person with a moral sense, with free will, with the knowledge of good and evil—even though he makes mistakes—and with complete responsibility. In Ibsen's world the individual, the private person, makes the decisions that matter, social customs and institutions flowing from them. Ibsen's idea of man is that he stands alone and makes his decision. Because of this his drama, although it embraces criticism of "society," is primarily a *critique of morality* pivoted on faith in the realization of a human ideal in the free individual.

For a drama that provides a criticism of society, in a stricter sense of the term, we may turn to Georg Kaiser's *Gas*. The people of this play, with one exception, exist only in functional relation to an organized mass, their salient characteristic being that they have lost their individual independence, both in character and actions.

Gas is not a great play; it suffers from stridency and over-emphatic style, and the feeling about "humanity" that makes it a violent rhetorical protest against certain tendencies in modern society remains crude and sentimental. Yet it is a very remarkable play because, using a bold and incisive method for the theatre, it projected an original vision of the society that was fast developing within the liberal bourgeois framework which was still what the surface showed. In the general development of this century the date of the play—1918—has significance as marking the end of World War I and therewith of the first stage of the transition from the liberal capitalist society of the nineteenth century to the socialized states and planned centralized societies of the following era. Kaiser's theme is the dehumanizing influence of technocratic social organization. His method is to portray such a society, bring catastrophe upon it from one of its own elements, and use a main character as a foil to point his moral. His picture shows a factory community, producing the most up-to-date form of energy, not only run with maximum scientific efficiency but also completely socialized, since its head, the Billionaire's Son, has renounced his wealth for the sake of the new ideal, by which the profits are shared. In this perfectly, even idyllically, arranged life an explosion occurs which by all the laws of science should not. Kaiser makes great play with the symbolic "formula" that represents the limit of scientific exactitude and yet still leaves something to the unexplainable and uncontrollable; so that there is a dangerous flaw not only in the formula but in the nature of the society which is built on the idea behind it. The Billionaire's Son learns his lesson from the destruction and suffering and turns away from a society and a philosophy that are at the mercy of such a catastrophe. If the factory with its formulae and machines is liable to such a breakdown why be enslaved to it? He recovers for himself the human sense of values of the pre-technological life and, finding a new ideal for his philanthropy, imagines a farming community in which men can be natural and human again. This vapid return-to-nature or agrarian philosophy is as weak as the picture of the futuristic worker-technician-factory culture is incisive.

This gospel he tries to preach to his factory workers, technicians, his chief Engineer, and industrialists; the play is a sequence of scenes in which he implores them to see the light. But no one does. The workers want their work back; they demand only the dismissal of the Engineer responsible for the breakdown to appease their sense of oppression and loss. The Engineer is also in opposition, deriving his particular form of stubbornness from professional pride. The industrialists have only one idea, which is to get the "gas" factory re-started so that their own concerns have power again. All these classes of men are united in their opposition to the Billionaire's Son because they are no longer conscious of any meaning in themselves except as parts of a machine and in their world all society has become a machine. Its denizens live wholly under the technocratic compulsion that enslaves every class of its servants. Their obtuseness and inflexibility are the signs of servitude. They have lost the conception of their own nature as something they might still have; they cannot think themselves out of their situation; they are all engaged in a constrained misdirection of their natural feelings, ignorant of how their humanity has already slipped beyond their reach.

Toller was to say in connection with his own technique that you can see men as "realistic human beings" but you can also see the same men, in a flash of vision, as puppets which move mechanically in response to external direction. The people in Kaiser's picture of society are puppets in this sense, with their meaning withdrawn from their humanness and concentrated in their function, for which one part of them may be alone of significance, their hand, or eye, for instance. In a sullen way these people are indeed aware that they are distortions; but great pathos (in spite of the overemphasis) derives from their inability to revolt and liberate themselves; so long as someone is "punished" for the explosion they are satisfied to let the process start again:

MÄDCHEN: Von meinem Bruder sage ich das!—Ich wusste nicht, dass ich einen Bruder hatte. Ein Mensch ging morgens aus dem Hause und kam abends—und schlief. Oder er ging abends weg und war morgens zurück —und schlief!—Eine Hand war gross—die andere klein. Die grosse Hand schlief nicht. Die stiess in einer Bewegung hin und her—Tag und Nacht. Diese Hand war der Mensch!—Wo blieb mein Bruder? Der früher neben mir spielte—und Sand mit seinen beiden Händen baute? —In Arbeit stürzte er. Die brauchte nur die eine Hand von ihm . . . Da frass die Explosion auch die Hand. Da hatte mein Bruder das Letzte

gegeben!—Ist es zu wenig?—Hatte mein Bruder gefeilscht um den
Preis, als man die Hand von ihm für den Hebel brauchte? Streifte er
nicht willig den Bruder ab—und verschrumpfte in die zählende Hand?
—Zahlte er nicht zuletzt die Hand noch?—Ist die Bezahlung zu
schlecht—um den Ingenieur zu heischen?—Mein Bruder ist meine
Stimme—: arbeitet nicht—ehe der Ingenieur nicht vom Werk ist!—
Arbeitet nicht—meines Bruders Stimme ist es!!

One realizes at this point that Kaiser has taken several steps beyond
the simple protests at the misery of underpaid workers, uninteresting
factory jobs, and slums, consequent on the industrial revolution. These
were familiar to the later nineteenth century, both in literature and
sociological writing. In drama the humanitarian protest at social misery
is well seen in Hauptmann's *Die Weber*. Kaiser's protest is not against
misery of that kind, held in abhorrence as an affront to human beings.
His socialized world has removed those things. He protests against the
loss of human status. The shrill nostalgia of the Billionaire's Son for
"den Menschen" would not be so excessive if it were a case simply of
suffering, for that brings human qualities and virtues into play. He
fights his battle against men who have lost the knowledge of what man
is. They are morally destitute because the private world is gone. A
wholly public world engulfs the human one. Every person is chained
to a function in a closely articulated mechanism; and when human
creatures exist as no more than a function within a whole, the whole
itself is not human.

The nature of Kaiser's vision of society in this play has not to my
knowledge been explicitly related to the conditions of 1917–18 in
Germany, when, under the stress of a war no longer offensive but
desperately defensive, the country was converted into a military machine. Here one might seek an embryonic model of what we have since
called the totalitarian society, and we remember too that World War II
made "total war" and "total mobilization" the rule everywhere. If *Gas*
is based on German society of 1917–18, as I think it is, it gives, however
"expressionistic" in method, a vision of reality. Clearly a process of
generalization is involved; but the play presents an image of the skeletal
structure of a certain kind of society. Although simplified, it is logical
and analytically true. And on this truth to something real rests its
power, because that provides some justification for an emotional atmosphere so intense as to border on hysteria. The pessimism is strong;

and with reason, when the end of the individual and his moral independence is involved.

At the side of this, Ibsen looks very nineteenth century. Great changes have occurred. If, as we said, "society" for Ibsen was the herd with its fears and stupidities, but still a human herd, here in Kaiser it is the product of economic and industrial forces which transcend the individual will. His drama is in consequence a *critique of society*, or social structure, in the twentieth century sociological meaning of the words. His picture, with its unnamed persons representing classes or functions, its elimination of the private man and his private life (the daughter and her officer husband who runs into debt and commits suicide are the faintest echoes of "bourgeois" life), its sharp stylizations streamlining the features of the technocratic culture, and its clipped, pounding verbal style, shows an adjustment of dramatic form not only to some extraneous principle of style or subjective expression but to the new social realities.

It is a noticeable feature of *Gas* that the nature and quality of *Menschentum* remain obscure. Kaiser's feeling is all concentrated in his protest, in the name of something referred to as humanity, against its elimination. Hence on the one hand we have a stark, metallic, glinting picture of the system criticized, and on the other an explosion of rebellious sentiment. The former we see to be analytically correct; the indignation and pity we take as a sign of good faith. But we are not given to feel in our minds or senses some quality of living, or thought, or sensibility, or character, recognizable as belonging to what we mean in an ideal sense by "humanity." In short, the play, although a strained expression of human resentment and nostalgia, contains no person, or situation, or words that vibrate, if only for a moment, with the ideal so constantly evoked in name.

Giraudoux' dramatic work, which belongs to the years 1928 to 1945, possesses the quality absent in Kaiser. It is saturated with the indefinable essence of humanity, understood as a delicate sense of the situation of human beings, living under the shadow of Fate, of gods and devils, amidst men and women of incredible complexity of character and given particularly to bellicosity, but also aspiring to happiness and goodness in a way that touches even those who do not know very much about such things. In one sense the dramatic pattern of a central focus-character in opposition to others, seen in both Ibsen and Kaiser, repeats itself in Giraudoux; it is by now conventional to discuss his "élues," as they are called. But such characters in Giraudoux do not incorporate in themselves a single idea of "the human person," as so many of Ibsen's, different as they are, represent the struggle for the true self. They are drawn, it is true, with psychological art and are real enough with their motives and emotions to fit into a story. But they are above all the vehicles of certain qualities admired by the ethical sensitiveness of humanity whose spokesman Giraudoux makes himself. Judith, with her great love, Electre with her uncompromising sense of justice, Alcmène, innocent, chaste, and faithful, Hector with his sense of brotherhood, La Folle with her unerring instinct for simple and good people—all of them are very human, and yet a little more than human, endowed by the abstracting imagination with an eloquence of person and function that derives not from themselves but from the human faith of their creator.

The use of a myth provides the perfect opportunity for setting such quasi-real persons in motion and making them the meeting-point for generalized ideals and the personal forms in which everything human has to appear. Hector in *La Guerre de Troie n'aura pas lieu* is such a person. In him and his attempt to prevent a further outbreak of war, struggling first with the established habits and beliefs of his family and fellow Trojans, then with the wilful bellicosity of Demokos and the warmongers, and finally with Destiny, there is concentrated the immense nostalgia for peace which flooded the hearts of Europeans in the thirties of this century. At that time the success of Fascism and National Socialism represented a counter-blow to all the post-1918 endeavors to organize an international society. The outstanding event of the twenties was the Treaty of Locarno; the symbolic act of hope was the institution of the League of Nations. It was in the late twenties that the "war books," mostly of pacifist intentions and headed by Remarque's *All Quiet on the Western Front*, burst on to the literary scene, focusing general feelings on the subject in a generation that had lived through the horrors of modern warfare from 1914 to 1918. The outstanding events of the thirties, on the other hand, were the victory of the National Socialists in 1933, the Abyssinian War, the Spanish Civil War, and the various unilateral acts of Hitler's foreign policy. It was the age of the "threat of war" and of paralyzed attempts to evade it. But the threat of war was simply the symptom of the problem as to how international relations should be organized, by federation of free peoples or centralization under a predominant power. The national problem of socialization here reached its international form, and the difference, both in time and theme, between Kaiser and Giraudoux reflects this logical development of the modern situation. For the vital theme now concerns the relations between the different branches of human society. What does man, within the brotherhood and unity of the human race, owe to man and to himself? The force of Giraudoux' play lies in the simplicity of feeling over the central issue; its delicacy, however, in the way the public theme is treated in connection with the complex passion of men and the play of fatality.

It would be profitable to examine in detail Giraudoux' adroitness of method in touching, through his persons and their discussions, on virtually all the factors that agitated people's feelings on this problem at the time. The brilliant satire on the procedures of international jurists in the Busiris passage may be adduced as an example. But we must be content to define briefly Giraudoux' method in contrast to that of Ibsen and Kaiser. The new pattern shows a public theme—in this play, peace and brotherhood in all their reasonableness—joined to a generalized ethical sensitiveness as to what constitutes "humanity." The problem is not in any sense a private one, as Nora Helmer's was; it concerns nations and humanity as a whole. The peculiar fictitiousness of Hector as a mythical character emphasizes this by contrast with the contemporary substantiality of Nora. Yet on the other hand it is not only a social question, as in *Gas;* for the distinguishing feature of Giraudoux' plays is a refinement of ethical feeling that only flourishes in persons as part of their essential individual character and human form, and can never inhere in impersonal "social" actions. And this is expressed in the fact that Hector, like other Giraudoux characters, in spite of being so obvious a device, assumes nevertheless the form of a person.

We perceive now that Giraudoux, using a framework taken from classical mythology, achieved a brilliant invention of method. His subject and emotions were absolutely contemporary, but of a kind that could not possibly have been treated realistically—you can only put modern politics and diplomacy into a play as caricature, as Shaw did in *Geneva.* Giraudoux extracts the myth from its own historico-religious context, fills the person with contemporary public meanings, and thus, creating a new form that is half myth, half allegory, makes it do service again, giving an aristocratic aesthetic quality to what might otherwise not have risen above propaganda or dull moralizing. Such is the character not only of *La Guerre de Troie n'aura pas lieu* but of other plays of this author. They avoid the particular reality of historical or contemporary events, substituting a quasi-real world, but only in order to clarify issues of contemporary urgency.

The drama of Giraudoux thus appears as a *critique of humanity;* that is, of the human kind. In a succession of plays he meditates, amidst all the fantasy, caprice, and wit of his theatrical style, on general ideals such as pity, charity, justice, loyalty, faith, and so on, which together constitute humanity understood as the characteristic form of existence separating man from the rest of creation. Ibsen's characters seek self in order to be real. The people in *Gas* are emasculated of both self and humanity. Giraudoux explores in his mythical fictions the nature of human quality and its place in the modern world. He is sensitive, not labored; skeptical and bewildered, but not without hope, and in no way a clamant castigator of morals. At the same time as his ethical idealism is diffused through his plays, so also is a sense of man's precarious situation, since he lives subject to chance and fatality. From these two things—the humanity expressed in ideals, and that witnessed in helplessness—emanates the tragic pathos of his work.

If a play like *Gas* leaves one with a feeling of something lost or abandoned, the work of Giraudoux gives the impression of embarrassment. Kaiser protests against a world in which humanity is eliminated; Giraudoux, gentle and civilized, is saddened by one in which humanity cannot make its values effective. Kaiser's persons are marionettes, those of Giraudoux fictions of the moral conscience battling against powers they cannot cope with or do not understand, like Judith with God and the priests, Alcmène with Jupiter, or Hector with the spirit of war. As individuals they find themselves involved in a public situation without being able to establish a harmonious relationship with it. The decisions their own virtues require for themselves are contravened by incalculable factors operating apart from individuals and their values, but not apart from human life. Thus the world of private values is not adjusted to the public situation, yet the latter is all-important. Giraudoux reflects with great accuracy what is a dominant feature of the modern situation as experienced by many people: the sense of good and noble qualities lives on in natural and perhaps philosophically ungrounded forms, while the dogmatic moral legislation that alone secures an adjustment of public and private forms is lacking.

One of the main impressions left by his work is of an aristocrat of mind and sensibility *commenting* on life. His mythical fictions give the semblance of drama, but they also express a withdrawal from true drama into that kind of dialogue which springs not from separate persons but from a divided self, or one that habitually ruminates on moral intricacies whilst others live by cutting the Gordian knot. The sense of the real in Giraudoux comes entirely from the author's personal voice. It is he, not "life," that we feel everywhere. His persons, like his fantasy and wit ceaselessly at work, are valid not as poetic intuitions but as vehicles of *his* sensitive meditation. Giraudoux ponders real situations, contemporary and public ones; he himself is real, uttering his thoughts; but his dramatic characters are shadows whose unreality reflects the unreality of the individual's situation in contemporary life—his being encased in a private world of values and victimized by a public world of events. Giraudoux' myths are in one sense a positive assertion of artistic form, in another a symptom of a maladjusted society.

The three authors considered up to this point work without orthodox religion. In that they differ little from most other dramatists of the period. The great exceptions are Hofmannsthal, Claudel, and Eliot, whose work might be expected to throw further light on the problem of private and social worlds. The two former yield less in this respect than Eliot, since their plays are devoted to more exclusively religious feelings and events. It is true that a play like *Das Grosse Welttheater* has a social meaning within its religious imagery; and one like *Le Soulier de Satin* has persons with very real human passions. Yet their action moves toward a moment when the merely human is transfigured with a divine meaning and at such a moment what we call the "social" has little relevance. Eliot, by contrast, observes constantly the social world, the plays extending an analysis begun in the earlier poems. He has himself emphasized that he wanted to portray in his plays people in contemporary circumstances. This no doubt constituted a problem for drama in verse but it was not an accidental or merely ambitious aim. Eliot has the modern situation deliberately under view, his analysis of it springing from a mind sensitive to the complexity of civilized issues in any modern society and interested in them all. The poet of *The Waste Land* and the *Four Quartets* wrote also *After Strange Gods*, the commentaries of *The Criterion*, and the *Notes towards the Definition of Culture*.

His plays have met with much hostile criticism and yet they have shown an astonishing vigor and power to move audiences, one reason being doubtless that they do succeed in touching modern life at so many points, not only by presenting contemporary people but in the manner of doing so, which shows the characteristic modern awareness of intricacy in psychology, sociology, manners, morals, religion, and culture. Sin, expiation, and martyrdom are in the center of his picture, ideas disagreeable to a skeptical and scientifically minded, or merely lighthearted, public. But they are not there as pure religion flung in the face of life. They fascinate and disturb because meaning falls from them on to aspects of modern life on which one might not think religion directly impinged, and in respect of which other current philosophies have notably failed to find meaning. A passage in the *Notes towards the Definition of Culture* provides an illuminating gloss on the characters of *The Family Reunion* (and *The Cocktail Party*):

> The reflection that what we believe is not merely what we formulate and subscribe to, but that behavior is also belief, and that even the most conscious and developed of us live also at the level on which belief and behavior cannot be distinguished, is one that may, once we allow our imagination to play upon it, be very disconcerting. It gives an importance to our most trivial pursuits, to the occupation of our every minute, which we cannot contemplate long without the horror of nightmare. When we consider the quality of the integration required for the full cultivation of the spiritual life, we must keep in mind the possibility of grace and the exemplars of sanctity in order not to sink into despair. And when we consider the problem of evangelization, of the development of a Christian society, we have reason to quail. To believe that *we* are religious people and that other people are without religion is a simplification which approaches distortion. To reflect that from one point of view religion is culture, and from another point of view culture is religion, can be very disturbing (p. 32).

Here we see promulgated a criterion for the quality, not of "humanity," but of the spiritual life, which may be taken to mean human life irradiated by a transcendent power, every feature of behavior coming finally under its influence. Against this criterion Eliot measures modern forms of culture. All the persons in *The Family Reunion* represent these forms, according to their character, tastes, gifts, possessions, and education, from the uncles and aunts to Amy and Mary, and then Agatha; and they are judged against the elected person at the center, a pattern repeated with variations in *The Cocktail Party*.

We may note in Eliot's work a degree of loathing of life that quite exceeds a realistic acknowledgement of corruption or native wickedness in man, and this no doubt gives rise to a despair that needs redemption and also to nostalgia for sainthood and the scarcely curbed contempt for anything lower than that. Yet such extremes of feeling cannot really impair the main structure of Christian belief nor the criticism of man and society deriving from it. This faith restores decisively to the individual both meaning and responsibility, and removes from the conception of "society" and the "social" the materialistic and secular meanings that have come to predominate. The terms we have used—private and public, even individual and society—cease to be strictly relevant, except as secondary distinctions, since a theological conception is primary. Ibsen's rebellious individual, Giraudoux' aristocratic and sensitive humanity, Kaiser's articulated society, all of which show what can only be a partial view of life and civilization, are here displaced by a conception of greater comprehensiveness. Extending our classification of these plays as critiques of man and society it is easy now to borrow from Eliot's own terms the word that describes his drama in relation to the others we have considered. It is a *critique of culture*.

It does not follow that because culture, in this context, comprehends more and deeper meanings Eliot's dramatic art is superior to that of the other authors here considered, for dramatic power does not depend on a well-ordered philosophy. But the kind of integration of dramatic forms attempted by Eliot in his plays corresponds to the degree of integration envisaged in his idea of true culture. For what he attempts to do is to portray a realistic scene—the family in the country house, the barrister with wife, mistress, and social circle—through which an underlying mythical pattern diffuses its meanings to the surface; so that the "real" becomes, without being negated or displaced, transparent, and through it the myth appears as the imminent meaning. In a drama based on such a view both realistic and mythical forms are authentic; the one is more than a preoccupation with limited aspects of social reality, and the other more than a modern aesthetic device. The symbolism of Eliot's characters is implicit because the personal form contains the meaning. Similarly, the mythical power inheres in the real human situation, since people like Harry and Celia, unlike figures from past myths, begin as ordinary persons leading ordinary lives and remain human even after the assumption of their distinctive functions. The incorporation of elements from primitive or ancient ritual, though not uniformly successful, is at least relevant, since it fortifies the endowment of the whole situation (especially in *The Family Reunion*) with its complex meaning. Eliot's considered technique of verse also makes an appropriate and organic contribution, pendulating between the realistic surface and the underlying myth, the verse that is very close to the prosaic, and that which draws on all the expressive sources, ancient and modern, of poetry.

It may be that the unifying of many strands of feeling and experience in the picture of life presented in Eliot's plays admits of approval in theory without being unchallengeably successful in dramatic practice. But the attempt to express this in drama by a combination of realistic modern setting and emergent myth is unique and, because of the range of experience and thought involved, infinitely interesting.

The examination of these four plays throws a vivid light on the relation of drama to contemporary life as expressed both in its themes and forms. For each springs from a distinct phase in the conditions of life in the past fifty or sixty years, and the originality of form is in each case seen to depend on an acute visionary assessment of the essential reality of the situation in both its individual and social aspects. Drama, like other literary forms, is always created by a particular imagination, but it is never simply a personal statement. It is always about men-in-society, and a dramatist must be interested in that in the same way as the general run of men, however much greater his insight or stronger his emotions. The four cases here examined show four dramatists with their finger on the pulse of events and social change. Ibsen's analytic realism, Kaiser's expressionistic imagery, Giraudoux' myth-fantasies, Eliot's ritualistic realism, are distinct dramatic forms for distinct visions of man in society and amidst historical change. They each contain a critique of the human situation at given moments, shaped by acuteness of feeling and perception working together; and it is to signalize their particular contributions within this general function that we have described them severally as critiques of morality, society, humanity, and culture.

The comparative method is especially fruitful, indeed essential, for this topic. The changes involved have been broadly similar in all European societies but they have not all been expressed, or not equally well, in any one literature; not in the Norwegian, nor the German, nor the French, nor the English, nor any other. National genius plays its part in these high points of expression; for the Protestant austerity of Ibsen, the strained emotionalism of Kaiser, the civilized intelligence of Giraudoux, the resort to verse drama in Eliot, to mention only a few features, all appear with peculiar appropriateness against the respective national backgrounds. The four plays to which interest has been directed were not chosen to make an argument; on the contrary the latter emerged from seeing the pattern into which they naturally fall. They are plays that have attained an uncommon fame throughout Europe, which seems to confirm that situations evolving everywhere were expressed best now in one country, now in another.